D0404534

PRINCIPLED PRACTICES FOR ADOLESCENT LITERACY

A Framework for Instruction and Policy

PRINCIPLED PRACTICES FOR ADOLESCENT LITERACY

A Framework for Instruction and Policy

Elizabeth G. Sturtevant
Fenice B. Boyd
William G. Brozo
Kathleen A. Hinchman
David W. Moore
Donna E. Alvermann

with

Patricia L. Anders • Thomas W. Bean • Judith L. Irvin
Gay Ivey • Guofang Li • Josephine Peyton Marsh
Elizabeth Birr Moje • Richard T. Vacca • George Hruby

LEA LAWRENCE ERLBAUM ASSOCIATES, PUBLISHERS
2006   Mahwah, New Jersey   London

Copyright © 2006 by Lawrence Erlbaum Associates, Inc.
All rights reserved. No part of this book may be reproduced in
any form, by photostat, microform, retrieval system, or any other
means, without the prior written permission of the publisher.

Lawrence Erlbaum Associates, Inc., Publishers
10 Industrial Avenue
Mahwah, New Jersey 07430
www.erlbaum.com

Cover design by Kathryn Houghtaling Lacey

Library of Congress Cataloging-in-Publication Data

Principled practices for adolescent literacy : a framework for instruction and policy /
Elizabeth G. Sturtevant . . . [et al.]; with Patricia L. Anders . . . [et al.].
    p. cm.
Includes bibliographical references and index.
ISBN 0-8058-5112-7 (cloth : alk. paper)
ISBN 0-8058-5113-5 (paper : alk. paper)
    1. Reading (Middle school)—United States.   2. Reading (Secondary)—United States.
3. Middle school teaching—United States.   4. High school teaching—United States.
I. Sturtevant, Elizabeth G.   II. Anders, Patricia L.

LB1632.P75   2006
428.4'071'2—dc22   2005053108
                                                                          CIP

Books published by Lawrence Erlbaum Associates are printed on acid-free paper,
and their bindings are chosen for strength and durability.

Printed in the United States of America
10 9 8 7 6 5 4 3 2 1

We dedicate this book to the students and teachers throughout the United States who welcomed the authors and contributors into their classrooms and willingly shared their knowledge and perspectives during this project.

Contents

Foreword

It has been a delightful experience to play a small part in the writing and development of this book. To the best of my knowledge, *Principled Practices for Adolescent Literacy: A Framework for Instruction and Policy* is the first of its kind to identify for school-based practitioners, scholars, and policymakers a comprehensive set of guiding principles underlying adolescent literacy practices. It is hard for me to imagine now that just 8 years ago most adolescent literacy educators were deeply concerned over the lack of attention and urgency to the literacy needs of children and youth beyond third grade. At that time, I was just completing my term as president of the International Reading Association. The second Clinton Administration had made education generally, and learning to read specifically, the United States' top domestic priority. Yet the developmental emphasis by political leaders and policymakers focused almost exclusively on literacy learning in the early grades. There existed in the public mindset a misguided notion that it was too late to teach students to read well beyond the primary school years. When George W. Bush became president in 2000, the emphasis on reading in the early years remained stronger than ever.

As we approached the new millennium, literacy professionals were among the first to recognize that a diverse, information-driven society such as ours could ill afford to marginalize adolescent literacy by pushing it to the edges of public debate and policy. As a result, the International Reading Association created the Commission on Adolescent Literacy to ignite a professional conversation on the literacy development of young adolescents and teenagers. Many of the authors, scholars, and practitioners who participated on the Commission have contributed substantially to the development of this book.

The Commission on Adolescent Literacy underscored the importance of viewing literacy learning as a developmental process that for all intents and purposes begins at birth and ends with death. Our goal as a Commission was not to bifurcate literacy learning and teaching into the early and adolescent years. Literacy learning and teaching must be viewed as a seamless, continual process occurring throughout one's life. Without question, early literacy is critically important in children's lives. Developing the ability to decode accurately, read with fluency, and comprehend a variety of age-appropriate texts is vital to the literacy growth of young children. Yet literacy tasks and texts become increasingly more complex and difficult as children grow into adolescence.

Results from the 2002 National Assessment of Education Progress (NAEP), for example, indicate that about 25% of 8th- and 12th-grade students read at "below-basic" levels. That is to say, one in four adolescents are unable to understand informational passages, identify main ideas, or extend ideas in text. Moreover, there are significant achievement gaps in reading achievement between White adolescent students and minority students. No wonder that nearly 50% of students in high-poverty, urban areas leave school without graduating.

The imperative today is to teach adolescent literacy—and to teach it well. Let us face it, adolescent literacy is "hot"—so hot that even national, state, and local political leaders are taking notice as adolescent literacy initiatives swirl around Congress and state legislative branches of government. The possibilities, after all, for the uses of literacy in school and nonschool settings are unprecedented in adolescent lives. The timing of *Principled Practices in Adolescent Literacy: A Framework for Instruction and Policy* could not be better. This is a book that belongs in the hands of every teacher, curriculum leader, and policymaker who is deeply concerned with making a difference in the literate lives of adolescent learners. Not only do the authors identify key principles associated with adolescent literacy, but they also provide a summary of the evidence base for each principle, instructional vignettes based on observations of evidence-based practices in action in classrooms across the country, and carefully wrought, rich descriptions of principled practices.

I am proud of my colleagues for fighting the good fight on behalf of the literacy needs of older learners. As an adolescent literacy educator for nearly 40 years, I have witnessed many ups and downs related to what was then called *secondary reading instruction.* I am also mindful of the reality that what is hot in the literacy field often is not when the momentum shifts to the next best thing. I do not think that will be the case with adolescent literacy. This is a movement whose time has come. Books such as *Principled Practices in Adolescent Literacy: A Framework for Instruction and Policy* ensure that the legacy of adolescent literacy will endure for generations to come.

—*Richard T. Vacca, Emeritus Professor*
Kent State University

Preface

Adolescent literacy is suddenly a hot topic in North America. Presentations on the literacy needs of adolescents gather large audiences at educational conferences, publishers find a ready market for programs designed to solve adolescent literacy problems, and policymakers garner public approval by demonstrating an interest in reading for older learners.

Yet there is much that is not known about how to develop programs that will effectively support 6th through 12th graders in developing the advanced levels of literacy that will serve them throughout their lives. Although literacy for older learners has been studied since the early part of the 20th century, the research literature is difficult to interpret because studies span a wide range of disciplines and use varying research methodologies. In addition, published professional opinion on effective school practices, including those related to literacy for 6th to 12th graders, is frequently embedded in documents related to content areas, such as social studies, mathematics, or science, or in materials for teachers of special populations, such as students with disabilities or students who enter school with limited knowledge of English. Few individuals have the time or background to make sense of this diverse and diffuse knowledge base.

PURPOSE

This book takes a step toward filling this gap by providing educators, scholars, parents, and the general public with a bridge to the knowledge base on adolescent literacy. It emerges from a unique collaboration of 14 adolescent literacy scholars who worked together over 4 years. First, six of us met together in intensive work sessions for a year to synthesize evidence from research and professional opinion, including the work of the numerous professional organizations that have published national standards. We then involved eight other prominent adolescent literacy educators in a nationwide effort to locate middle and high school classrooms where excellent instruction was occurring. Together we made observations in 28 settings and developed the *Eight Guiding Principles* for adolescent literacy that appear in this book. These principles provide educators, parents, and the general public with a foundation for developing programs that support adolescent literacy within their own contexts.

IMPORTANT TEXT FEATURES

The book is divided into 11 chapters. Chapter 1 presents the *Eight Guiding Principles,* which are related to the contexts, instruction, and learning opportunities adolescents need to continue to grow in literacy during their middle and high school years. The *Principles* are broad enough to encompass a variety of contexts and student needs, yet specific enough to support those involved in program development or policy decisions. Chapter 1 also provides an explanation of the rationale for using *Guiding Principles* to develop a program that fits local needs.

The book continues with chapter 2—a review of the research base in adolescent literacy. This chapter also provides vignettes of youth in a variety of settings to draw the reader into a deeper understanding of adolescent characteristics and needs. It ends with questions for personal reflection or discussion.

Chapters 3 through 10 follow a similar pattern: First, one *Principle* is presented, along with a brief explanation of the research base for the *Principle* and a sample of national standards that support it. Next, each chapter moves to one or more extended case examples that provide readers with an indepth look at the *Principle* in action. These case examples span a wide variety of disciplines, grade levels, and local conditions. Finally, a well-known adolescent literacy expert provides a response to each case example. This response gives readers an informed view of the importance of the *Principle,* how it is enacted in the case or cases, and examples of other work that relates to the *Principle.* Following this expert response, readers are again provided with questions that can be used for individual reflection or group discussion.

Finally, chapter 11 addresses school structures that support adolescent literacy. This chapter emphasizes the idea that school-wide backing is needed to develop curriculum and instruction that effectively serves diverse adolescent learners. As in earlier chapters, chapter 11 also provides questions for personal reflection or discussion. This chapter is followed by the final sections of the book, which provide references and additional resources.

Acknowledgments

Numerous individuals have contributed to this project. First, we thank the educators in districts across the United States who welcomed us into their schools and classrooms as observers. We equally thank those who prefer to remain anonymous and those who allowed us to state their names. A list appears at the end of this section.

We also acknowledge the graduate assistants who provided support in various phases of the project and book development. In particular, we are indebted to George Hruby (formerly at the University of Georgia, currently a faculty member at Utah State University); Anna Safi, Kristine Calo, Grace Kim, and Kelley Christian (George Mason University); and Richard Gerber, Joo Young Lee, Natalya Vinogradova, Janka Szilagyi, and Debbie Ma (University at Buffalo–SUNY). We also thank Paul Sturtevant for the graphics in chapter 6.

Additionally, we wish to acknowledge the important contribution of Andrés Henriquez and the Carnegie Corporation of New York, who provided the financial and conceptual support that led to the development of the technical report on which this book is based. In addition, Barbara Gombach (Carnegie Corporation) offered ideas and feedback on early drafts of the technical report, Catherine Pino (Carnegie Corporation) put us in contact with district personnel in the Schools for a New Society initiative, Margaret Honey (Education Development Center, Inc.) put us in contact with schools in Union City, New Jersey, and Dan French (Center for Collaborative Education), Ellen Guiney (Boston Plan for Excellence), and Fred Carrig (Union City Board of Education) invited us into their districts for the purpose of observing firsthand some of the principled practices we include in this book. We also thank Evelyn Jacob and Joseph Maxwell (George Mason University), who served as research advisors, and Robert Jiménez (Vanderbilt University) and Ruth Schoenbach (WestEd), who provided valuable feedback on the original report.

We are also indebted to our editor and associate editor at Lawrence Erlbaum Associates, Naomi Silverman and Erica Kica. We thank them for encouraging us to move from the original project to development of this book and for guiding us through the publication process. We also thank our reviewers, including Nancy Guth, Stafford County Public Schools, and Richard T. Vacca, Kent State University.

Finally, we wish to thank the International Reading Association for having the foresight in 1997 to create the Commission on Adolescent Literacy. The Commission brought us and other colleagues together to collaborate on initiatives to improve the literacy and lives of adolescents; the result, including this book and a wide variety of other initiatives, has been far reaching.

SCHOOL-BASED EDUCATORS WHO PARTICIPATED

Educators from school districts in Arizona, Florida, Massachusetts, Michigan, New York, New Jersey, Virginia, Tennessee, and Nevada participated in this project. Those listed here granted permission to be personally identified.

Sarah Blanusa, Dorchester, MA
Val Bringle, Henderson, NV
Juanita Clay Chambers, Detroit, MI
Donna DeSioto, Syracuse, NY
Karen Engels, Boston, MA
Sonia Felix, Brighton, MA
Sarah Freedman, Boston, MA
Nancy Guth, Stafford, VA
Scott Harlan, Dorchester, MA
Joyce Harding, Boston, MA
Steve Kahill, Boston, MA
Denise Karpelenia, Las Vegas, NV
Ann Kennedy, Arlington, VA
Gwen Larson, Boston, MA
Cheryl Machac, Peoria, AZ
Richard Martin, Boston, MA

Michael A. McCarthy, Boston, MA
Constance Monastra, Woodbridge, VA
Ed Murphy, Glendale, AZ
Kathy Murphy, Boston, MA
Martin O'Brien, Boston, MA
Christina Patterson, Dorchester, MA
Deborah Peek-Brown, Detroit, MI
Stephanie Pettengill, Stafford, VA
Thana Vance, Fairfax, VA
Craig Whitley, Henderson, NV
Kim Wilson, Syracuse, NY

List of Figures

Chapter 1

Why Principled Practices?

Literacy is widely acknowledged as a powerful influence in the lives of youth. Adolescents who have strong and flexible reading, writing, and communication abilities are equipped with important tools for achieving their goals. In contrast, those who struggle to acquire the literacy skills required by schools, communities, and workplaces may find their options limited in our fast-paced technological society.

Despite the importance of ensuring high levels of literacy for adolescents, until quite recently most public discussions of reading and writing instruction have ignored the needs of this age group (Vacca & Alvermann, 1998). Although educators who work with adolescents have recognized since at least the 1920s that older learners have literacy needs (Moore, Readence, & Rickelman, 1983), it is still a common public impression that reading and writing instruction are—or should be—completed by Grade 3 or 4.

Research and reports of large-scale national assessments of reading progress, however, demonstrate the importance of providing well-designed literacy instruction for students throughout middle and high school. Recent studies (Alvermann, 2002; New London Group, 1996) show that literacy is complex, consisting of an array of abilities—or literacies—including reading, writing, and other forms of communication that must be developed and applied in a wide variety of content areas and contexts. When literacy is viewed as a tool for communicating and learning at advanced levels, the logic of providing environments and instruction that enhance adolescents' literacy development becomes obvious.

What is less obvious to educators, however, is how to develop effective adolescent literacy programs that will serve the needs of a diverse range of students in any school or district. Educational publishers offer dozens of text-books and programs with widely varying approaches, while educational journals often provide suggestions for specific teaching strategies or lessons. State and federal mandates may require adherence to "scientifically proven" approaches. Yet comprehensive guidelines that provide adequate support for making curricular decisions about adolescent literacy programs are not readily available. This book, based on a project that explored adolescent literacy instruction in depth, was developed to provide support for teachers and other educators who are designing adolescent literacy programs to meet the needs of learners in their own schools and districts.

HISTORY OF THE PROJECT

The collaboration on which this book is based began in 1997. At that time, the International Reading Association established the Commission on Adolescent Literacy, with the goal of focusing increased national and local attention on the literacy needs of adolescent learners. Under the leadership of Richard Vacca (Kent State University) and Donna Alvermann (University of Georgia), approximately 30 school- and university-based adolescent literacy educators from across the United States and Canada began meetings and e-mail discussions. This collaboration, which eventually extended over 8 years, resulted in numerous publications, a Web site, educational forums held in several cities throughout the United States and Canada, conference institutes, and, perhaps most notably, a widely circulated position statement related to the types of instruction adolescents need ("Adolescent Literacy: A Position Statement" at http://www.reading.org/resources/issues/positions_adolescent.html).

After the Position Statement was published (Moore, Bean, Birdyshaw, & Rycik, 1999), the research subcommittee of the Commission on Adolescent Literacy decided it was essential to take the concepts it presented a few steps further. The Commission had received many questions about curriculum and program development across various contexts and disciplinary areas. Although the Position Statement was very helpful in providing a general overview of the most important issues, teachers and administrators indicated a need for more specific and elaborated information related to evidence-supported practices. Staff developers and teacher educators were also asking for case examples or illustrations that would provide a sense of what an exemplary literacy program for adolescents might look like in a particular context. They believed this was especially important for content area teachers in middle and high schools because most teachers had never experienced a curriculum that would support adolescent literacy development in their own secondary school years or during their student teaching experiences.

Subsequent to the publication of the Position Statement and after learning the need for more specific information, the six authors of this book undertook a 1-year project to review three types of evidence related to instruction that would enhance adolescent literacy: the research on adolescent literacy across several fields (such as literacy, special education, content area instruction, and bilingual education), expert opinion from major education organizations in a variety of disciplines, and observations in the classrooms of highly regarded teachers in a variety of contexts. We received financial support from both the Carnegie Corporation of New York and the universities where we worked at the time of the project (George Mason University, University at Buffalo-SUNY, University of Tennessee, Syracuse University, Arizona State University-West, and the University of Georgia).

Our goal in reviewing the evidence related to adolescent literacy was to identify principles that would assist educators in developing effective curricula to meet the needs of diverse adolescent learners. We emphasize that our goal was not to find the "one best way" or to develop a "program" that schools could purchase and put into place irrespective of local conditions. We concur with the International Reading Association's (2002) *Position Statement on Evidence-Based Instruction* that ". . . there is no single instructional program or method that is effective in teaching all children to read. Rather, successful efforts . . . emphasize identification and implementation of evidence-based practices" (p. 2).

In adopting the concept of *principled practices* (Smagorinsky, 2002), we sought to move away from a "one-size-fits-all" model of instruction, preferring instead to focus on what teachers and schools can expect to accomplish given the evidence that is available as well as their particular circumstances and available resources. We chose the notion of principled practices to undergird our work because of our strong belief that educators and others participating in curricular decisions should be supported in their efforts to plan excellent adolescent literacy programs specific to their own contexts.

After studying the evidence related to adolescent literacy, we developed eight principles that can be used as guidelines when designing programs. The principles describe what students in middle and high school classes are able to do when their teachers implement instruction that appropriately supports their literacy and learning development (see Fig. 1.1).

Principled Practices for Adolescent Literacy: A Framework for Instruction and Policy provides background, support, and further explanation for the eight principles. Following this introductory chapter, chapter 2 provides an overview of the research on adolescent literacy. Chapters 3 through 10 offer a unique structure designed to engage readers in small- or whole-group discussions. These chapters, each featuring one of the eight principles, begin with an explanation of the featured principle as well as specific evidence

Principles related to contexts for learning:
1. Adolescents need opportunities to participate in active learning environments that offer clear and facilitative literacy instruction.
2. Adolescents need opportunities to participate in respectful environments characterized by high expectations, trust, and care.

Principles related to instructional practices:
3. Adolescents need opportunities to engage with print and nonprint texts for a variety of purposes.
4. Adolescents need opportunities to generate and express rich understandings of ideas and concepts.
5. Adolescents need opportunities to demonstrate enthusiasm for reading and learning.
6. Adolescents need opportunities to assess their literacy and learning competencies, and direct their future growth.

Principles related to connections between literacy in and out of school:
7. Adolescents need opportunities to connect reading with their life and their learning inside and outside of school.
8. Adolescents need opportunities to develop critical perspectives toward what they read, view, and hear.

FIG. 1.1.   Principled practices seen in instructional settings that support adolescent literacy growth.

that supports the principle from the research literature and content-related professional organizations. Each chapter also includes one or more case scenarios based on observations in classrooms in middle and high schools in different parts of the United States. We use these because, as Seidman (1998) noted, narratives can be "tool[s] for understanding complex issues" (p. 102). Some of the cases specifically illustrate the work of a particular teacher, whereas other cases represent composites of teachers with whom the authors have worked in the past.

Directly after the case scenarios in each chapter, a reflection related to the featured principle is presented. The eight reflections are written by adolescent literacy experts who are well known for scholarship in the field. These eight experts were not part of the author team, but participated as consultants to the Carnegie-supported project. Their responses provide additional perspectives on adolescent literacy issues based on their own extensive research and experience. Following each expert's reflection, several discussion questions are provided with each chapter.

The last chapter of the book (chap. 11) changes course and presents information on structures, which, if in place at the school and district levels, should provide needed support in implementing the eight principles. Finally, the appendixes contain information on useful Web sites as well as other resources.

In summary, *Principled Practices for Adolescent Literacy: A Framework for Instruction and Policy* is a call to reform without simple quick fixes or prescriptions. It avoids injunctions that demand certain behaviors of teachers and administrators. It neither critiques nor endorses any particular program or method. Instead, it advocates on behalf of upper grades literacy reform by presenting a realistic interpretation of the evidence in the research literature, work of multiple content area organizations, and observations of classrooms.

This book is intended for anyone who is concerned about adolescents' literacy needs—teachers, families, administrators, policymakers, community members, or adolescents. You may be new to the issues presented here, or, like members of our author and consultant teams, you may already have spent a career considering the needs of adolescent learners. Either way, we hope you find this work useful as you discuss and plan actions you can take in your own classroom, community, or beyond to meet the literacy needs of adolescent learners.

Chapter 2

Research on Youth's Literacy Development: An Overview

Morgan and her friend, Jacqui, throw backpacks and gym bags into the car waiting outside the school doors. They climb into the back seat, talking about the game they'd just won for their high school volleyball team. Teammates, honor society members, and friends since seventh grade, they are now seniors.

Jacqui is dropped off at her apartment after practice each day by Morgan's mother, who picks the girls up on her way home from work. She enters the front door and is attacked affectionately by a much younger brother and sister who have been waiting for her. She goes to the kitchen and begins to prepare a simple supper of hot dogs and canned beans. Her mother arrives home at 8 p.m. from a second job, eats, helps Jacqui wash the dishes, and collapses into a living room chair. Jacqui puts her brother and sister to bed and returns to the kitchen, sitting at the kitchen table and doing homework until 11. She glances at the application to the local community college on the top of her homework pile and sighs, too tired, again, to figure it out. She goes to bed.

Morgan arrives home with her mother and checks the mail pile for thick envelopes to indicate her acceptance into yet another college. She sits down to a dinner of fish, salad, and brown rice that was prepared by her father, a teacher who arrives home at 4 p.m. She puts her practice clothes in the washing machine and goes to her room, turning on her computer to finish homework. She sends an instant message to an older brother who is away at college and another to a boyfriend before settling down to work as her parents put dishes into the dishwater and watch TV in another room. Soft music plays in the background as she works.

Morgan and Jacqui will soon be graduating from high school. Morgan, who is not sure what she wants to major in, has always believed that she would go to college and, with the help of an application consultant, has so far been accepted at three schools, although none yet is her first choice. Her parents set up a college savings plan for her at her birth to which they have regularly been contributing.

> *Jacqui wants to be a lawyer, and her single mother's limited income means that she likely qualifies for generous financial aid. But she has not been exactly sure how to choose a school or apply. No one in her family has experience that might help her to figure some of these things out, while her high school guidance counselor is responsible for advising over a hundred students. She and her mother do not understand financial aid packages, but they think she can afford the local community college if she works a part-time job at the same time.*

The preceding fictitious youth, Morgan and Jacqui, are complex individuals who participate a bit more in the larger society with each passing year. The ways in which they will participate across their lifetimes are not predetermined. Yet inherent, environmental, and accrued factors converge in unique combinations to influence their development and opportunity over their life spans. Consider the differences in opportunities that appear available to Morgan and Jacqui, as well as for other youth who may have greater interest in more marginalized activities not endorsed by school.

Today's young people are often critiqued on all fronts. Complicated individuals with much life experience and expertise, they are often trivialized as "not yet adults," "at an awkward stage that will soon pass," "egocentric," or "irresponsible." As it does for all of us, the world around our youth transforms in rapid and complex ways relative to who they are and how they see themselves. Like all of us, they are faced with a series of tremendous and ongoing physiological, cognitive, emotional, and social challenges. When they are lucky, young people are supported through these challenges with the caring and wisdom of others in their community as they assume increasing responsibilities within this community.

Unfortunately, schools in the United States have not always recognized and made use of the very real but widely disparate abilities of our nation's adolescents. Their diversity, the result of individual differences and life trajectories, as well as community differences and cultural backgrounds, are too often seen as liabilities rather than the helpful opportunities for education that they can be. Despite a growing body of scholarship on the intellectual, emotional, and social worlds of teenagers (e.g., Alvermann, Hinchman, Moore, Phelps, & Waff, 1998; Larson, Richards, & Moneta, 1996; Lesko, 2000), most schools have not employed the curricula and instructional methods this work suggests.

The purpose of this chapter is to provide an overview of what research suggests about literacy instruction in schools serving students in Grades 6 to 12. This research supports literacy development using a comprehensive approach—one that includes both teacher-directed and student-centered instruction and makes use of a variety of specialists and support personnel. Its success is marked by a school culture that cares about its students and expects them to do well.

RESEARCH ON PREADOLESCENT
AND ADOLESCENT LITERACY

Educators of young adolescent students are struggling to meet the literacy needs of learners who, by the time they reach the intermediate grades, are faced with increasingly difficult texts as well as greater content learning expectations. Even students who were successful readers in the early grades may experience difficulty during this period of time commonly referred to as the *fourth-grade slump* (Snow, 2002). They may become discouraged during this period and begin to do less well academically (Kos, 1991; McCray, Vaughn, & Neal, 2001). Unless addressed consistently through efforts of schools and families, this dip in academic achievement can lead to disastrous consequences, especially at the high school level when students may choose to leave school. The situation is especially serious for students who may have struggled with reading as young children or who are learning English at the same time they are required to master the content of their subject matter classes (G. E. Garcia, 2000).

Although a recent administration of the National Assessment of Educational Progress (Education, 2002; *USDOE,* 2002) finds that a majority of upper elementary and middle-school students are able to decode words that follow predictable spelling patterns and answer factual-level questions about simple passages, far fewer students have reached the proficient or advanced levels of reading that are necessary for comprehension of complex subject-matter texts. There is also concern that middle-school students may not possess adequate knowledge of content subjects such as U.S. history. Data reported in *The Nation's Report Card: U.S. History 2001* revealed that less than 20% of middle-school students comprehend at or above the proficient level, and there remain significant achievement differences favoring nonminority over minority students, students in rural and suburban schools over those in urban schools, and students from higher income over lower income homes (Lapp, Grigg, & Tay-Lim, 2002).

The research literature that addresses the perceived gap between basic and more advanced levels of reading development among preadolescents and adolescents is generally focused on comprehension, inquiry, and discussion. Another body of research looks at students' motivation, self-efficacy, and identity construction in learning from and with text. A third research area focuses on contexts of literacy instruction, and a fourth on students' use of multiple literacies both in and out of school.

Each of these areas is discussed next, with particular attention given to research that has been compiled and published in the *Handbook of Reading Research: Volume 2* (Barr, Kamil, Mosenthal, & Pearson, 1991), *Handbook of Reading Research: Volume 3* (Kamil, Mosenthal, Pearson, & Barr, 2000), the *Report of the National Reading Panel* (2000b), the RAND Reading Study

Group's *Reading for Understanding* (Snow, 2002), *Reading Next: A Vision for Action and Research in Middle and High School Literacy* (Biancarosa & Snow, 2004), *Adolescent Literacy Research and Practice* (Jetton & Dole, 2004), and *Bridging the Literacy Achievement Gap, Grades 4–12* (Strickland & Alvermann, 2004). This research is reviewed to provide empirical support for the eight principles described in this text, *Principled Practices for a Literate America: A Framework for Literacy and Learning in the Upper-Grades,* and the practices they engender, as captured in the classroom vignettes in the chapters that follow.

Text Comprehension, Inquiry, and Discussion

> Mikel is a sixth grader who is well loved by teachers and administrators at his school. He is outgoing, not afraid to ask questions. His class is presently engaged in the study of the Great Plains region of the United States. Students are previewing the day's reading selection as the teacher explains the importance of such anticipation to comprehension.
>
> Mikel is focused on the teacher-led comprehension mini-lesson, but his furrowed brow indicates that he does not understand the discussion. He raises his hand and asks, "But how do they get all those farms onto the plains?" He does not understand what a "plain" is in this context, his listening ears confusing "plane" and "plain," betraying a lack of exposure to the latter term. Luckily, he is motivated and outgoing enough to ask a question that allows a caring teacher to help him adjust his understanding. Sadly, many children are not so outgoing. Perhaps they do not participate in classrooms that encourage asking such questions or that provide opportunities for inquiry learning. Even more basically, they are not taught the technical meanings of words that can unlock content learning in their disciplinary subjects.[1]

The preceding anecdote connects vocabulary understanding to comprehension. It hints of the importance of sensitivity to students' backgrounds, existing insights, and motivation for learning. It advocates an instructional context within which students can talk out their understandings with others, get feedback on what they say, and modify insights accordingly. These connections between comprehension growth and variables such as vocabulary development, background knowledge, and opportunities to inquire and get feedback through class discussion are well documented in the literature. Although instruction in decoding multisyllabic words and other word study techniques is important, most of the research that has been conducted on these elements of comprehension instruction has focused on the early grade levels, so it is less helpful for this review. What is known from re-

---

[1] Kathy would like to thank her colleague, Mary Ann Zelinski, for sharing the plane/plain anecdote from her urban teaching experiences.

search at the secondary school level is the importance of motivating and showing students how to comprehend the texts they are assigned to read as part of the regular curriculum (Guthrie & Humenick, 2004; Hinchman, Alvermann, Boyd, Brozo, & Vacca, 2004).

According to the RAND Reading Study Group (Snow, 2002), a great deal is known about the prerequisites for successful reading comprehension, including comprehension at more advanced levels. For example, drawing on the work of numerous literacy researchers and the *Report of the National Reading Panel* (2000), commissioned by the U.S. Congress to assess the availability of evidence-based research on reading instruction for classroom application, the RAND Group concluded that:

- Effective reading instruction provides students with a repertoire of strategies for fostering comprehension.
- Strategy instruction that is embedded within subject-matter learning, such as history or science, improves students' reading comprehension.
- Effective strategies for teaching students to comprehend complex materials include self-questioning, comprehension monitoring, representing information using graphic organizers, making use of different text structures, and summarizing.
- The more explicit teachers are in their strategy instruction, the more successful low-achieving students are in their reading and learning.
- Vocabulary knowledge is strongly related to successful text comprehension, and it is especially important in teaching English-language learners.
- Exposing students to various genres of text (e.g., informational, narrative, poetry) ensures that they do not approach all reading tasks with the same purpose in mind.

Inquiry-oriented comprehension instruction provides students with opportunities to critique and discuss information gained through interacting with texts of many kinds (e.g., print, visual, audio, digital). For example, using an experimental posttest-only design (Ghaith, 2003) found statistically significant differences favoring the experimental group that was provided comprehension instruction in think-alouds that taught students to read critically. Echevarria (2003) examined secondary-level students' knowledge construction and scientific reasoning when presented with anomalies found in simulation software on Mendelian genetics. Qualitative and quantitative data analyses showed a significant shift in students' mental models of dominant trait transmission at the end of the 3-week inquiry unit. Applebee et al. (2003) conducted a year-long naturalistic, classroom observation study of 64 middle- and high school English classes in 19 schools located in five states. Using a series of hierarchical linear models, Applebee and his colleagues found that discussion-based approaches were effective (controlling for fall performance and other background variables) across a range of teaching situations for both low- and high-achieving students. Like Applebee et al., Greenleaf and her colleagues studied the effects of academic literacy instruction in natural settings. Their year-long study of an urban, culturally diverse ninth-grade class revealed that explicit instruction in Reciprocal Teaching, think-alouds, sustained silent reading (SSR), note-taking strategies, graphic organizing, identifying text structure, and vocabulary strategies led to significant gains on a nationally normed assessment called the *Degrees of Reading Power* (DRP). Students started the year at late seventh grade on the DRP and finished at late ninth grade (a gain of 2 years' growth in reading proficiency in only 7 months).

The research on comprehension, inquiry learning, and discussion tells only one part of the story of how students learn in the content areas. There is also ample evidence to suggest that understanding students' motivations to read (including their sense of self-efficacy in certain reading tasks), plus being attentive to the types of identities they construct for themselves as readers, are other important pieces of the story.

Motivation, Self-Efficacy, and Identity Construction

Donna recently worked with a young man named Grady, an African American boy in the ninth grade who was reading at the fifth-grade level and wrote about his participation in an after-school media club in the *Journal of Adolescent and Adult Literacy* (Alvermann, 2001b). Donna described the insights she was able to gain from observing how Grady's self-esteem was tied to purposeful literacy pursuits:

> My earlier assumption that Grady would go to great lengths to avoid any activity involving reading proved wrong. We [Margaret Hagood and I] observed him reading and responding to our e-mail messages about his club project. Using e-mail, he also began to write freely about his frustration with Metal Gear and his growing interest in Pokémon. This new interest came as a surprise to both Margaret and me, for although we knew very little about Pokémon we had assumed that it appealed primarily to kids much younger than Grady. Also, we noted that beyond offering players the option of advancing to different levels of proficiency, Pokémon and Metal Gear seemed to have little in common. Whereas Metal Gear carried the "Parental Advisory" warning label (a point I had discussed with Grady's father at the time I purchased the game), Pokémon featured characters that simply fainted in battle—only to regain consciousness at the hands of skillful players, or trainers, as they are called in Pokémon.

Grady was to become just such a trainer. . . . He was glad to have the Pokémon book over Thanksgiving break because he was able, in his words, "to get ahead." He explained that the way he used the book was to read something that interested him (e.g., a special move or training skill) and then try it out. During club meetings when we observed Grady playing Pokémon, he appeared to use the Pokémon book as a source of reference. When he got stuck, he would put the game on pause and turn to an appropriate page in the book for help. After finding the information he needed, he would close the book and go back to the game. (Alvermann, 2001b, pp. 685–686)

During adolescence, as well as later in life, it is the belief in the self (or lack of such belief) that makes a difference in how competent a person feels. Grady came to feel quite competent within Donna's after-school media club, and we can theorize regarding how such competence might be extended to self-efficacy in academic tasks.

Although the terms *self-concept* and *self-efficacy* are sometimes used interchangeably in the research literature, they actually refer to different constructs. For example, an adolescent boy may have a good self-concept of himself as a reader, but his answer "Not very" to the question "How confident are you that you can solve a word problem using algebraic expressions?" would indicate low self-efficacy for that particular task. A statement of self-concept is domain-specific, whereas self-efficacy is task-specific. Moreover, the two constructs need not relate to one another. For instance, an adolescent girl may feel highly efficacious in an American Literature class, yet experience few if any positive feelings of self-worth partially due to the fact she may not value excelling in that subject area (Pajares, 1996).

Perceptions of self-efficacy are central to most theories of motivation, and the research bears out the hypothesized connections. For example, providing students who are experiencing reading difficulties with clear goals for a comprehension task and then giving feedback on the progress they are making can lead to increased self-efficacy and greater use of comprehension strategies (Schunk & Rice, 1993). As well, creating technology environments that heighten students' motivation to become independent readers and writers can increase their sense of competency (Kamil, Intrator, & Kim, 2000). The research is less clear, however, on the shifts that occur in students' motivation to read over time. Although decreases in intrinsic reading motivation have been noted as children move from the elementary grades to middle school, explanations vary as to the cause, with a number of researchers attributing the decline to differences in instructional practices (Eccles, Wigfield, & Schiefele, 1998).

In an extensive review of how instruction influences students' reading engagement and academic performance, Guthrie and Wigfield (2000) concluded that various instructional practices, although important, do not directly impact student outcomes (e.g., time spent reading independently, achievement on standardized tests, performance assessments, and beliefs about reading). Instead, the level of student engagement (including its sustainability over time) is the mediating factor, or avenue, through which classroom instruction influences student outcomes. Guthrie and Wigfield's conception of the engagement model of reading calls for instruction that fosters student motivation (including self-efficacy and goal setting), strategy use (e.g., using prior knowledge, self-monitoring for breaks in comprehension, and analyzing new vocabulary), growth in conceptual knowledge (e.g., reading trade books to supplement textbook information, viewing videos, and hands-on experiences), and social interaction (e.g., collaborating with peers on a science project and discussing an Internet search with the teacher).

Perhaps one of the best-known studies for helping struggling readers to construct positive identities for themselves as learners is Carol Lee's (1997) cultural modeling project. In an empirical study framed within a culturally based cognitive apprenticeship, Lee tested her theory of how to teach literature to students who struggle to read texts that are part of what is known as *the canon.* On temporary leave from her faculty position at Northwestern University, Lee taught ninth graders in an inner-city Chicago high school how to use what they knew about their everyday language—the language with which they identified—to comprehend texts that heretofore had been inaccessible to them. She accomplished this by combining her deep understanding of how English literature is structured with her appreciation for her students' cultural knowledge. Specifically, Lee used signifying, which is a form of talk widely practiced within the African American Vernacular English (AAVE) speech community, to scaffold or facilitate her underachieving high school students' literary responses to the mainstream canon. Although signifying is valued for language play in its own right, Lee used her students' tacit knowledge of their everyday discourse and the culture with which they identified to help them hypothesize the meanings of various tropes, ironies, and satires found within the school curriculum's canonical texts. By the end of the year, her students demonstrated statistically significant gains in reading achievement when compared with a control group (C. D. Lee, 1995). This study as well as Hynd, Holschuh, and Hubbard's (in press) research on helping students think like historians provide evidence of the importance of building on students' ability to identify with the content they are expected to learn. In a similar vein, the work of Vyas (2004) and Moje and Hinchman (2004) attests to the importance of studying how students construct their identities so that literacy instruction can be made culturally responsive. As important as identity construction is in teaching all students, there is research to suggest that it alone is not sufficient for turning students into life-long readers and learners. For that to happen, educators must give equal attention to the contexts in which students become literate learners.

Contexts for Literacy Instruction

Dante and Joseph are Spanish-speaking English-language learners in a seventh-grade mathematics class that is reviewing how to calculate percentages
as they explore the value of sales tax to their community. They begin their
unit of study with a teacher-led mini-lesson that explains the calculations one
needs to determine how much a visit to a restaurant will cost, including how
to calculate the percentages needed to determine tax and tip. The teacher is
not bilingual, but the boys listen to her explanation and then turn to one another to work as a Spanish-speaking pair to complete a restaurant simulation
in which they estimate total, tax, and tip for what they wish to order to be sure
they have enough money to pay the bill. They discuss how much to tip and
whether and why tips and taxes are needed before setting up a proportion to
determine the needed percentages and reaching their conclusions about
what to order.

After this, Dante and Joseph participate in an English class discussion
about the relative value of taxes and tips given the cost of such meals, listing
pros and cons for each. In connection with a social studies class, they move on
to a study of state legislation and local newspaper accounts regarding merits
of state and local sales taxes so that they can present an argument regarding
their value to the class as well as see the value of percentages to these calculations. They and other class members participate in an organized debate, inviting local legislative aides to ask questions and critique their efforts.

Inspired by Kathy's observation of colleague Debbie Walker's seventh-
grade mathematics class, Dante and Joseph's story suggests what can happen when two young men learn to apply what they are learning in mathematics class to situations they will encounter throughout their lives. The research literature shows that when school systems make a concerted effort—
one that involves teachers, students, parents, and community leaders—the
nature of the schooling process can change dramatically. For example, data
from work conducted as part of the Coalition of Essential Schools (Sizer,
1996) and case studies of elementary and high schools engaged in reform
efforts that explore the personalization of instruction, student engagement, and ongoing holistic assessment (Darling-Hammond, Ancess, & Falk,
1995) suggest that it is possible to reform schools given an appropriate set
of initiatives and a targeted focus.

Other successful reform efforts include the work of a national teacher-
researcher network of English and social studies teachers and university faculty (Freedman, Simons, Kalnin, Casareno, & Teams, 1999). This network
focused its reform efforts on classroom-based research related to learning,
diversity, bias, and inequality. Efforts led by individuals working without the
benefit of a network have also resulted in schoolwide reform. Meier (1995),
working alone and within her own high school, championed the achieve-

ments of urban youth and families by advocating radical innovations in the public schooling process.

In a synthesis of the qualitative research on adolescent literacy instruction, Moore (1996) showed that (a) the type of strategy taught is less important than the nature of the context in which it is taught, and (b) engaging students in cooperative learning activities is conducive to subject-matter learning. Not surprisingly, the RAND Group (Snow, 2002) found similar support for these practices in the experimental and quasi-experimental research literature on comprehension instruction. Teachers working within contexts that are conducive to learning provide students with adequate background information and relevant hands-on experience as a way of preparing them to read a textbook, view a video, or listen to a tape on content particular to their subject areas (Alexander & Jetton, 2000). They also look for ways to integrate reading and writing because they know that each process reinforces the other and can lead to improved comprehension and retention of subject area content (Tierney & Shanahan, 1991).

Multiple Literacies

In a recent study published in Reading Research Quarterly, Kelly Chandler-Olcott and Donna Mahar told the story of Rhiannon, a 13-year-old young woman who created numerous Web sites on the Japanese animated film characters known as anime. Chandler-Olcott and Mahar (2003b) wrote:

> Rhiannon's anime fandom provided her with raw material—visual, linguistic, spatial Designs of meaning—for her online composition. It also provided her with what activity theorists call an object or purpose for that authorship: in this case, to communicate with and connect to other WebTV-using anime fans. To that end, her websites featured various fan-related elements where, for example, visitors could comment on which anime characters they most admired or download images from picture galleries of "bishonen" (a Japanese term anime fans use to refer to male characters they find physically attractive). Several sites also featured fanfictions (i.e., episodic stories Rhiannon wrote using characters and settings from favorite cartoons and video games).
>
> Because these stories incorporated material from existing media texts, they made the intertextuality of Rhiannon's writing clearly visible. In fact, readers' ability to construct meaning from [Rhiannon's] fanfictions depended on having a certain level of familiarity with the anime texts that inspired them, because Rhiannon rarely gave much attention to setting, character descriptions, or back story. Melding characteristics of various genres, including fantasy, science fiction, "teen buddy" movies, and romance, Rhiannon's writings also provided good examples of "hybridity," the New London Group's (1995) term referring to the creation of new meanings and new genres through Designing. (p. 371)

That Rhiannon demonstrated a wealth of reading and writing competence was evident in Chandler-Olcott and Mahar's rich qualitative analysis of her literacy practices. Street (1995) was among the first to theorize that individuals, like Rhiannon, develop multiple literacies suited to the varied texts of our complex social lives. Such literacies include reading, writing, speaking, listening, and other performative acts, allowing us to produce and respond to the host of texts we encounter each day. The New London Group used the term *multiliteracies* "as a way to focus on the realities of increasing local diversity and global connectedness" (p. 64). They continued,

> Dealing with linguistic differences and cultural differences has now become central to the pragmatics of our working, civic, and primate lives. Effective citizenship and productive work now require that we interact effectively using multiple languages, multiple Englishes, and communication pattern as that more frequently cross cultural, community, and national boundaries. Subcultural diversity also extends to the ever broadening range of specialist registers and situational variations in language, be they technical, sporting, or related to groupings of interest and affiliation. (p. 64)

The New London Group theorized that we develop multiliteracies to communicate in such complex and competing worlds. We shape and are shaped by the processes involved in acquitting and using discourses specific to our varied, overlapping, social affiliations, including those tied to gender, race, class, academic discipline, neighborhood, and other affinity groups.

In addition to Chandler-Olcott and Mahar's description of middle-school girls' tech savviness, a variety of qualitative researchers have taken stances toward exploring the manner in which youth manifest multiple literacies in and out of school. Examples include Hagood (2000), who theorized that youth bring many literacies, developed outside school, with them to their classrooms; Blackburn (2003), who explored the ways Queer youth read and wrote to both challenge and reinforce power relations evident in their worlds; Leander (2002), who described how one youth came to be viewed as "ghetto" by others who constructed identity artifacts that stabilized in practice across space and over time; and Schultz (2002), who studied youth's in- and out-of-school writing practices, arguing that, "When teachers take their experience with students in the classroom as the sum of their knowledge of students' interests and abilities, they are taking a narrow slice of students' lives and treating it as the whole" (p. 356).

The New London Group recommended that the "what" of pedagogy to promote multiple literacies would include a focus on design of new and hybrid literacy practices suited to our increasingly global purposes. The "how" of such teaching would necessitate situated practice, overt instruction, critical framing, and transformed practice. Researchers have begun to explore such notions, proposing a host of theoretical constructs to explain youths' multiple literacy practices. Moje and her colleagues (2004) orchestrated scientific inquiry and related literacy tasks anchored in urban middle-school youths' funds of knowledge. Rex (2001) explored the co-construction of a reading culture to support one youth's efforts to come to see himself as a reader. Rush (2004) detailed her use of Freebody and Luke's (1990) Four Resources Model to enhance youths' development of multiple literacies in a summer intervention program.

Teachers create effective contexts for literacy learning when they provide students with opportunities to weave their own experiences, feelings, and interests into various learning activities. Through hypermedia projects, peer-led discussions, and journal writing, adolescents find ways to make textbook reading and studying less dry or boring. At the same time, teachers learn from student-generated texts about preadolescents' and adolescents' everyday literacies and the competencies they exhibit when reading, talking, and writing about things that matter to them (Alvermann, 2001a; Bean, 2000; Knobel, 1998; Wade & Moje, 2000).

SUMMARY

Although much is known about effective literacy instruction, the challenge lies in implementing this research base in ways that make sense to busy administrators and that meet the needs of teachers and students. This is no small matter. In fact, remarking on the gravity of the challenge, members of the RAND Group (Snow, 2002) noted that, despite a fairly well-articulated knowledge base on the value of strategy instruction that fosters reading comprehension, such instruction continues to receive too little time and attention in typical subject-matter classrooms. In addition to helping students read strategically, teachers need to consider students' perceptions of their competencies as readers and writers, their level of motivation and background knowledge, and their interests. To be effective, content literacy instruction must be embedded in the regular curriculum and make use of multiple forms of texts read for multiple purposes in a variety of contexts. It must also take into account preadolescents' and adolescents' everyday literacies in ways that enable them to engage actively in meaningful projects that both extend and elaborate on academic literacy.

This book is organized to help readers understand empirically supported principles of practice that can be used to address literacy concerns in today's urban schools. Following are chapters that illustrate and discuss each principle.

Discussion Questions

Reflect on your own reading and learning during adolescence and today as you consider the information presented in this chapter.

1. What types of materials or texts did you prefer as an adolescent? Did this change for you in adulthood? Why or why not?

2. What did your middle- and high school teachers do to encourage literacy? Could they have done more? How?

3. What types of literacies (uses of reading, writing, and other forms of communications) do you believe are most important for adolescents? Why?

4. Do you think the literacy needs of adolescents have changed since you were a teenager? Why or why not?

Chapter 3

Principle 1: Adolescents Need Opportunities to Participate in Active Learning Environments That Offer Clear and Facilitative Literacy Instruction

This principle relates to the overall environment that best supports adolescents' literacy and learning. Active learning environments are those in which students participate as players rather than as spectators (Hinchman et al., 2004). In active classrooms, talk is distributed among class members rather than centralized in the teacher. Dialogue among students and between students and the teacher is encouraged. Class members engage in various types of discussion, such as those involving partners, small groups, or the whole class. In addition, thoughtful questions—often questions with more than one right answer—are posed and answered by both teachers and students (e.g., Kuncan & Beck, 1997). This type of environment stands in contrast to a teacher-centered environment, in which a teacher lectures or conducts a recitation and students are called on to answer oral, testlike questions (Vacca & Vacca, 2004).

Within an active learning environment, literacy instruction can take on a variety of forms. All teachers will continuously assess student needs and provide clear and specific lessons that build student competence as readers, writers, and learners (Sweet & Snow, 2002). For content area teachers, the competencies addressed in these lessons will generally relate to students' uses of literacy within a particular discipline. For example, a history teacher may conduct a mini-lesson, or short lesson, on how to take notes during reading as part of a continuing plan to increase students' comprehension of history materials. A mathematics teacher might provide modeling and specific guidance on how to interpret word problems or vocabulary specific to statistics. An English teacher might help students improve their comprehension of literature by teaching them to create graphic organizers related to story structure. Teachers working with students with special needs in literacy might provide individualized or small-group instruction in word recognition or vocabulary development. These teachers also could help students develop techniques for learning new vocabulary in a variety of subject areas.

Within an active learning environment, teachers can facilitate literacy development and learning through assignments that require students to use their literacy in a wide variety of ways (Hynd, 1999). For example, students might use reading, writing, and other communication skills in a collaborative mathematics and science project in which they study the causes and effects of pollution in a local stream. During such a project, students might read scientific and newspaper articles on water pollution, take measurements using scientific instruments, make mathematical calculations tracking change in pollution over time, create charts and graphs, take notes on observations, participate in discussions and debates, and write reports. Such a project could also be easily linked to other disciplines, such English, social studies, technology, health, and the arts through the inclusion of texts, questions, and assignments related to those areas.

Overall, students' active participation in the school curriculum across all of their subject areas will tend to increase their uses of literacy and their development of multiple forms of literacy (or *literacies*; Alvermann et al., 1998). Their active participation is important in classes, in co-curricular or extracurricular activities, and in opportunities to link learning at school to learning outside of school (Alvermann, 1998). In all of these venues, adolescents can use reading, writing, and communication in ways that enhance their own learning as well as their active participation in school and life activities (Moje, Young, Readence, & Moore, 2000).

In national standards documents and other position statements of professional organizations, we find that educators across many disciplines concur with this principle. The National Council of the Social Studies (1994), for example, advocated that teachers should facilitate communication by "plan[ning] sequences of questions that allow for numerous responses and stimulate reflective discussion" (p. 168). Teachers of English for Speakers of Other Languages (2001) encouraged teachers to help students "use appropriate learning strategies to construct and apply academic knowledge" (Goal 2, Statement 3, Paragraph 1). The International Reading Association, in its Position Statement on Adolescent Literacy, asserted that adolescents "deserve expert teachers who model and provide explicit instruction in reading comprehension and study strategies across the curriculum" (Moore et al., 1999). Across these and other disciplines, educators have found that adolescents' learning and literacy are enhanced when they are given opportunities to participate in active learning environments that include specific attention to their strengths and needs.

We now turn to a extended vignette that further illustrates this principle.

VIGNETTE 1: SEVENTH-GRADE STUDY:
OUR COASTAL REGION

Susan Fleener teaches seventh-grade environmental science at Eagle's Nest Middle School. Eagle's Nest is located in a town near the Atlantic coast, where many community members are involved in occupations related to the fishing industry or tourism. The community is also home to military families stationed at Navy and Marine bases in the area. The school is about 3 miles from the oceanfront. A large salt marsh, or wetland, extends for many miles near the coast and is within walking distance of the school. Although much of the salt marsh is protected as a national wildlife area, there are few restrictions on building in areas near the marsh. Waterfront vacation homes, hotels, rural homes and small farms, a new development of suburban homes, two small strip shopping malls, and a golf course are all located within the school's attendance area.

Recently, the community has experienced a sudden expansion in the building of vacation and permanent residences due to a drop in real estate interest rates. This has caused the school population to grow and has also raised concerns about the environmental impact of the new construction on the wetlands. Concern heightened 2 months ago when a large chain department store applied for permission to build a store near the marsh. The town council has been considering this proposal for several weeks.

Students at Eagle's Nest come from a wide range of home backgrounds and income levels. However, a commonality is their familiarity with and knowledge about the shore area. For some, this knowledge has resulted from long hours spent on fishing boats helping their parents earn an income or chats with grandparents about tides and the best types of crab traps. Others may have volunteered in "Save the Sea Turtle" activities sponsored by the local marine science museum or just enjoyed the ocean through swimming and surfing.

At Eagle's Nest, students take classes with teams of about 125 students who share the same group of teachers. Susan's team, called the *Ospreys*, mixes seventh graders of varying achievement levels in each class. The team also includes 12 students with identified learning disabilities who are mainstreamed into the regular classes and receive extra support from a learning disabilities specialist teacher who is part of the team. In addition, an English-as-a-Second Language (ESL) teacher provides support for 10 students.

Over the past year, Susan has worked with Sam Berger, the art teacher on her team, to implement a project that encompasses goals in both curriculum areas related the characteristics and importance of the local wetlands. Susan suggested the project because the topic is required by the state's guidelines for seventh-grade science. She also believes it is essential that her students come to better understand the value of the wetlands to the environment especially in light of the recent growth of their community. In addition, in past years, Susan has found that the topic elicited a great deal of student interest.

Sam decided that a unit on the wetlands was a good choice for collaboration because he could think of many ways to link the art curriculum to the study of the salt marsh and local region. He also had contacts in a local community of artists who focused their work on wetland scenery and species and knew he could call on them as advisors and guest speakers.

After 2 months of planning, the unit began in November with a field trip to the local marine science museum, which contained live displays of the habitats of local plants and animals as well as a scale model of the salt marsh and nearby coast. In science class the day before, Susan prepared the students by using a strategy called a K-W-L (Ogle, 1986). First she wrote K (What We Know), W (What We Want to Know), and L (What We Learned) on the chalkboard. She explained that before visiting the museum, students would complete the K and W columns, and, after the visit, they would complete the L column. Susan then asked students what they already knew about the salt marsh located between their school and the ocean. Students met first with partners and then shared their prior knowledge with the whole class, while Susan wrote what they said on a chart. She next asked students what they wanted to know and filled in Column II of the chart. Susan told students that for the museum visit they would each receive a printed copy of the chart, and that she wanted them to see how many answers to their "Want to Know" questions they could find at the museum. She also suggested that they check the accuracy of their "Know" column by looking at exhibits and talking to the museum naturalists, and that they should add additional information to their chart if they learned something that was not related to their list of questions.

In the art classroom, Sam also prepared students for the visit to the museum. First, he arranged for a local photographer who focused on salt marsh animals, birds, and landscapes to speak to his classes and share slides of her work. The photographer, who was a member of an environmental protection group, captivated students with her photos of a wide range of local wildlife from egrets to bull frogs and baby fox. She shared with students why she choose to focus on the local wetlands and what she had learned during her work about both the salt marsh and photography.

The day before the trip, Sam also asked students what they expected to see at the museum, explaining that artists must develop keen observational skills. Some students had visited the museum earlier and were able to give partial answers. However, because some of the museum visits changed monthly, none of the students had seen all of them. Sam then gave out sketch pads and pencils and asked that students bring these on the museum visit to sketch one animal or plant they found interesting in the displays related to salt marshes. He also told students he would bring the school's digital camera along. Several students who had come after school to learn to use the camera would be invited to take photographs of different species.

THE MUSEUM VISIT

At the museum, the students were split into groups and visited the exhibits for 1 hour; they also participated in rotating small groups in a hands-on presentation by a naturalist about the plants and animals that live in the wetlands in their area. During the morning, students filled in the "L" section of their charts, adding new information they had learned. After lunch, each also took 30 minutes to 1 hour to make drawings in their sketch pads. They labeled the drawings with the scientific names of the wildlife as well as brief descriptions of the habitat in the museum display. Several students also took photographs.

Follow-up

Back at school the next day, each of the teachers debriefed with the students about the museum visit. Susan started her classes by asking students what they put in the "L" section of their KWL charts. As her students shared, Susan wrote their answers on her computer, which was connected to a projector. Students followed along and made notes from the image on the wall. This formed the first page in their notebooks on the coastal wetlands. After each class member had shared at least one idea, Susan posed two follow-up questions that required students to summarize what they had learned. She first asked, "What is a coastal wetland?", and then asked, "Why is a coastal wetland important?" Susan discussed both questions with the class for a few minutes and then indicated that these central questions would form the basis for the rest of their study of the wetlands.

The next day, Susan took her students to the library, where the media specialist had pulled out a large variety of books on wetlands and related topics and placed them on several tables. Students were invited to browse the books and select one or two they found interesting. The books included nonfiction trade books that ranged from easy to difficult. For example, one book for easy reading was *Life in a Wetland* (Fowler, 1998). Another was *Wetlands* in the Exploring Ecosystems series by Lisowski and Williams (1997). Another was *The Great Marsh: An Intimate Journey Into a Chesapeake Wetland* (Harp & Horton, 2002). After students returned to the classroom, Susan provided time for them to begin reading their books and indicated that they would be using the books to find answers to the key questions she posed earlier. These questions were now posted on the bulletin board.

In Sam's class, students shared their drawings and discussed ways that both art and science were helpful in studying nature. Sam showed the students PowerPoint slides he had made using the photographs that had been taken the day before, and then he took students to the computer lab to introduce them to software that allowed them to scan in their drawings. After several tries, every student had a scanned image of the drawing they had made at the museum that they could use in the art project that would begin the next week.

The unit continued for two additional weeks. In science class, Susan led students through several inquiry activities related to the two central questions. After reading their self-selected books, students wrote answers to the two key questions on index cards and posted them on the bulletin board by the appropriate question. They also wrote the name of their source on the back of the card. Susan took each of her classes on a walk through the salt marsh area near the school to make observations and collect water samples. Back in the classroom, the students learned to use microscopes to observe water samples from different parts of the salt marsh and made diagrams of what they saw in their water samples. They compared the diagrams to pictures of microscopic life that appeared in their science text. They also took notes and made diagrams in a journal, and they wrote up a lab report with a partner.

In her planning and in daily class sessions, Susan worked with the specialist teachers to provide support for students with special needs. The media specialist located taped versions of several of the more difficult books so that all students could have access to them. The English learners were encouraged to make their notes in both their native language and in English, and they were encouraged to learn the names of the plants and animals in the marsh in both languages with the help of their dual-language dictionaries.

Vocabulary was a special emphasis for all students because the unit included complex scientific vocabulary such as *ecosystem, wetland, marine wetlands, estuarine wetlands, salt marsh, bog,* and the names of various species that inhabited the wetlands near the school. In pairs, students looked for definitions for these terms in the various books in the classroom as well as on the Internet. Susan and the specialist teachers reviewed the meanings of the terms with small groups, and they also posted the words on a "word wall" on the bulletin board so that students had easy access to them for writing and spelling. In addition, Susan taught students to use the computer program "Kidspiration" to create webs, which illustrated the meanings of words and relationships between them.

Family volunteers also provided vital assistance with the project. At the beginning of the unit, the teachers sent home a questionnaire asking family members if they could volunteer to speak to students about some aspect of the marsh or recommend someone in the community who could. The teachers were surprised by the response. One student's mother was a member of the town council and came in to discuss the policy-related issues of the proposal. Another student's grandfather shared the duck decoys he had been creating for many years and answered questions about the history of the community. Students were especially interested in stories about a hurricane in the 1940s, which led to questions about weather on the salt marsh and the wildlife there. In addition, a parent connected with the Army Corps of Engineers could not attend, but sent printed materials and information about a relevant Web site. One article he sent, published by the Army Corps of Engineers, was entitled "The Young Scientist's Introduction to Wetlands." Susan made a class set of the article and also asked a parent volunteer to tape record the article so students who needed extra support could listen to the tape while they read.

Art Project

Down the hall in the art room, Sam developed a project for his classes that helped students learn to communicate using their original artwork and writing. Students were asked to create a trifold brochure to inform visitors to their area about the beauty of the wetlands as well as scientific information about the value of the wetlands to the environment.

On the first day of the project, Sam explained that students needed to think about their intended audience and consider the messages they were trying to communicate. He brought in samples of various types of brochures, including simple newspaper advertisements as well as more detailed brochures advertising vacation resorts. In small groups, students looked at the advertisements and discussed the ways the designers had used artwork, text, and other elements of design to communicate their message. Each group then selected one ad to show to the class to share what they had discovered.

Over the next few days, students designed and printed their brochures. While each student developed his or her own brochure, they met first with a partner to brainstorm ideas. They then drafted a mock version of the brochure and selected artwork or photographs they had made either at the museum or on the trip to the wetlands. The final brochures were created in the school computer lab using the digital photos students had taken or scanned images of their drawings. Sam reminded students throughout the project that this was an open-ended assignment and he wanted them to think creatively. However, he also required that each brochure include at least two accurate scientific facts about the wetlands and original artwork or photographs. Susan gave students time during science class to use reference materials and the Internet to check the factual scientific information they were including on their brochures.

Unit Wrap Up

To conclude the 4-week unit, Susan and Sam gained permission from the school principal and their other team members to involve students in designing and sharing their work at a "Salt Marsh Museum" exhibit in the school library. Each student was asked to select two pieces of their work from the unit and join with others to create a display related to the two central questions: What is a Salt Marsh? and Why is a Salt Marsh Important?

First, within each class, students gathered in groups of four, developed answers to the central questions, and used these as titles for the displays. For example, under the title, Why Is a Salt Marsh Important?, one first-period group, Talia, Alan, Jorge, and Alexandra, wrote, "Salt Marshes are Incubators for Young Animals" and decided to display their photographs of baby animals that lived in the marsh. Other groups made displays of their science lab reports containing drawings of microscopic life and entries from the observational journals they completed on their walks through the marsh. Several groups also made short PowerPoint presentations using information from their brochure or journal as well as the Internet. During and after school, both Susan and Sam met with the small groups to discuss what they had selected for their display and provide guidance.

On the day before the museum exhibit opened, students hung their work on display boards in the library. The next day and evening, other students, parents, and community members came to visit the display and asked students questions about what they had learned.

At the end of the unit, Susan and Sam both felt it had been a success in terms of student learning and motivation. Of course each had ideas about what they would do differently next time—everything from moving the unit earlier in the year (marsh hikes were sometimes a little difficult in January!) to providing more specific instructions to students for some of the projects. However, they believed that students had made important progress in understanding their own environment both scientifically and aesthetically, and they had gained important skills and concepts in the process.

A SCHOLAR'S RESPONSE
Judith Irvin, Florida State University

> Principle 1: Adolescents need opportunities to participate in active learning environments that offer clear and facilitative literacy instruction.

With increasing pressure to "cover" the curriculum and "meet" state standards, teachers are sometimes fearful of taking too much time to implement a unit that involves projects and field trips. Unless students engage in the learning events, however, everyone involved may be just going through the motions of lessons presented, tests taken, content forgotten, and moving on to the next lesson or unit. Guiding Principle 1 is essential to both learning content and developing and improving literacy.

The example presented in this chapter illustrates many components of effective instruction. First and foremost, Susan and Sam chose an important topic, both to meet the state guidelines and to the members of this community. Although there was no mention of involving students in the choice of the unit of study, I suspect they would have embraced the idea enthusiastically given the significance of the wetlands to their community.

Susan activated and built prior knowledge using the KWL strategy, and she facilitated oral communication through sharing prior knowledge with partners and then the entire class. She focused students on what they wanted to know, thereby connecting to their interests and their motivation for learning. Susan modeled organizing information by listing what students learned after the museum visit. She also provided visuals through use of the projector and by printing a copy for students. The two central questions helped students focus on and summarize what they were learning about the wetlands. She provided students with choice about the books they would read—an important element in student motivation to read (Ivey & Broaddus, 2001). In addition, she provided leveled books for students of all reading abilities and made accommodations for ESL and special needs students. Susan explicitly taught key vocabulary that was important to the content and choosing words that students would meet in other contexts. She also involved parents and community members in the unit.

The photographer that Sam invited to the classroom not only brought visual images for students, but also her passion and commitment to the wetlands. The sketches helped students with their observational skills and served as a visual in the brochure students created later. Sam also cleverly incorporated the use of technology in the PowerPoint slides, digital camera, and construction of the brochures. It would have been a natural extension if the brochures were copied and given to the local Visitor's Center to give students an authentic audience.

Do these descriptions represent good literacy instruction? Do they represent good content area instruction? The answer is both. In fact they are intricately linked. Students were reading, writing, sketching, observing, speaking, listening, thinking, predicting, asking questions, determining importance, organizing information, making inferences, and visualizing. Both Susan and Sam scaffolded instruction so that all students participated and modeled important literacy abilities. When teachers do this, students learn to become more literate and learn much more content.

Langer's (2002) study has influenced my work and confirms Guiding Principle 1. This 5-year study involved 25 middle- and high school English programs in Florida (Miami), New York (New York City and Hudson), and California (Los Angeles), all large schools serving highly diverse and ELL populations. Eighty-eight (88) classrooms and forty-four (44) teachers were studied over a consecutive 2-year period. The purpose of this study was to specify features of instruction that make a difference in student learning by comparing high- and underachieving schools that are otherwise similar. Three populations were compared:

1. *Effective Teachers in Effective Schools* were teachers whose students were "beating the odds" and were in schools that were "beating the odds" or scoring higher than students in demographically comparable schools.
2. *Effective Teachers in Typical Schools* were teachers whose students were beating the odds, but they were in schools that scored typically when compared with demographically similar schools.
3. *Typical Teachers in Typical Schools* were teachers whose students scored typically and they were in schools that scored typically. These were not "bad" teachers or "bad" schools, just typically scoring.

Although Langer studied English/Language Arts teachers, I think the implications for other content teachers are clear. She found that effective teachers:

- integrated skill instruction and test preparation within meaningful content such as a unit on the wetlands,
- connected learnings "among knowledge skills and ideas, across lessons, classes, and grades, as well as in-school and out-of-school connections" (p. 23) such as the community resources and the collaborative work between the art and science teacher,
- overtly taught enabling or learning strategies such as the use of the KWL and pushed for deeper understanding of content, and
- viewed social activity as an important aspect of learning and engaged students in thoughtful dialogue.

Few would argue that this unit taught by two talented teachers does not represent excellent instruction and opportunities for student learning in both literacy development and content knowledge. But I question: Is this a pocket of excellence in this school or is this type of excellent instruction available to all students? In the field of adolescent literacy, I think we have finally reached the point where we can recognize good content area instruction that develops student learning and literacy. Many examples exist in schools across the country. But I think we stop short of saying that this quality instruction is consistent across a school or across a district, is part of the culture of the school, and is sustainable if key people leave the school. Langer stated that

> . . . the teacher cannot do it alone—the program makes all the difference. An excellent teacher without a well-coordinated program can do only so much. In these situations, even the best of teachers can offer students only isolated moments of engrossed learning and rich experience in an otherwise disconnected series of classes. (p. 11)

I have had the privilege of working with many schools and districts across the country to develop school-wide and district-wide literacy plans, working with administrators to build the capacity of teachers and other educators so that the literacy improvement efforts are sustainable and available to all students. The quality instruction that Susan and Sam displayed is laudable and should be encouraged school and system wide so that all adolescents have the opportunity to participate in active learning environments that offer clear and facilitative literacy instruction.

Discussion Questions

As you reflect on the information presented in this chapter, consider the following questions as they relate to your own teaching and/or your experiences in schools:

- In your experience, to what extent do schools provide active learning environments for adolescents?
- Do you think the types of instruction or the collaboration presented in this vignette presented is unique or unusual? Why or why not?
- Compare and contrast the views of the expert responder to your own views.
- What dilemmas must teachers, schools, and others solve to implement Principle 1?

Chapter 4

Principle 2: Adolescents Need Opportunities to Participate in Respectful Environments Characterized by High Expectations, Trust, and Care

Like Principle 1, Principle 2 focuses on the environment in which learning takes place. This principle foregrounds the concept that students learn best in schools and other situations where they feel accepted, cared for, and challenged. Educators and communities must strive diligently to provide such environments because it is not an easy task. Unfortunately, some middle and high schools—both today and in the past—have been characterized as places where students feel inadequate, marginalized, unsafe, or unwelcome. This type of negative environment seriously undermines any effort to improve student learning and achievement. However, schools with positive environments are often seen by young people as havens from difficult outside circumstances in neighborhoods or families. These schools build respect—they enable youth, their families, community members, and educators to work together to develop a feeling of belonging so that all students can achieve high levels of literacy and learning (Lipsitz, 1983; Moje, 1996).

School leaders can take essential steps toward developing a respectful environment by ensuring that their school is a safe place, both physically and emotionally. First, the school community must welcome and include students from all backgrounds, achievement levels, and cultures (Finn, 1999; Jiménez, 2004). Additionally, the curriculum must be designed to provide the maximum challenge as well as support for each learner (Payne-Bourcy & Chandler-Olcott, 2003). Finally, steps must be taken to ensure that the achievements and special needs of all learners are honored.

Teachers also have an essential role in developing a respectful environment and can take numerous steps within and beyond their classrooms to develop competence and confidence in students. English/language arts teachers, for example, can involve all students in a class in the study of an excellent piece of literature, with supports such as tape recordings for those who need extra support in reading. At other times, the same teacher could provide students with choices among multiple text sources with differences in level of difficulty and format (Ivey & Broaddus, 2001). Such variations can enable students to learn both together and individually. This type of instruction also helps class members realize that help will be there as they move to new levels of reading and learning.

Students, community members, and families also have important roles to play. Students can encourage one another, for example, by providing informal and formal assistance to their peers through peer mentoring programs. Students can also learn to work together in class toward mutual goals, and they can learn to provide one another the same level of trust and care the teacher shows for them. In this type of environment, confusion and errors are expected; they are viewed as opportunities for understanding rather than mistakes susceptible to ridicule.

A positive school environment requires close ties with the community outside of the school. Families and community members are invited to take an active role in the school, participating in decisions and serving as resources for students and teachers. This connection can provide extra support to students (e.g., through tutoring) and can also enable teachers to understand, appreciate, and link their curriculum to the varied cultures of the students. Students can also be encouraged to serve the community, providing valuable assistance for others as well as important learning for themselves beyond the walls of the school.

A key aspect of this principle is that schools must support students while holding high expectations (Moore et al., 1999). One way to accomplish this is to nurture students' interests and provide a variety of challenges. These challenges might range from encouraging students to enter science fairs, try out for debate teams, or compete in rap contests sponsored by recording companies. Additionally, teachers' assessment practices can help students learn to self-assess their own performance and progress. Well-crafted self-assessments can encourage and motivate students to take the next steps in their own learning.

For this principle to be enacted, teachers must get to know their students as individuals and as members of families and communities (Sturtevant, 1997). They need to be able to provide instruction that builds on the interests, skills, and abilities students have developed both in and out of school. They also need to create a classroom community in which everyone is responsible for helping everyone else be successful. Such an environment encourages leadership in both individuals and groups. This leadership might be connected to classroom-based projects, such as work on Internet research related to curriculum objectives, or community-based projects, such as a buddy reading program, neighborhood cleanup, or nursing home project. Overall, in a respectful environment, youth have a voice in their own education: They participate in making plans for themselves, they choose among options; they learn to work effectively with others, and they become increasingly competent as learners (Alvermann, 2002).

A variety of professional organizations explicitly support this principle in their standards documents. For example, the International Reading Association and National Council of Teachers of English (1996) suggested that English/language arts teachers should help students to "develop an understanding of and respect for diversity in language use, patterns, and dialects" (p. 3). In addition, the National Council of Teachers of Mathematics (1991) suggested that teachers should "display sensitivity to, and draw on, students' diverse background experiences and dispositions" (p. 25).

FOUR VIGNETTES

This chapter presents four brief vignettes based on observations of actual classrooms throughout the United States in rural, suburban, and urban areas. All of the teachers described here believe strongly in creating a positive and respectful environment for adolescent learning and literacy growth.

Vignette 1: Whole-School Reading Program

Sheffield Middle School is located in a rural area about 40 miles south of Washington, DC. The district, which has six middle schools, is known for supporting the literacy needs of its students. Over the past 10 years, the reading/language arts supervisor has implemented a comprehensive program that places licensed reading specialists in all middle schools and then supports them through ongoing professional development. The reading specialists serve in a variety of roles and take leadership of their school's literacy programs.

Susan Williams has been the reading specialist at Sheffield for 4 years. Students at Sheffield Middle School are encouraged in their reading in numerous ways, and Susan has been highly instrumental in creating a respectful and positive school environment that supports individual growth. One step she has taken has been to create a reading center that students can visit individually and with their classes. The reading center holds about 25 computers and a wall of books for students and teachers. Before school each day, Susan is present in the reading center for about 30 minutes to welcome students who want to use computers for writing, research, or to take computer-based assessments. Students and teachers also stop by to chat or borrow books at this time. One student, selected to read the morning announcements on the school's closed-circuit TV system, regularly visits Susan during the early morning period to read over her presentation. Susan notes that this student has not always been a strong reader, and the daily practice has helped her build fluency.

Later in the morning, Susan visits classes, working with students on reading strategies and modeling effective literacy practices for their teachers. She notes that she serves as a coach for teachers in the school, providing support for their efforts to include literacy instruction within their curriculum areas. In this role, Susan works informally with teachers who request assistance; she also presents inservice workshops to small groups of teachers and runs a study group of teachers who are reading a book related to students' literacy development.

As the only reading specialist in her large school, Susan focuses on sixth grade. She works hard to learn every sixth grader's name and gets to know their interests and needs. She also regularly spends time with students who have transferred to the school during seventh or eighth grade. Over time this practice has enabled Susan to know all of the students in the school. She also makes special efforts to meet students' family members, and she encourages them to visit the school or work as volunteers on committees or in classrooms.

Susan explains that a particular concern she has at the middle-school level is student motivation, as she has found that students' motivation to read often declines at this age. Susan believes that teaching practices can hold the key to motivation, noting that, "If they're not motivated it's because they're not being successful." She works with teachers and administrators to ensure success for each student, which she believes relates strongly to a positive attitude: "For success, attitude is as important as ability."

The principal at Sheffield as well as the district's reading supervisor work closely with Susan to ensure that teachers and students have the strategies and materials necessary for success. For example, the principal has budgeted funds to provide a wide variety of books for students, so all have excellent reading material at the appropriate level. The school also participates in the Virginia Young Readers Program, which encourages students and staff to read a wide variety of books each year. Families are also included in this activity through an open house and festival.

Vignette 2: ESOL in an Alternative High School

During a Friday lunch hour at Glebe Alternative High School near Washington, DC, a visitor finds Alison Jones and many of her students engaged in book discussions with content teachers, the school principal, and two public librarians. Students have selected and read books intended for teenage beginning readers; they are actively engaged in talking about what they have read as they eat pizza and cookies.

Alison's students are enrolled in an alternative high school program for older adolescents who have recently immigrated to the United States. Their home countries are widespread, with the majority arriving from Central and South America, Africa, and the Middle East. Many of Alison's students have lived through extreme conditions of war, poverty, extended family separations, and other hardships; some are attending school for the first time when they enter her classroom at age 16 or older. Alison has worked in this urban district for over 20 years and is certified as both an ESL teacher and a reading specialist. She also has strong connections with faculty at a local state university, where she occasionally teaches classes and has recently completed a doctorate.

The lunch discussion group is one part of Alison's continuing effort to help her diverse students learn English and improve their reading abilities through an immersion in books. She started the program by applying for a small grant with the librarians at a branch of the city's public library, which is attached to her school. The grant funds are used to buy easy-to-read books that appeal to older adolescents as well as teenage-friendly food for the lunchtime discussions. Alison says that an important key to the success of the program, which is completely voluntary for students, is that teachers personally encourage each student to attend. They also provide a friendly environment by permitting students who are less comfortable with reading or talking about books to attend and listen to others for a few weeks before plunging in. Alison is very pleased with the students' growing participation in the book discussion groups, but says she is concerned because she cannot find enough easy books that they would be interested in even though she has explored a wide variety of publishers. She is considering writing new books herself or thinking of a way to involve her students in writing books for the project.

After lunch, students in Alison's first-level ESL/reading class discuss a science workbook selection on the Venus flytrap. Students write answers to questions related to a short selection they read the previous day, and then they share their answers in a small group. Alison also works with the class to review vocabulary meanings and sentence punctuation. Students then make drawings that compare different types of plants, and Alison uses these to elicit more class discussion.

Later, all of the students attend a once-per-week computer class where they have been taught to use computers for the first time in their lives and are permitted time to explore Web sites they find interesting. Many enjoy finding Web-based newspapers and music sites from their home countries. Others can be seen carefully going through employment ads and studying clothing catalog Web sites. One student decides to do a search on the Venus flytrap, the subject of the earlier science lesson. He finds a Web site that includes beautiful photographs and shares it with the other students. Alison and the computer teacher are both very pleased that the students are using computers and learning through all types of visual and auditory texts. However, they also mention that some teachers in the school disapprove of the flexibility they give students and advocate a computer curriculum that is linked specifically to the state's subject-specific competency tests. Alison believes, however, that her flexibility respects the students' natural inclination to learn through the use of the computers. She also notes that "what helps her most" to be an effective teacher is the support of the school principal, who encourages her to be creative in designing a reading curriculum to meet the needs of her students.

Vignette 3: Algebra in the Southwest

Ana Sanchez teaches at La Paz High School, which serves 2,150 students in a large southwestern city. The large school is almost new and is located in a former citrus grove with spectacular mountain views. Ana's algebra class includes 20 students from Native American and Hispanic backgrounds. The room is welcoming and colorful; the walls are covered in student artwork and mathematics posters in English and Spanish. Ana's classroom, as well as all others in the school, is outfitted with white boards and a computer, projector, and screen for instruction.

Announcements blare over the loudspeaker as class begins. During the announcements, students notice their "bellwork"—an assignment on the overhead projector that they are to complete as class begins. The bellwork assignment is a review of statistical principles that will be included on a test the next day. These are the instructions: (a) Make a stem-and-leaf plot; (b) Find the median, mean, and mode of the numbers; (c) Mark a box and whiskers plot; and (d) Label the quartiles.

As students work on this assignment individually, Ana circulates around the room, checking work and assisting those who are having difficulty. She uses both English and Spanish in conversing with students. Students also are quietly helping each other as needed.

Ana then explains to students that during the rest of the class period they will create pamphlets they can use as study guides during their test the next day. As a model, she passes out examples of commercially produced pamphlets. Using both Spanish and English, she asks students what features they notice in the pamphlets. Students mention pictures, graphics, and colors. Ana explains that their study guides can include all of these features, plus definitions of terms and examples of problems. Students then get colored paper and markers and proceed to create personalized study guides. Ana reminds students that they can talk to their table partners about their ideas for the study guides, and that each pamphlet must be three-sided. Most of the talk between the partners occurs in Spanish.

Toward the end of the class, Ana indicates that students should show their pamphlet to their partner and explain the problem examples they have given. She then asks for volunteers to share with the whole class and uses this opportunity to review the main concepts that will be on the test. As students leave, Ana collects their "credit slips," which are part of a record-keeping system in which students record their own class points and track their progress. Ana also mentions to a visitor that students in her classes have extensive mathematics portfolios in which they collect and reflect on their work in class. These portfolios are perceived as being very powerful in advancing students' learning and self-monitoring.

Vignette 4: U.S. History

Carlos Buendia has been teaching history at Washington Irving High School, located just across the river from Manhattan, for over 20 years. Carlos teaches mostly juniors and seniors who are taking U.S. History. He teaches six classes per day, with students divided into sections designated as "regular," "honors," and "Advanced Placement." Irving's school community is primarily Hispanic, and the district reports that over 90% of the students are eligible for free or reduced lunch.

One of Carlos' primarily goals is to make his curriculum meaningful to his students and help them increase their critical thinking and writing abilities. He structures his lessons and units so they include a wide variety of print and nonprint resources. Students read primary source documents, political cartoons, magazine articles, and a wide range of Internet sources in addition to their textbooks. An example of a resource he located recently that students found both interesting and thought provoking was a book of political cartoons that were created by Dr. Seuss during World War II.

In discussions with his class, Carlos works to link students' experiences to history. For example, several months after the World Trade Center towers were attacked, he talked with students about their feelings and how these might be similar to or different than feelings of Americans during World War II. The World Trade Center attack was extremely relevant to his students due to their location, which is very close to Manhattan; some Irving students had even witnessed the event through windows of the school. Carlos also helps students understand the meaning of historical events through role-playing assignments that include extensive reading about a particular perspective, writing an essay, and enacting the role of a character in a particular time period.

Like others in his school, over the past 10 years, Carlos has greatly expanded his use of technology in his teaching and assessment. Several years ago, his district was the recipient of a large grant that provided computers and Internet connections to both schools and homes in the school community. Computers are now widely available in Irving classrooms, in a school library computer lab, in public libraries within walking distance, and in students' homes. Carlos' classroom includes eight computers, all with Internet access.

Carlos explains that the computers have been very useful to him and his students for research, writing, assessment, and record keeping. He uses a Web-based system provided by the school district in which students have individual work folders that they can access from any Internet-connected computer. Students write most assignments on computer and submit them by depositing them in their folders. Carlos reads student work directly on the computer and then provides detailed written feedback to each student by inserting comments directly within their documents. Carlos notes that he has gradually increased writing requirements over the past few years in all of his classes, and he mentions that he has seen his students' writing proficiency improve greatly. He notes that district scores on state writing assessments have also gone up.

In discussion after class, Carlos explains that he believes that his use of technology and, in general his teaching proficiency have expanded as a result of staff development opportunities the district has made available to him. Carlos values the opportunity to make choices in selecting staff development opportunities and in making professional decisions about designing instruction that will help students' meet learning goals.

Discussion

These four teachers, while taking different approaches, engage students in using literacy for learning and personal growth within a positive and respectful environment.

Susan Williams developed a strong middle-school reading program that provides support to both students and teachers and includes families. Ana Argules' Algebra students create portfolios and test study guides, and they are asked to set goals for their own learning. Alison Jones' alternative high school students become immersed in lunchtime book discussions and explorations of a wide variety of English and native language texts on the Internet. Carlos Buendia's students connect their lives to the lives of Americans in past generations through the use of multiple sources, including the Internet, extensive writing, role-playing, and class discussion. Throughout days, weeks, and months, students in all of these settings gradually build their content area knowledge and skills as well as their ability to use literacy in multiple ways.

Each of these four teachers has created positive learning contexts that make it possible for students to support one another in their efforts to become better language users, gain new knowledge, and think critically. These teachers facilitate learning with both high expectations and caring environments that build self-confidence and a sense of community. Solving problems in groups, working with partners to provide input and feedback on assignments, and role-playing with others are just a few examples of the ways these teachers help foster relationships that support student participation and achievement.

A SCHOLAR'S RESPONSE
Guofang Li, University at Buffalo - SUNY

> Principle 2: Adolescents participate in respectful environments characterized by high expectations, trust, and care.

Providing a positive learning environment for adolescent learners, especially learners from diverse cultural and linguistic backgrounds, is a necessary catalyst for successful school experiences. Research has concluded that for learners to engage in meaningful learning, it is important for schools to establish a respectful environment where school curricular and teachers' pedagogical practices affirm students' linguistic and cultural identities and respect students' personal knowledge as strengths (Li, 2006; Nieto, 1999). As the principle of this chapter states, a respectful environment should be characterized by high expectations, trust, and care. In my view, central to building such a respectful environment is the notion of *authentic caring*, in which teachers initiate and nurture reciprocal relations with students through engrossment in their welfare and emotional displacement (Noddings, 1992; Valenzuela, 1999). As Valenzuela (1999) pointed out, such a pedagogical practice "accords moral authority to teachers and institutional structures that value and actively promote respect and a search for connection, between teacher and student and among students themselves" (p. 21). When students feel they are cared for and respected as who they are, they are more likely to reciprocate their trust in schools and teachers, are more motivated to participate in learning, and therefore are more likely to achieve. Without such reciprocal relationships, students are not only reduced to the level of objects, they may also be diverted from learning the skills necessary for academic achievement (Valenzuela, 1999).

How can teachers and schools establish this kind of authentic caring environments for students? The first requisite, I believe, is that teachers must have positive attitudinal predispositions toward students, especially those of different cultural backgrounds. Teachers who have a deficit view of minority cultural differences often assume that minority students lack ability in learning or have inadequate parenting or both (Pang & Sablan, 1998). Teachers with this perspective often do not build on students' skills and knowledge or affirm students' cultural identity; this often results in "subtractive schooling," which reinforces the existing home/school dichotomy and limits children's access to school learning and achievement (Li, 2005; Valenzuela, 1999). However, teachers who view minority cultural differences not as barriers to overcome, but as resources, usually have a positive attitude toward students' ability to achieve and often see students' personal knowledge as assets. Teachers with this perspective often develop culturally relevant and linguistically congruent instructional approaches to translate school and home differences for minority students (Li, 2005). As the vignettes in this chapter demonstrate, the teachers in the different urban and suburban schools all held positive attitudes toward their students and their ability to achieve despite their diverse sociocultural, racial, and gender backgrounds. Such positive predisposition is essential for establishing a reciprocal caring relationship with students who need to master a higher level of learning to become successful in the larger society.

The belief that minority students are capable of learning is of paramount significance because it implies that caring teachers will not set low standards for students from minority backgrounds. Instead they hold high expectations for all students and believe that students have the talents and strengths to meet these high expectations (Nieto, 1999). At the same time, these teachers will set high standards for their own teaching. They do not just water down the curriculum. Rather, they set high standards and demands on their own teaching by creating inclusive learning communities and developing effective teaching strategies for diverse students so that they can all better achieve these high standards. The teachers in the four vignettes in this chapter, for example, did not just follow a rudimentary, rigid curriculum. They created different learning opportunities such as an open reading center, a lunch book discussion group, a pamphlet project, or a history class discussion that connected students' own experiences. These creative or flexible teaching practices reflect the teachers' authentic caring for the students' welfare, including their need to engage in different challenging tasks and achieve academic success.

The next step for teachers in establishing a caring environment is the need to take into consideration students' affective filters, especially factors related to their motivation for learning. Teachers need to create a safe and nonthreatening learning community in which students feel comfortable participating and in which students develop confidence that they can learn and achieve high academic standards. Research has shown that a strong connection among students, teachers, and schools has a positive influence on students' motivation to learn (Abi-Nader, 1993). Nieto (1999) argued that forging strong identification with teachers and schools is a fundamental ingredient in student learning because it helps students define schools as places that can give them an academic identity with which they can relate. A strong teacher–student alliance can also foster students' sense of belonging to the learning community and their positive self-image as academically capable members of the community.

To forge a strong teacher–student connection requires that teachers establish a classroom community that is "fluid and humanely equitable" (Ladson-Billings, 1994). Such a classroom is characterized by maintaining standards of excellence while taking into consideration student diversity and individual differences in students' development. Authentic, caring teachers develop different kinds of strategies, utilize an array of materials, and engage students in a variety of learning activities to ensure student success while addressing cultural and individual differences. In Susan Williams' and Alison Jones' classes described in this chapter, the two teachers both engaged students in activities that were fluid, flexible, and friendly. Students were welcomed anytime, and participation was voluntary. They were not pressured to achieve when they were not developmentally or psychologically ready. In addition to rewarding students with open, flexible activities, teachers also need to try their best to individualize instruction and pay close attention to students' personal growth. The teachers in the four vignettes all emphasized the importance of flexibility in program and task planning and of addressing individual differences by attending to students' personal growth. When teachers establish personal relationships with the students and know who the students are, and when they personally encourage each student to participate, students are more motivated to become part of their learning program. That is, when teachers show students that they respect them as capable individuals and care about their growth, students will reciprocate with more investment in their own learning—that they too care about their own school success.

Last, creating a respectful and caring environment requires teachers to cultivate relationships beyond the boundaries of the classroom (Ladson-Billings, 1994). As discussed in other chapters in this book, a recurrent theme is that students' out-of-school lives matter. Teachers must reach out to the community to establish school–home partnerships. Teachers and schools can involve parents and community members in the school setting through a variety of strategies and resources to address student concerns or learn about students' particular cultural ways of learning. By constantly involving parents, teachers and parents will become true partners and collaborators in finding culturally relevant and educationally beneficial ways to achieve a common goal—that is, to provide quality, caring, and respectful learning environments for all (Li, 2005).

Discussion Questions

As you reflect on the information presented in this chapter, consider the following questions as they relate to your own teaching and/or your experiences in schools:

- In your experience, to what extent do schools provide respectful, caring learning environments for adolescents?
- Do you think the vignettes presented here are unique or unusual? Why or why not?
- Compare and contrast the views of the expert responder to your own views.
- What dilemmas must teachers, schools, and others solve to implement Principle 2?

Chapter 5

Principle 3: Adolescents Need Opportunities to Engage With Print and Nonprint Texts for a Variety of Purposes

This principle, as well as the three that follow, focus on the instructional opportunities available to adolescents.

All adolescents, regardless of ethnic and cultural background, academic ability, or experience, need to be able to read a wide variety of print and nonprint texts in school and their daily lives (Ivey & Broaddus, 2001; Moje, Young et al., 2000; Smith & Wilhelm, 2004; Tatum, 2000). Living in an era where information is readily available at the click of a mouse makes it imperative that every adolescent is prepared to have successful personal, social, and economic lives in a burgeoning global and technological economy. Preparation for engaging with print and nonprint forms of communication requires adapting ways of thinking for multiple and different texts, different contexts, and different situations, as well as learning to become critical literacy thinkers and learners. Adolescents, in everyday occurrences, experience a variety of materials such as visual media (Eken, 2002), hypertexts (Bolter, 1998; Purves, 1998), and other complex and sophisticated technological texts. Adolescents are motivated by the array of information and entertainment opportunities available in these print and nonprint forms (Alvermann & Hagood, 2000; Worthy, Moorman, & Turner, 1999). These opportunities require families and teachers to take on the responsibility of assisting adolescents to be critical consumers of different text types (Ridgeway, Peters, & Tracy, 2002). They must develop a sense of the multiple perspectives one might take toward problems to be solved and issues that can be debated. They must also learn to use these abilities for personal as well as academic ends to become engaged readers of symbols, as well as the word and the world (Freire, 1970).

What might the use of multiple types of print and nonprint texts and practices look like according to grade level and subject-matter emphases? Unequivocally, it is no small feat for teachers or students to engage in teaching and learning with different types of texts. Although numerous types of texts are readily available to youth on a daily basis, only a small number are commonplace in classrooms. This principle implies that those responsible for guiding adolescents to be critically literate individuals should assume a proactive leadership role.

Within their own classrooms, teachers can engage in ongoing professional decision making that will result in more complex and sophisticated levels of literacy for the adolescents with whom they work. Thus, in a seventh-grade English language arts classroom, the teacher, while conducting a unit on a historical civil rights event, might include memoirs, pictures, documentary, and docudrama as interdisciplinary, print, and nonprint resources to enhance and enrich the study of literature of the time period. Another teacher might share various kinds of information sources with students, including Web sites, documentaries, and magazine articles. In another classroom, students might be invited to identify their own print and nonprint sources of information and to bring these to the classroom to share with the teacher and their peers. The classroom library in a high school automotive class might contain magazines, manuals, and reference books to be used for a project while the assembly of a motor engine is being completed. The classroom library in a middle-school biology class might include book-marked Web sites, picture book references, topic-directed expository texts, and other alternative textbooks, to be used as students complete observations during a laboratory assignment.

In essence, teachers in all disciplines can make reasonable decisions about introducing multiple resources given the demands of their content domain. The guiding principle of this chapter challenges teachers to develop dynamic and highly interactive learning contexts (Sweet & Snow, 2002); when participating in these contexts, students can become dynamic and highly interactive learners.

The teaching and learning standards of many professional organizations support this principle. The National Science Teacher's Association, for example, suggests that, "activities encourage the critical analysis of secondary sources—including media, books, and journals in a library" (National Reading Conference, 1996, p. 33). The National Standards for the English Language Arts state that students should "read a wide range of print and nonprint texts"; "read a wide range of literature"; and "use a variety of technological and informational resources" (International Reading Association & National Council of Teachers of English, 1996). In addition, the National Council for the Social Studies (1994) recommends that teachers "use a variety of instructional materials such as physical examples, photographs, maps, illustrations, films, videos, textbooks, literary selections, and computerized databases." The National Council of Teachers of Mathematics (1991) notes that teachers will enhance discourse by encouraging the use of "computers, calculators, and other technology; concrete materials used as models; pictures, diagrams, tables, and graphs; invented and conventional terms and symbols; metaphors, analogies, and stories; written hypotheses, explanations, and arguments; oral presentations and dramatizations."

Following this introduction are two vignettes that reveal what providing adolescents with opportunities to engage with print and nonprint texts might look like. We begin first with a look into a biology lesson, and later we turn to a seventh-grade English language arts classroom.

VIGNETTE 1: GUIDING PRINCIPLE IN ACTION DURING A BIOLOGY LESSON

Kenneth Petty is an experienced teacher of 15 years who has spent most of his career at Clarke Central High School, located in a mid-size city in the southeastern United States. Clarke Central is designated by its school district as a science and technology magnet school, and students throughout the county are encouraged to apply. However, most of the students at Clarke Central live in the surrounding neighborhood. Eighty-three percent of Clarke Central's students are African American, and 90% of the students meet federal guidelines to receive a free or reduced lunch.

Kenneth is a teacher who always operates with principled practices in mind. One of his goals is to enhance his students' learning opportunities by teaching biology in ways that encourage interaction among and between students as well as between the students and teacher. Another goal of Kenneth's is to use multiple text types, including the Internet and authentic Young Adult (YA) literature. In addition to these goals, Kenneth believes it is important to model the use of technology as a tool for enhancing students' learning opportunities. In Kenneth's classroom, modeling technology includes providing minilessons using PowerPoint and using WebQuests to focus on an inquiry project of environmental issues such as diversity of species.

Kenneth's 90-minute block class has 24 tenth-grade students with a range of academic abilities. As students saunter into the room, Kenneth makes last-minute preparations for today's lesson by setting up his laptop computer for his PowerPoint presentation. The title of today's minilesson is "Population Ecology and Fluctuations," which Kenneth has projected from his computer onto a large screen in front of the classroom. Kenneth begins class with the 10-minute minilesson, which defines *ecology* and the areas of study typically conducted within the field. He calls students' attention to *bi-*

otic and *abiotic* factors by explaining the definitions of the words. As a matter of review, he defines and characterizes populations for the students, highlighting points such as the existence of organisms within populations including cycles of birth, physical development and maturity, reproduction, and death. Kenneth notes the concept of community and explains that, within the community, organisms interact with populations of other species. He brings his point closer to his students' reality by calling their attention to the community in which they live and describing how various ethnic and cultural groups live and interact within the same community, often depending on each other for supply and demand of goods and services.

After the introduction, Kenneth then moves to talk about population fluctuations and the causes and effects of this concept. First he notes that there are factors which contribute to population fluctuations among organisms due to the density and dependency among organisms in the community. He teaches his students that if the population is small, the birth rates are high and the death rates are low. Therefore, the population may increase; however, predation also increases. That is, when one species of organism kills and eats another, the result is a high death rate of those organisms serving as food. Kenneth brainstorms with his students to gain their insight into what situations might enhance predation. Students respond with possibilities such as competition for resources, disease transmission among organisms, and food availability. Kenneth transitions to another activity for this lesson, but not before he notes a person named Thomas Malthus—an individual about whom students would later be responsible for researching information.

After his minilesson, Kenneth asks students to work in pairs to seek out as much evidence and as many examples as they can find of population fluctuation among various organisms. Students are able to use a wide variety of print and nonprint resources available in the classroom or on the Internet, including literature, the Smithsonian Magazine, WebQuests, and a variety of science texts. Kenneth projects the assignment description on the screen, and students are given a recording sheet to document their research. On the sheet are specific guidelines for completing the assignment in a satisfactory manner. As the students pair up to collaborate on the assignment, Kenneth walks around to monitor, answer questions, and offer assistance, guidance, and encouragement to all students.

Keisha and Jamaal begin the in-class assignment by thumbing back through the nonfiction book, *Never Cry Wolf* (Mowat, 1963), which the class had been reading aloud. These two students comment on how they are ready to move to the arctic after reading Mowat's humorous and humble account of his life among the wolves. *Never Cry Wolf* is a true story in which the author and naturalist, Farley Mowat, is left in the Canadian Wildlife reserves to investigate the reasons that wolves were killing arctic caribou.

Mowat writes about his summer of living in the frozen tundra alone study-ing the wolf population and consequently developing a deep fondness for the wolves. Keisha and Jamaal write down information related to the au-thor's description of what happens to the wolf population when too many wolves are killed or relocated.

Next, they move from the nonfiction book to the Internet and find a Web site devoted to problems related to overpopulation of humans. Jamaal remembers something he had seen in a magazine related to human over-population; he goes to the bookshelf and returns with a copy of the "Smith-sonian Magazine." Together, Jamaal and Keisha look through the article, taking turns reading aloud interesting and relevant points. They take notes on the left side of their double-entry journal as they continue to skim through the information. Jamaal and Keisha save the right column of their journals to synthesize information and put what they are reading and learn-ing into their own words. Finally, these students use one of the scientific ref-erence books in the classroom to look up information on Thomas Mal-thus—a person Kenneth mentioned in his presentation—for more leads about population fluctuations. Within the class, other students are seen us-ing similar source materials. Although there is a general biology textbook, only a couple of students consult it for information.

Similarly, Charles and Tamaria had scuttled to the computer the minute Kenneth finished giving directions for the assignment. They pull up the Google search engine and type in *population ecology* in the search field. They find a Web site that outlines this topic and quickly scroll through to skim for information. As Charles points to things he notices on the computer screen, he comes across two colorful pictures juxtaposed. One picture ex-hibits a lemming, the other a carnivorous bird that preys on lemmings. Tamaria notices the pictures as well and reads aloud the information on population fluctuations of the lemming and the long-tailed jaeger written above and below the pictures. She reads aloud with expression,

> Perhaps one famous example of population fluctuations is the interesting tundra animal, the lemming or the lemmus trimucronatus. This animal has population fluctuations that oscillate within a three or four-year period. The boom population may be 50 or 100 times that of the bust population. "Wow!" It is not yet known precisely which factors contribute to the boom and bust periodicity, as they are still being studied. Certainly as herbivores eating grasses and sedges, there could be food limitations and, since these are boreal animals, the cold winters and cool summers may make grass recovery from herbivory slower than one might find at more southerly latitudes.

As Tamaria continues to read aloud to Charles, he jots down notes. When she finishes, she gently reminds Charles to write down the Web site address so they can cite their source of information and give appropriate credit about this well-known example of population fluctuation between the lemming and long-tailed jaeger. As Charles follows through on Tamaria's reminder, she draws a connection between the overview information that Mr. Petty provided and what she reads on the Web site. She says:

> When we were brainstorming with Mr. Petty reasons for why animals prey upon other animals, we mentioned food availability—or in some cases the lack of food, and birth rates and deaths. Look at what it says here: "So as the population of lemmings rises, the jaegers are more successful in finding and eating them. Jaegers now can reproduce and their population rises. As the population of jaegers rises, the predation may now drastically increase the death rate leading to the crash in the lemmings' population. Now the jaegers starve and their population crashes. Of course with the jaeger population low, the lemmings now have very low death rates and their population rises." So it's just like Mr. Petty was teaching us, the predators and prey populations are so like linked together in such an interesting and gross way!

VIGNETTE 2: ENGLISH LANGUAGE ARTS CLASSROOM

Deborah Howe is a veteran teacher of 15 years, presently teaching seventh-grade English language arts at a private independent school in upstate New York. Founded in the late 1800s, the school is co-educational and includes Grades 5 to 12. Small classes are the norm, with approximately 18 students per class and an overall 8:1 student to teacher ratio in the school. Many of the students transfer in from local parochial and public schools in the metropolitan area.

For the past 2 weeks, Debbie has been teaching a series of minilessons to build background knowledge for the unit of study for *Warriors Don't Cry* by Melba Pattillo Beals (1994). One minilesson was a meaning vocabulary activity that included the following words: (a) *resister,* (b) *rescuer,* (c) *perpetrator,* (d) *victim,* (e) *collaborator,* and (f) *bystander.* To help her students better understand the words, Debbie asked them to develop skits to role-play the meanings of the words. For example, one student might play the role of a resister and the other a perpetrator. Students collaborated in teams to write the brief skits and then acted out their roles while Debbie videotaped them. This vocabulary strategy was a preview for what students would later read in *Warriors Don't Cry*; the strategy prepared them to better understand the roles of the Little Rock Nine and the segregationists who prevented the integration of Central High School in 1957.

Today, Debbie is moving her unit to a study of Beals' memoir by briefing her 11 students on what they will address during class time. She decided to enhance this unit by using a variety of primary sources related to the Little Rock Nine and the integration of Central High School in Little Rock, Arkansas. Debbie is very enthusiastic about this unit. She has taught it at least two times before, and through her reflections over time she has carefully selected multiple texts types to optimize the learning opportunities for her seventh-grade students. What is also worth noting is that by reading and studying *Warriors Don't Cry* with students, Debbie is carefully crafting an interdisciplinary study between English language arts and social studies; teaching students to read and think critically about multiple texts (e.g., memoirs, photos, movies) while studying a significant and historical civil rights event.

Debbie has *Warriors Don't Cry* in her hand as she talks with her students about the interactive lesson and activities. Point of view is the topic for this lesson, and she begins by posing a question to students: "Why do you think they [the African American community in Little Rock, AK] chose these nine kids to go to Central High School?" The seventh graders respond by saying that the kids were smart and the Black community wanted to send their best. "Yes," says Debbie. So in a sense, the Little Rock Nine were representing the whole race. The African American community in Little Rock wanted to send the most courageous nine students and those who would represent themselves well academically. At the time, Central High School was recognized as one of the best high schools in the United States. Sending African American students who could endure the political, social, psychological, and academic pressures they would encounter was necessary to fulfill a mission of school integration in the 1950s.

Debbie reminds the students that the homework assignment for the previous evening was to read chapters 5 to 7 because she wanted them to understand that whole first day and night in Melba Pattillo Beals' life, where the nine students try to go to school and were kept out by the Arkansas National Guard. She lets her students know that she is aware that reading chapters 5 to 7 was a long assignment, but they will see that it was well worth their time and effort to read it all at once.

In addition to discussing the chapters, Debbie informs the students that they will be doing something very different in class over the next 2 days; they will be looking first at a photograph and then at a film of this civil rights event. She carefully emphasizes that they will be learning how to look carefully at photos and film to interpret what might be really going on in the selected images. That is, while using film and a photograph, the students will take a closer look at events and situations that they had already read about in *Warriors Don't Cry*. Because it is typical for seventh-grade adolescents to think that looking at a movie and a picture can give them a sense of story, Debbie further explains the rationale behind reading chapters 5 to 7 first, and then enhances their knowledge with movie clips and photos. She states,

> The purpose of doing the reading first is it makes you a bit of an expert, and then you will have some knowledge with which to come to the photo and to

the film. The book boosts your background knowledge because without some sense of what the event is about, just looking at a photo isn't very meaningful. So, we're gonna' be looking at a photograph today that became really a symbol—it became a famous photo of the civil rights movement and of this event. It made the national newspapers, and the international press. It was shown all over the world. Um, photos are really important in terms of how people remember history. This is a small. . . . I don't know how big this event will seem to us 50 years from now, but right now we're in the middle of the Iraqi war. What video image or photo do you think is most likely to be the one people are going to remember?

Debbie raises a critical question when linking a photo from the civil rights movement to a current international conflict—the Iraq war. Viola, one of Debbie's seventh graders, states that one of the pictures people would remember is how the Iraqi people were tearing down the statue of Saddam Hussein when U.S. soldiers invaded Baghdad. Chester believes that people will remember the emotional things such as women and children crying. Debbie augments the contributions made by Viola and Chester and summarizes her thoughts by noting pictures of wounded people and how those pictures tend to stick in the minds of people because they are so graphic. Debbie states,

> But that video of the statue toppling to symbolize the downfall of the government in Iraq is a picture that people will associate with that time in history. So it's interesting when we listen to your thoughts about how those images from the news give us impressions and feelings about what we think and what we remember of the war we're currently in.

Debbie continues with her minilesson by bringing her students' attention back to the photo at hand for today, a picture of Elizabeth Eckford, a student who was one of the Little Rock Nine. She explains that they have already seen the picture because it is in their Warriors book, but it is considered a very famous photo because it is symbolic of the racial hatred that overshadowed everything in the United States at the time. As Debbie directs them, students look at the white board while she orally describes the four things she wants students to do with the photo of Elizabeth Eckford in conjunction with what the words mean on their photo analysis think sheet. The terms on the board are *observation, knowledge, interpretation,* and *additional questions* (see Fig. 5.1). For each term or phrase, Debbie describes what students should do when critically examining the photograph for this particular lesson. She says to students:

> Observe—We look at a photo to observe; telling exactly and precisely what the eyes see. Um, when we looked at the video clip yesterday of Central High,

OBSERVATION Describe exactly what you see in the photograph so that someone who has not seen the photo can visualize it. What people and objects do you see? How are they arranged? What other details do you see?	**KNOWLEDGE** Summarize what you already know about the situation and time period shown. State what you know about the people and objects that appear.	**INTERPRETATION** What is happening in this picture? What can you conclude about this event or time period?

ADDITIONAL QUESTIONS
What is missing in this photograph? What would you like to see? What would you like to hear?

FIG. 5.1.   Photo analysis.

if you say, "The hallways were long and dark," that's something you can visually see. You're trying to put a picture in other people's minds.

Knowledge is the information in your brain about what this photo or what a film might mean. When you were looking at the picture of Central High School, you looked at it with the knowledge that that was the famous school that African American students integrated in 1957. So that's the information from your brain that adds to the picture so you know what you're looking at and why it has meaning.

Interpretation. Hmm, the best way I've found to think about this is interpretation is when you try to guess what the people were thinking and feeling. Interpretation really has to do with putting meaning to something whether it's something that you read or looking at a photo, but that's kind of vague. If you try to look at the photo and guess what the people were thinking and feeling, you're beginning to interpret.

Additional Questions. Let's think about asking more questions, and the questions I'm gonna' keep asking you are what do you wish was in this photo? What do you wish you could see more clearly? If this photo had sound to it, what would you like to hear?

After an explanation of the terminology, Debbie proceeds by giving the students a photo analysis think sheet to be completed in class. The knowledge box is filled out together as a class because all students read the same chapters (e.g., 5–7) for homework. Debbie directs the students to make a summary statement in the knowledge box to say that they know the photo is of Elizabeth Eckford walking to Central High the first day, and that is the background knowledge students bring to the photograph. Debbie explains that they would study the photo and silently observe to think about what they see, other people they see surrounding Elizabeth, at what and whom the people seem to be looking, the nature of their facial expressions, and how their bodies are arranged or positioned in relation to Elizabeth Eckford. Any observations made as described should go into the box labeled *observation*. Debbie continues to explain the activity by saying, "When you start trying to guess what the people were thinking or feeling, that guess goes into the box labeled 'interpretation,' and when you start wondering, 'Man . . . one of the questions I had is what are the soldiers saying? The soldiers' mouths are open. I'd love to know what they were saying.' So you might have other questions like that, which you would put in the question box." After asking whether everyone understands the assignments, Debbie waits for a cue from her students.

Next, Debbie redirects students' attention to another individual in the same photograph. She explains:

Now we're going to concentrate on Hazel Bryan. She is the one with her mouth wide open screaming, and looking very angry. And when I passed around this book yesterday to look at a sequence of photos, someone said that she almost looks like she's growling in some of the photos. Her lips are curled; her face is very angry. But she spoke very, felt very differently about this event, even six years after it happened and she was interviewed for this book [A Life is More Than a Moment] in 1997 for the 40th anniversary, and I'm going to read what the author of this book says and I will tell you when it's exactly Hazel's words. . . . The author confirms what Ann Thompson says, that the majority of the crowd was adults; only a few of them were high school students. And that's why it's so interesting to hear from these students. There actually are three and I'll go around once more to show you. Ann talks of the blonde girl and the girl with the black dress and the white kind of school tie. Her name is Sammy Dean and she becomes the major harasser and leader of the bullies, essentially, throughout the school year. And there's Hazel and it's kind of a good picture because you can see her kind of scowling. Those are the three girls. But most of the crowd, according to the author was adults. Where were most of the students? You already kind of heard that. They were in school—they were going through the soldier lines and going into the school. These three girls here are following Elizabeth Eckford. Now, this is what Hazel has to say, or actually what the author says about, first of all the background. "Only a few of the segregation resisters that tried to block the black student's entry in 1957 were of high school age. One of those teenagers, Hazel Bryan, now recalls that she went along with her parents to Central High on the morning the black students were scheduled to enroll to protest the racial integration of the school that she was scheduled to attend. I felt very religious at that time," this is her own words now, "I attended church every Sunday morning and night as well as Wednesday nights. While no one at church said we should protest school integration, we got the feeling that it would be a good thing to do." So pause for a minute we're looking at Hazel and what role is she playing right now?

As Debbie poses this question to the students, she brings them back to the vocabulary words they studied at the beginning of the unit. One of Debbie's students argues that Hazel Bryan might be playing two roles—the resister and the perpetrator. Debbie probes by asking from whose point of view is Hazel Bryan the resister and what specifically was she resisting? "Letting the black students into the school," responds the student. Debbie confirms the student's response by stating that Hazel Bryan is a resister because she is reacting from the point of view of the segregationists. Yet for the people who are trying to integrate Central High School, she becomes the perpetrator. Debbie continues to examine the roles that Hazel Bryan plays by asking students to continue to think. Another student offers an explanation by stating that Hazel might be a corroborator. "Yeah, who's she corroborating with?" asks Debbie. "All the people who are joining her," states the student. Debbie notes that Hazel is corroborating with the mob of segregationists and that in class she and the students had talked about that point previously.

Skillfully, Debbie continues to explore point of view by exploiting situations she deems ironic in both of the texts (i.e., *Warriors Don't Cry, A Life Is More Than a Moment*), as well as the historical event being studied. She points out that the segregationists in Little Rock, Arkansas, often quoted the *Holy Bible* as their source for why Black and White people should not live in the same neighborhood, and thus why Black and White students should not attend the same school. She notes,

Her religion, which is kind of ironic if you realize a lot of the civil rights leaders were ministers, but I unfortunately did not keep this clip with a movie, but there's one clip in *Eyes on the Prize* where white segregationists are quoting from the Bible to show that the Bible says we should be segregated people, and of course there's a lot of information in the Bible about people living as different tribes because that was the society of the time, but Governor Faubus uses it to defend segregation.

So her [Hazel Bryan's] religion made her feel this was the right opinion to have. We also are told that because her parents did not want her attending school with only nine blacks scheduled to attend Central High, Hazel transferred to a different school a few weeks after she was photographed as a central figure taunting Elizabeth Eckford. So what does that tell you about what's influencing her opinions about race and integration?

Students clearly state that Hazel was influenced by her parents and her religion, as Debbie emphasizes that Hazel would have been attending school with only 9 Black students and 1,950 White students.

Before ending the lesson, Debbie brings students' attention to another incident related to the photograph of Elizabeth Eckford and Hazel Bryan. In the book, *A Life Is More Than a Moment* (Counts, 1999), it is revealed that in 1963, six years after the photograph is taken, Hazel Bryan contacted Elizabeth Eckford at her father's home and apologized for her actions in the mob on that September morning in 1957. Debbie reads from the book because she believed that the sentence was very important, to let the students know that Hazel Bryan wanted to apologize to Elizabeth because she continued to feel like the poster child for the hate generation trapped in the image captured in the photograph. In the interview, Hazel Bryan acknowledged that she knew her life was more than a moment. Before students complete their photo analysis think sheet, they, along with their teacher, contemplate what Hazel must have been feeling about herself when she looked at the infamous photograph 6 years later.

ON USING MULTIPLE TYPES OF TEXTS

The vignettes described in this chapter, along with the national standards documents and research in literacy, offer insightful ways to teach content subjects such as biology and English language arts using multiple text types. To execute the strategies exhibited by Kenneth Petty and Deborah Howe, teachers need relevant knowledge, skills, and dispositions. Also, teachers should be willing to take reasonable risks to encourage students to do likewise, as well as provide learning opportunities to engage students with print and nonprint materials for a variety of literacy learning purposes.

One way Kenneth exhibits his own knowledge and skills is by using PowerPoint in his teaching; this serves as a model for using technology as a tool for teaching and learning. Care in the planning and design of his PowerPoint presentation and minilesson enabled Kenneth to focus his stu-

dents' attention on the content presented in PowerPoint, rather than daz-
zling them with animation and sounds that can often be a distraction to
learning. Kenneth was also skillful in facilitating collaborative learning and
inquiry among his students. Having no boundaries, inquiry-based learning
experiences are authentic and promote multiple and varied ways to explore
the world. As noted by Harvey (1998),

> Nonfiction inquiry starts with one condition, and it simply will not lift off with-
> out it: wonder. Teachers must find and fuel student curiosity into a state of
> wonder and a need to know more. The most likely place to unearth such won-
> der is in the realms where the person already has a passion, interest, or devel-
> oping knowledge. (p. 208)

The inquiry-based opportunities Kenneth Petty fostered for the topic of
population fluctuation support this theory.

In addition, Kenneth employs resources including YA literature and the
Internet. *Never Cry Wolf* (Mowat, 1963) is a piece of nonfiction that gives details about a particular topic (e.g., wolves) that cannot be thoroughly realized in a science textbook. Harvey (1998) asserted,

> the best nonfiction writing emerges from topics the writer knows, cares, and
> wonders about and wants to pursue. Nonfiction inquiry demands that learn-
> ers select a real topic that interests them, develop some questions about it,
> read for information, search for answers through research, report informa-
> tion, and ultimately gain new insight. (p. 4)

In the biology lesson vignette presented in this chapter, we see that Kenneth is teaching his students the significance of consulting resources other
than textbooks to gather information and read to learn.

Like Kenneth, Debbie was also strategic in using print and nonprint
texts to teach her lesson, which centered on point of view. Students studied
and discussed a photograph in conjunction with *Warriors Don't Cry* and *A
Life Is More Than a Moment*; both are nonfiction texts for teaching social justice issues. Debbie's strategic teaching methods resulted in several different
facets of literacy learning including: (a) interdisciplinary study of a historical civil rights event, (b) an in-depth critical analysis of a photograph, (c)
the emergence of complex questions for critique of print and nonprint
sources, (d) exploration of point of view as a way to enhance comprehension skills, and (e) reading and writing connections through the use of a
photograph analysis think sheet. Photographs are primary sources that can
assist in situating students within some historical contexts. The picture used
by Debbie not only enabled students to visualize what Melba Pattillo Beals
was talking about in her memoir, but also gave them an opportunity to ad-

dress experiences of a similar nature that they had encountered as adolescents (e.g., bullying).

A SCHOLAR'S RESPONSE
Gay Ivey, James Madison University

> Principle 3: Adolescents need opportunities to engage with print and nonprint texts for a variety of purposes.

It is clear from research that reading materials, both print and nonprint texts, are critical to the literate experiences and development of adolescent learners (Ivey & Broaddus, 2001; Worthy et al., 1999). Key to the principle addressed in this chapter, I believe, is the concept of *engagement*. To say that "adolescents need opportunities to engage with print and nonprint texts" suggests more than providing students with a variety of materials. Making available a range of texts that address curriculum standards and students' personal interests is a sound and necessary beginning, but it does not guarantee that students will read purposefully, enthusiastically, and with understanding. What Kenneth Petty and Deborah Howe show in this chapter is not just the use of alternative texts, but also the role of the teacher in facilitating involvement in the subject matter through those texts.

Given my experiences and research in middle and secondary classrooms, what concerns me most is the scarcity of situations where *all* students have the opportunity to experience true engagement in worthwhile texts. Here I am suggesting *engagement* as Guthrie (1996) defined it—that is, the motivated use of strategies for reading or thoughtful reading stemming from the personal desire to know. Guthrie's distinction of *engagement* from the concept of *compliance* is an important one:

> When children read merely to complete an assignment, with no sense of involvement or curiosity, they are being compliant. They conform to the demands of the situation irrespective of their personal goals. Compliant students are not likely to become lifelong learners. (p. 433)

I am afraid that in most secondary classrooms, the fit between available reading materials and adolescent learners does not even facilitate compliance with reading, much less engagement. When I ask my preservice teachers to recall their experiences with content area reading in high school, most confess that they were able to circumvent the reading assignments and still score high on tests and report cards. One can imagine that the situation is much more severe for students who still find reading difficult. Even in high-quality classrooms with expert teachers, what is the likelihood of real engagement in a variety of texts for struggling readers, language-minority students, and special education students?

This will remain our continuing challenge as educators of older students. It is highly doubtful that our least competent readers and writers in middle and secondary classrooms will become skillful, engaged readers if they are limited to a narrow scope of reading materials, such as the textbook or whole-class novels, that are too difficult, too tedious, or both (Allington, 2002). True engagement in a variety of texts for these students requires that we turn our attention to several matters. First, schools will have to bolster the sheer volume of reading materials available to teachers and students. One or two books on a subject or concept, regardless of difficulty level or quality, will not suffice in meeting the needs of the wide range of readers who will exist in any secondary classroom, nor will they provide enough information for students to become even mildly expert or interested in that subject.

Rather than relying solely on classroom libraries, schoolwide initiatives will be needed to build extraordinary collections of appealing, readable texts connected to the curriculum and to students' interests. At Thomas Harrison Middle School in Harrisonburg, Virginia, for instance, the literacy coordinator, librarian, and content area teachers worked together to create a vast collection of reading materials centered on the state standards and students' reading preferences (Ivey, 2002). When a science or social studies teacher in this school is ready to begin a certain unit of study, they may find as many as 100 or more books on their topic spanning both difficulty levels (primer level to high school level) and formats (journals, historical fiction, field guides, poetry, primary sources). This kind of commitment to materials is surely the only way that struggling readers and all students in a class will have real access to a variety of texts that seem worth reading and actually make sense to them.

Second, we need better ways to help teachers become experts on alternative reading materials within their subject areas. Content area methods courses and professional development opportunities of the past have focused on strategies for reading difficult text, mainly the textbook. New plans for secondary teacher learning should include a vision for changing texts, rather than creating new tools for reading the same old materials. It is highly improbable that anyone will devise a new strategy that will help struggling readers access materials that are too far beyond their reach. Trade books, primary sources, electronic texts, and other alternative materials spanning the gamut of difficulty levels and genres must become the centerpiece of instruction and learning rather than serve as supplementary resources. This will also require us to create and describe rich descriptions of how secondary content area teachers use diverse materials for instruction, particularly when, for example, 25 students in a class may be reading 25 different texts to learn about a particular concept.

Third, we need to use a variety of texts to change teachers' and students' perceptions of reading to learn. Traditional textbooks and other curriculum materials may actually mask what is interesting about a particular subject and make content area reading seem unappealing and even disruptive to learning. Alternatively, certain diverse reading materials that include intriguing details and multiple perspectives may help some students develop curiosity about school-sanctioned topics they never imagined possible (Ivey, 2004). In other words, the right reading materials can help build interest in areas where there seems to be no interest.

Fourth, we need to consider ways that teachers can help individual students actually engage in a variety of texts, particularly inexperienced readers. Teaching from the front of the class will probably not lead to engagement for students who have not already connected with texts on their own. For struggling readers and language-minority students in particular, this will mean working up close and personal with students to find a text that matches students' needs and interests, help them get started, or help them navigate a text (Worthy, Broaddus, & Ivey, 2001).

Discussion Questions

As you reflect on the information presented in this chapter, consider the following questions as they relate to your own teaching and/or your experiences in schools:

- In your experience, to what extent do teachers use multiple text types in classrooms, including nonprint as well as print materials?
- Do you think the case presented here is unique? Why or why not?
- Compare and contrast the views of the expert responder to your own views.
- What dilemmas must teachers, schools, and others solve to implement Principle 3?

Principle 4: Adolescents Need Opportunities to Generate and Express Rich Understandings of Ideas and Concepts

While studying content area subjects, great potential for understanding new ideas and concepts can be achieved when adolescents actively participate with teachers and peers. An understanding of ideas and concepts assists students in constructing meanings in the process of a lesson or explanation. Active participation assumes that there are specific and observable criteria (e.g., providing evidence that one is listening to the ideas of others by responding) that will allow adolescents to build on their own background knowledge as well as contribute to the learning of others. If opportunities to express rich understandings of ideas and concepts are to occur in content area subjects, both teachers and students must perform critical and formative roles so that all participants involved acquire knowledge (Gavelek & Raphael, 1996). Analytical approaches to teaching and learning are necessary for improving students' understanding of concepts and ideas in content area development within a social context; it is an approach that is critical to treat learning as an active, constructive process (Cobb, 2000).

When adolescents actively participate in subject area explorations, they also can become excited about understanding new ideas and concepts. Such teaching involves interactive responses between teachers and students—a process where both teachers and students actively listen and participate. Active participation enables students to learn why ideas and concepts work the way they do and how to represent their learning in varied ways. Students also gradually gain a better understanding of what they know and why they know it.

There is great variability in the ways teachers might assist students in using their literacy skills for generating and expressing new understandings.

For example, high school mathematics teachers can orchestrate a conceptual discussion as students learn generalizations regarding problem solving. Students can also use a variety of types of writing to understand ideas and concepts (e.g., Birken, 1989; Chapman, 1996; Ganguli, 1994). Chapman (1996), for example, used journal entries in algebra with her sophomores to first diagnose and trouble-shoot students' misconceptions. Reading students' journals enabled Chapman to gain insights and plan instructional strategies that assisted her students in understanding complex mathematical concepts. Because mathematics is a highly symbolic language, strategies that combine writing with classroom dialogue can assist students in learning new information. As Davis and Gerber (1994) argued, students "process information using language as they read, write, speak, and listen" (p. 55). When students use various forms of language to process mathematical concepts, they will be on a path for better understanding.

Middle- and high school teachers in every subject area can also facilitate students' learning through inquiry projects. For example, teachers working with students who are learning English can organize cultural studies that include the expertise students and their families bring with them to classrooms. Teachers who work with students with exceptional needs might identify overarching concepts to be explored by all students and then vary expectations for the learning of details depending on students' knowledge and expertise.

Many professional standards support the tenets of this principle. For instance, the National Council of Teachers of Mathematics (1991) state that "Students will use discourse to listen, respond, and question; explore examples" and "try to convince themselves and one another of the validity of particular representations, solutions, conjectures, and answers" (p. 45); and will "clarify and justify their ideas orally and in writing" (p. 35). The National Science Education Standards (NSES) state,

> Students need the opportunity to present their abilities and understanding and to use their knowledge and language of science to communicate scientific explanations and ideas. . . . Writing, labeling drawings, completing concept maps, developing spreadsheets, and designing computer graphics should be a part of science education. (NRC, 1996, p. 144)

Similarly, Teachers of English to Speakers of Other Languages (TESOL, 2001) asserts that students should "use English to obtain, process, construct, and provide subject matter information in spoken and written form" (Goal 2, Statement 2, Paragraph 1).

The guiding principle of this chapter and the support of the professional standards across disciplines convey that understanding new ideas and concepts entails more than a style of teaching where teachers transmit information and students passively learn. It requires more than asking questions that require a "yes" or "no" answer or an I–R–E (Initiation, Response, Explanation) pattern of response (Cazden, 1988). For students to actively participate and reveal how they understand new ideas and concepts, they must first know that they are free to take risks as they grapple with information and themselves as learners. Cobb (2004) argued that in mathematics, for example, "students' development of a sense of affiliation with mathematical activity and thus the cultivation of what might be termed their *mathematical interests* is essential" (p. 335). A learning environment that encourages students to take risks requires that teachers take time to scaffold student learning and be aware of various learning styles as well as students' needs and interests.

The following illustration is mixed between vignette and transcript, and conveys how teachers might create a favorable learning environment (Alvermann & Phelps, 2002) so that adolescents can take risks to express their understandings about conceptual information. In this illustration, we focus on ninth graders in the process of developing a formula to calculate their teacher's water bill. The first part centers on a minilesson where the teacher offers a detailed description and explanation of the concepts necessary for understanding what is needed to develop the formula. The second half is a transcript and conveys the ninth-grade students' collaborative effort to create a formula so they can determine how much water their teacher used in a 30-day period.

VIGNETTE 1: HOW MUCH WATER DO WE CONSUME AND WHAT DOES IT COST?

Richard G. is an experienced teacher of 14 years who has spent most of his career at a high school located in a large urban district in the northeastern United States. Currently, Richard is pursuing his doctorate in mathematics education. Because of his doctoral studies and his proactive and progressive stance on issues related to math education, Richard spends time at the library reading peer-reviewed journals to learn more about current research in math education. In Richard's newest venture, he is seeking ways to implement writing in his math class, making annotations that will be useful when he later implements strategies based on research and practitioner articles. He uses his annotations of the articles to refresh his memory of the ideas and concepts, and he says they also help him think about the theoretical rationale for particular strategies before he decides to use them.

Richard begins his lesson today with a minilesson on generating linear equations. He then leads his ninth graders through an examination of water consumption and the total cost from his water bill. First, he writes the basic formula $y = mx + b$ and a set of coordinate axes on the white board. He then plots a point, explaining, "The coordinates of this point would be the (4, 7). For some relationships when we have an input of 4, we get an output of 7. So, some rule could generate that relationship; obviously an infinite number of rules could generate that pair. What are some of those relations or rules?" (see Fig. 6.1).

Debbie:	Add 3.
Richard:	What do you mean?
Debbie:	Add 3 to the input.
Richard:	To . . . ?
Debbie:	. . . to get the output.
Richard:	Good. Others?
Janka:	Times two minus one.
Richard:	What would the equation be?
Janka:	Two x minus one.
Richard:	. . . equals?
Janka:	. . . y, two x minus one equals y.
Richard:	Write it for us.

As the student writes $y = 2x - 1$ on the white board, Richard continues to seek additional information from his ninth-grade students. Debbie asserts that $3x - 5 = y$, and Elena offers a different equation, which states $4x - 9 = y$.

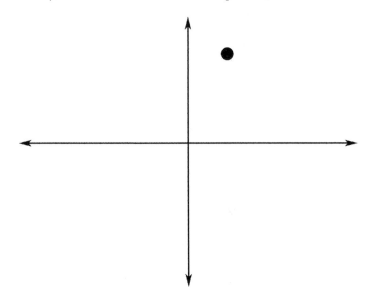

FIG. 6.1. Axis with point.

As Richard acknowledges his students' correct statements, he continues with his explanation: "A very standard algebraic form of a rule for a linear relationship or line, which, remember, is just a set of solution pairs or ordered pairs, is called the slope-intercept form." As he points to the y = mx + b, on the white board, he draws a line through the points (4,7) and (0,1) on the graphs (see Fig. 6.2). "What is the slope here? It's the rate of change. So the slope of this line is how much the output changes for every unit change in the input. So if we had a . . . let's look at two lines like this . . . OK this line is very steep. This means every time I go from here to here, that's the output for that input, and this is the output for this input" (see Fig. 6.3). As Richard continues with his explanation of the slope, one student interrupts to ask a specific question for clarification. "So that's more?" [Pointing to the steeper slope.] Richard responds by letting the student know that it is a lot more. He continues with,

> Where here if we look at these two places, alright for this input we have that output, and for this input we have that output so it's just a little bit more. So we'd say there is a high rate of change or a larger slope here; low rate of change, lower slope. What is the change in input and output between these two points?

Students give Richard the answers he is hoping for, signaling their understanding. "Four. And the output is six . . . the change is six. So the slope is one and a half."

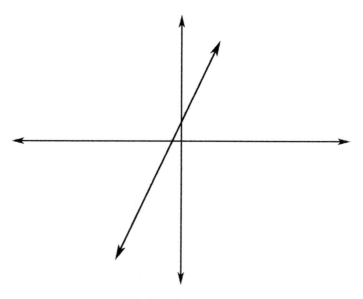

FIG. 6.2.   Axis with line.

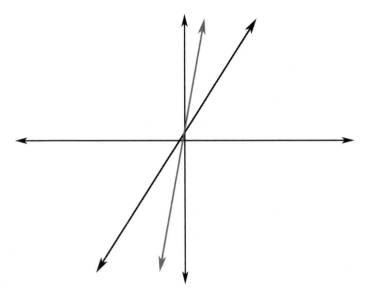

FIG. 6.3.   Axis with second line.

Richard continues: "If we talk about the input zero as the starting point {points to the point (0, 1)} what's the output, when the input's zero? OK. And that's just one way to talk about it." A student says, "The output is where the lines intersect? Is that . . ." Richard notes that "The output, the y value or the second term in the ordered pair. So if I said ah, 'books are five dollars each.' OK. And I ask you how much money you spent? So you would say, well, I bought four books so the input's four, the number of books you—bought the output then would be . . . ?"

The student becomes excited that she knows the answer and interrupts her teacher, saying, "How much I paid for four books!"

"That's correct," notes Richard. So,

How much you paid for 4 books, say at 5 bucks each, so $20 is the output. So, in that sense if you bought zero books, the output would be zero. OK, so that's the output when the input's zero. I'm calling it the starting point, and that's my own terminology, I don't think it's in any books. Now remember the output at the starting point does not have to be 0. It can be negative or positive. OK. So, that's the general schema of what's going on. We call the input, usually, I refer to it as x but you can use any symbol—it's the independent variable. And then that makes the output the dependent variable, because it depends on what the input is. So the amount you would spend on the books would depend on how many books you bought. Now this m is representative of the slope, the larger it is, the steeper the slope. In the example we just talked about the slope is the cost of one book $5; every time we buy another book the output goes up $5. And the number that multiplies a variable is gen-

erally called a coefficient. When you have something like this, we refer to the
5 as a coefficient: it's a constant that multiples the variable term. This term b is
also gonna' be a numerical constant because for this given line, we only cross
the y-axis at one point. So this is also some constant term. So we have two variables, x and y, the input and the output; and two constants, m and b, the rate
of change and the starting point. We use these symbols to represent the gen-
eralized statement of this type of relationship. So this is a whole class of relationships, right? And every straight line—no matter which way it goes—fits
into this class of relationships. OK. Follow?

As Richard passes around a handout of his water bill, one student laughs
at his question and says, "Yea. I'm following so far."

"Alright so now let's talk about this . . . and this is probably where the interesting part is now because we're all going to talk about this water bill,"
Richard informs his students (see Fig. 6.4).

We pause for a moment in this vignette to provide a few explanatory details about Richard's purposes and goals. As a teacher who is reflective
about his math instruction and makes changes based on students' performance, over time Richard has learned that it is better to have a long conversation about his water bill before requiring students to go into the exercise.
The conversation between Richard and his students has some influence on
the direction the activity will take. Therefore, as the teacher, it is important
that he brainstorm with his students about concepts necessary for successful
completion of the activity. One of Richard's goals is to connect his students'
intuitive sense of the everyday concept of spending money to the scientific
concepts embodied in the relation y = mx + b. His theoretical base for this
goal stems from Vygotsky's (1986) notion that talk or the social interaction
among people enables them to solve practical tasks. It is the junction of
multiple perceptions, voices, actions, and the understanding of various
mathematical concepts among students that enables them to generate and
express their rich understandings of ideas and concepts about an abstract
mathematical problem. Vygotsky argued:

> The most significant moment in the course of intellectual development,
> which gives birth to the purely human forms of practical and abstract intelli-
> gence, occurs when speech and practical activity, two previously completely
> independent lines of development converge. (p. 24)

Early in his career, Richard had always left it up to his students to have
conversations about the math problem at hand without taking the opportunity to observe the quality of the students' discussion. Over time, however,
he began to realize that the depth of students' discussions about this exercise, in addition to their expressions of understanding, were important for
his assessment of what and how they were learning. Consequently, Richard

Math 110
Relations Exercise

Below is a copy of my water bill. I never use more than 3000 cubic
feet of water in a billing period. Using the information given, write a
function for my water bill. That is, write an expression that displays
total cost as a function of cubic feet used.
1. Assign variables
2. Write expressions for each component of the bill, including meter
   capacity charge.
3. Combine the expression into an equation
4. Represent the equation as a function
5. In words, describe some of the problems you had and why you made the
   decisions you made.

THIS ACCOUNT HAS A .58 INCH SIZE METER THE
METER CAPACITY CHARGE FOR WATER WITH THIS
SIZE METER IS $14.07

METER QUARTERLY WATER CHARGES
FIRST 9 THOUSAND CUBIC FEET
$11.26 PER THOUSAND CUBIC FEET
OVER 9 THOUSAND CUBIC FEET
TO 36 THOUSAND CUBIC FEET
$10.03 PER CUBIC FEET
OVER 36 THOUSAND CUBIC FEET
$7.66 PER CUBIC FEET METER QUARTERLY SEWER
CHARGES
$11.09 PER THOUSAND CUBIC FEET
MINIMUM CHARGE OF $48.30

CHARGES	WATER	SEWER
CURRENT	26.91	48.30
ARREARS	0.00	0.00
SPL. CHGS.*	0.00	
COLL. FEE*	0.00	
COLL. COMM.*	0.00	0.00
RET.CK. FEE*	0.00	
INTEREST	0.00	0.00
CREDITS	0.00	0.00
TOTAL	$75.21	

METER READING		
PRIOR READING	CURRENT READING	COMSUMPTION
5580	6720	1140

IMPORTANT INFORMATION

**PAYABLE WITHIN 10 DAYS
OF BILL DATE**
WHEN PAYING BILL IN PERSON, PLEASE
BRING ENTIRE BILL

UNPAID WATER BILLS ARE A LIEN ON THE PROPERTY.

NONPAYMENT OF BILL MAY RESULT IN THE SHUT
OFF OF WATER

TOTAL PAID SINCE LAST BILL $71.15

SPECIAL MESSAGES

For rapid processing use the enclosed envelope when paying your bill.
Please pay each property with a separate check. Each month when bills are sent out
our phones are invariably busy. When calling please be patient, your call will be
answered in the order it was received.   Seq. 12485

FIG. 6.4.   Math 110 relations exercise.

changed his methods so that in this lesson he engages with and monitors students' discussions as they struggle with abstract ideas and concepts to develop a formula during the water bill activity.

Now we return to Richard and his students as they talk to understand the concepts and ideas presented for this activity.

Richard: Now we're talking about what sorts of things are gonna vary here; we want to know what's the input and output? And you could define this situation in a lot of ways, but the traditional way would be the output is gonna be what you pay. So, that's gonna be . . .

Meloni: It's like the books . . .

Richard: Yea, it's like the book. What about the books?

Meloni: Oh, the total cost of the books. Right?

Richard: And so that would be dependent on what?

Meloni: That would be dependent on the [pause] input, which would be the constant price or cost?

Richard: Well, that's one of the things it's gonna be. Right? It's gonna be dependent on the constant. It's also gonna be dependent on not just what the cost is, but . . . the $5 was the constant with these books in this situation, but what could change?

It is important to note here that a common problem exposed by Meloni is the difficulty of mapping the components of a situation to the terms in the formula. In this student's mind, the price of a book can change, so the price should be a variable. It could be, but for this exercise Richard wants to stress that the unit cost is a constant.

Meloni: How many I buy?

Richard: How many you buy? So what's gonna be the thing that changes here? What am I buying?

Meloni: How much water you use.

Richard: How much water. So how much water you use is . . . ?

Meloni: The independent variable.

Richard: Does that make sense? So that's your input.

Meloni: How much water I use, how many books I buy?

Richard continues with his explanation in further detail:

Yep, so there's a nice literal mapping there. And then your total bill in dollars is your output or your dependent variable. And we're gonna see now that as we use more water our bill's gonna get bigger. OK. Now this is really the hard part for you . . . getting that down because you don't see any variable on this water bill. You don't see any equations, only verbal explanations and numbers and you have to decipher the relationships described in those explanations and the roles of those numbers. So even though you may understand y = mx + b algebraically, to actually apply it to this situation is difficult if you don't have a real flexible mental image of the relationship.

Richard knows that, in general, his students only have the symbolic image of the formula. So it is usually hard for them to take a situation and line the pieces up to realize that the consumption reported on the bill is one possible value of the independent variable—the number they are going to use to generate the output. In other months, the variable terms will have different values assigned to them if water consumption varies, but the relationship will stay the same. Because this is often a difficult concept for students to understand, and it is critical to their understanding of the task, Richard often spends additional time talking about and encouraging his students to talk as they collaborate to generate a formula. For example, on this day he says to students: "Let's say, for example, there's a holiday season where family members and friends come to visit. More people are taking showers, and the family is cooking more and, you know, all of that would have an impact on the consumption of water."

Richard later explains the difficulty his students experience to a colleague:

> Students often see y = 2x + 3 over and over again, and so they know that if x = 4 then y = 11, so it's always just been some number and this is one solution. So they have this ordered pair, and we could say x = 5, right? And that makes y = 13, so we have this ordered pair (5, 13). So they're always thinking the variable, has to be some number or it's taking the place of some number. Therefore, it's tough for students to get the idea that the number can vary. To apply it we have to think that it's more than a number, that number represents some value, or some measurable quantity. And I think that's something that has to come into the discussion, that it's not just this list of numbers, but these numbers have units; they have meaning, you know, if they're ever going to apply this. And likewise, they look at this and say, "how is that a variable?" It's a number. I think in the future I may give students bills from two different time periods so they can see which numbers have changed.

After the minilesson, Richard asks his students to form groups and discuss the problem. The following is a discussion among one group of students coming to grips with some of these issues.

Debbie: OK, well it says that we should assign and label variables.

Janka: It just says using the information . . . ?

Charles: The total's $75.21.

Debbie: Um-hmm, so where should we put that?

Katy: We need to find the input and the output.

Debbie: He said the water was the input.

Charles: What water?

Debbie: The 1140.

Charles: But if it's a constant why do we need a function?

Debbie: So if the water changes, then the cost would change, it gets
              bigger.

Charles: I don't know . . . the more you use the cheaper it is?

Debbie: But the total bill gets bigger.

Janka: Well, let's see what we know. Let's gather all the information
              that we know.

Katy: It also says that it doesn't use more than 3,000 cubic so that
              should be . . . ? Because it's first 9,000 so this 3,000?

Debbie: We have to think about the units too.

Janka: So what do we know?

Katy: The water used is different every month. We know that the
              more you use the more you pay.

[students laugh]

Debbie: That is . . . will be $11.26 by a certain amount of . . . ?

Charles: By a certain amount of what?

Debbie: Um, cubic feet.

Charles: Cubic feet, so does that mean, that's one of our variables?

Students: Yeah.

Charles: So what do we want to call that?

Janka: W.

Charles: W? So W is equal to what? Water use?

Janka: Number of thousand cubic feet.

Charles: Number of thousand cubic feet of what? So that's one of our
              variables. What else do we know?

Katy: Well we know that for every thousand $11.26 will be paid.

Charles: [writing] What else do we know?

Janka: How much we use.

Charles: OK. How much we use.

Debbie: 1.14 hundred . . . a thousand

Charles:	Well then, 1.14 thousand, but, well then what's our other variable?
Katy:	Do we need the other variable?
Charles:	The function, aren't there two? Like you're gonna . . . an input and output?
Katy:	Like the books, total cost.
Charles:	Yea, so the output . . .
Janka:	But we already know the cost.
Charles:	Do we know the output? That's the $75.21 right?
Debbie:	And that depends on the amount that you use by the cost.
Charles:	But, we aren't gonna use the same amount every time right?
Katy:	Yea, that's why we use a variable?
Charles:	So that means it's not gonna cost the same every time.
Katy:	Yeah.
Charles:	So?
Katy:	The cost will depend on how much you use?
Charles:	So the cost is gonna be a variable too right?
Katy:	Yea, but if they ask us to find the function, we usually have to ask like what it costs to do something, and then x is to something you know. So what's the output?
Janka:	How much we spend?
Debbie:	The total of the bill every month.
Charles:	Ok, so what are we gonna call that T? T = the total we spend. Alright. So is that our function? So then you have to come along and say OK, let's let w = [cubic feet of water used].
Katy:	W standing for water?

As the students mull over their ideas to come up with a formula, their teacher reenters the discussion. Richard says,

> Water, that's gonna be our consumption, and we can say consumption, but we want the units, so we have to clarify things. We can't just say consumption, but gallons, or cubic feet, of consumption. So we want to make sure that we have the units. And that adds something concrete then to this pretty abstract idea of what this variable is. That's gonna be our input, or independent variable. Then we could say, a lot of times we use T = total cost in dollars. And that's our output. Does that make sense?

His students acknowledge that they understand.

Richard continues:

So that's all this is asking you to do? But while this part of [may seem] really easy, it's getting to understand which piece of this whole thing is the input, which piece is the output and what is the relation between the two described on the bill. In that discussion we were talking about just a little while ago, a key issue [was] getting you to understand this is the input variable and that's the output variable [pointing to x and y on the white board]. These are just one representation of it [pointing to consumption and cost figures on the water bill]. That's the hard part.

Janka joins the conversation, indicating that she needs clarification:

So the first part of the assignment is for us to understand that there is an input and output amount of water that's consumed in cubic feet, and the total cost of it depends on how much is used. And we have to assign . . . OK, so how are we supposed to know um, oh, I got it, I think I got it. [laughs] I was gonna' ask you Mr. G., how are we supposed to know how many variables we should work with, but if you have two concepts, the input . . . the independent variable, and the output, the dependent variable, then that would let us know how many?

Richard responds to Janka's query with a detailed clarification.

Right. And just to reiterate, it's a linear equation in two variables, but that's a very good question because often students want to say . . . because they do see this formula this way, students do see this all the time and they want to think that these are variables also [pointing to m and b]. You want to think the m and the b are variables because from one representation, out of this whole class, to another representation out of this whole class, the m and the b can change. You know we can have y = 2x + 3 and we can have y = 5x − 7 . . . you know these are both in the same class of linear equations, two variables, but the m and the b have changed. But these are two completely different relations now. And so it's kind of a struggle sometimes for students to look at something like this, and not think of the rate of change and the starting point as something that can change, so what many of you might want to do is assign more than two variables. So that has to become part of your discussion too. So how do we know that there are only two variables? Well, we have an input and we have an output OK. Where do these other things come in? And you can have relationships that have three, four, or more input variables. For example, think about all the different things, you could think about that affects grades in math class. Well your attendance factors in, your test grades, homework grades, quiz grades, and your project grades. All those different things you could think of as inputs. So you can have any number of variables, but in this case we're talking about just the two. So you have to have this discussion on whether or not this will change, will this $14.07 change when consumption changes?

Debbie answers: "Let's see now, this account has a .58 inch size meter, the meter capacity charge or water with this size meter is $14.07. OK so no matter how much water is consumed, it's going to cost $14.07 per period."

What Debbie is pointing out is not clearly explained in the handout of the water bill and the directions.

Richard tells his students,

We're talking about my house, it's about me [laugh]. So that's [the meter capacity charge] never gonna change, I hope. So this becomes part of the b; this is the starting point. Katy asks Mr. G. if he's talking about the $14.07 and he answers "right" as he continues, "So even if I don't use any water, even if my input is 0, my consumption's 0, I'm still paying that $14.07. OK?

Debbie asks, "So that would be the minimum you would pay even if you didn't use any water whatsoever, not even a glass" [laugh]?

"Not even a leaky faucet! I still pay $14.07. And actually even more because of the sewer charges that are on the bill too," states Richard.

After this in-depth tête-à-tête, students read through the quarterly water charges on the water bill. The first 9,000 cubic feet is charged at $11.26 per thousand cubic feet. Richard informs his students that closely reading the water bill is a real exercise in reading directions. He reiterates that he never uses more than 3,000 cubic feet. Richard lets the students know that mathematically this is a matter of limiting the domain. So the only part they have to be concerned about is the first part of the description, which can be a little tricky. In any event, Richard makes his students aware that one of the things he likes about this water bill activity is that many rich mathematical concepts come into play.

Kathy wants to know if the 1140 means 1.14 cubic feet. Richard answers,

No, it's 1.14 thousand cubic feet. And they [the county water board] charge by the thousand cubic feet. So this is like an exercise in units now, too, and place value comes in here. Alright, you have to pull in a lot of your background knowledge here. Right, this is the same as saying one thousand one hundred forty, or eleven hundred forty. OK. So this is the rate of change; every time I use another thousand cubic feet, my bill goes up $11.26. So that's in here. Then we get to this next part, and we look up here and that might help us look for more, and it says, the meter quarterly sewer charges are $11.09 per thousand cubic feet with a minimum charge of $48.30. So I'm using 3,000 cubic feet at $11.09, what do I pay?

Janka says that the minimum is $48.30, but qualifies that Mr. G. still has to pay that regardless. Richard continues, "So, I have to pay that. So for me, [since I] never use more than 3,000 cubic feet, is this a variable or a constant charge?" Janka states that it is a constant.

Richard continues, "So that falls under the *b*. That is part of the starting point. So now I can say, given everything that we've talked about, we can say, my total cost is equal to my rate of change times my consumption, plus my starting point. So this is what I hope you get to." Janka wants to know whether Mr. G. would still have to pay $62.37 if he did not use the maximum amount of water.

Richard explains,

> Well yea, you can also say it . . . even if I use no water at all I'm still paying this. Does that make sense? And then so what's gonna' happen . . . is [that] as input changes, output's gonna change, if this gets bigger, that will get bigger [pointing to *x* and *y*]. But the total cost will never get below $62.37, because you'll never have negative consumption. You might have zero consumption, but not negative. What's an interesting thing to know is, if you generate electricity, the power company has to . . . if you generate more than you use the power company has to take it back. So with the electric bill, you could actually have negative consumption, but not the water bill. We assign the variables and write expressions for each component of the bill including the meter capacity charge. And so the components of the bills are, the water, the sewer, and the meter capacity charge.

Kate inquires as to whether the complete water bill represents three different amounts. Richard acknowledges there are three different quantities that are part of the relationship between input and output.

> So decide how to calculate each one. What I'm looking for you to do, is break this down into pieces . . . and then the final one is total cost, which we're just gonna call T. OK, so here're all the pieces now. These are each expressions for everything that contributes to your bill. So now how do we combine them? So that's what I'm asking you to do here and here.

The following transcript shows the students' discussion in which they further examine the impact various parts of the water bill play in the construction of the linear equation.

Janka:	So T = $11.26 times W.
Charles:	Cool.
Katy:	What do you think for W again?
Janka:	Number of one thousand cubic feet of water.

Charles:	Alright, so does that . . . yea, but this doesn't make sense. Because look at what the total bill is here, and look at how much he used. Doesn't this teacher ever shower? [students laugh] 'cause look. If x is equal . . . we're saying that's how much he used. Then here is 1.14 thousand cubic feet right. So we multiply that by the 11.26. That doesn't give us 75.21.
Janka:	But we didn't take into consideration all the other charges that we have to pay above the water we use.
Charles:	Alright, and that's what this says. Write the expressions for each component of the water bill including meter capacity charge. So is it supposed to be y = mx + b? What's b?
Janka:	That's the 14.07.
Charles:	OK, so what's that? $14.07 is the meter capacity charge. Is there anything else?
Janka:	What is that sewer charge? What does that mean?
Charles:	I don't know. Let's see what does it say? Meter quarterly sewer charges 11.09 per thousand cubic feet.
Janka:	But we should have added that to the $11.26 and multiply our x.
Charles:	So you think it should be 11.26 + 11. 09 right? So that's 22.35 right?
Janka:	Um-hmm.
Charles:	Alright, does that . . . plus the $14.07 somewhere.
Janka:	Yea, that goes plus . . .
Charles:	So y = 22.35(x) + 14.07. Alright, so 22.35(x) 1.14 is gonna' be somewhere around 25 right? Plus 14, it's still not 75.
Janka:	What else is there? Let's see. Maybe there was a leak.
Katy:	No, but it says that the minimum sewer charge is 48.
Charles:	For . . . but he's over that. He's 75.21 already.
Janka:	Oh, for the sewer charge there's a minimum. Yea, so it's not always included in here. We don't always have to multiply.
Charles:	So we don't always have to multiply by that. So where do we put it?
Janka:	Wow. [long pause]
Charles:	Let's see. We have an expression for the capacity charge right? And that's just the 14.07. And we have an expression for the water used. Right, that's the 11.26(x) right?
Debbie:	He never uses more than 3,000 right? So if you have 3 by 11.09 that wouldn't be more than 48.30 which is added on instead of multiplying again?

Charles: Add on what?

Debbie: 48.30.

Janka: That's a good idea.

Charles: Oh. So he always pays that, 'cause he doesn't shower.

[students laugh]

Charles: So for number two we just say that that's the sewer charge? Call it 48.30.

Janka: Yea.

Charles: OK, sewer charge, 48.30.

Janka: We don't have to multiply by that big number but . . .

Charles: So we want to combine the expressions and then the equation. So y = . . .

Debbie: . . . 11.26(x) + you would have the 14.07 right? + 48.30 for the sewer.

Charles: Well, let's see if it checks? So the 48.30 and the 14 that's about 62 and then 11.26 x 1.14 that he used that's gonna be around 75 right? So . . .

Janka: It looks right now.

Charles: So . . .

Janka: Now what?

Charles: Well, can we add those two together?

Debbie: Yep.

Charles: So we get y = 11.26(x) + 62.37. So that's saying the total cost is equal to . . . what was x?

Debbie: Cost per thousand cubic feet, or the number of thousands. It's the amount of water.

Charles: So it's the number of thousands times . . . the amount of water in thousands times 11.26 + this . . .

Janka: . . . 62.37 which covers the sewer charge and the . . .

Debbie: . . . the meter capacity charge.

Janka: Yea, so but we cannot use more than 3,000 cubic feet of water.

Richard steps in to say,

Now what number four is about, it's just about a different type of notation. We tend to talk about relations and equations as functions, and as we would use the terminology, we would say total cost is a function of consumption. And the way we notate that is "T = f of W," that's the way you would say that. And this reads total cost is a function of consumption: "T = F of W." And then the rest of it would just be the same. This notation adapts better to computer technology. And then if we say for this case I use this much, I would say F of 1.14 equals 5.21 so when I input 1.14 thousand cubic feet, I should generate a total cost of $75.21. We can look at that in terms of an ordered pair (1.14, 75.21). That's my ordered pair for this billing period; that's my input and my output. . . . [Richard then gives an explanation of how to graph the variables.]

The class continues with a discussion of function notation, with students grappling with the concepts and eventually writing a formula representing the water bill. At the end of the discussion, students address a question Richard has posed that asks them to reflect on their learning experience. Charles begins by reading the reflective question.

Charles:	[The question is] . . . Describe some of the problems you had and why you made the decisions you made. Oh no! Alright, so what kinds of problems did we have?
Debbie:	We didn't necessarily read all the directions [unclear] before we started?
Charles:	OK. Now write that down, Janka.
Janka:	Say that again?
Debbie:	That we didn't read everything before we started.
Charles:	That's kinda what you [Janka] were telling us to do at the beginning, get all the information.
Janka:	That's how we gotta start.
Charles:	What else did we have trouble with?
Janka:	The sewer.
Charles:	The sewer yea. So why did we make the decision we made about the sewer?
Katy:	[unclear] like we first looked . . . we came back and found this gap and then [we] looked [it] up [and found] that he doesn't use more than 3,000, so it's always . . . [unclear]
Janka:	For me it was that I didn't read that. I thought it was a different line. I didn't even read it.
Debbie:	We don't get the f of x thing.
Charles:	Yea. What is that f of x thing? What's different?
Janka:	Something expressed is a function of x.
Charles:	Is a function of cubic feet used. Oh, well, maybe he'll answer it for us. What other problems did we have?
Janka:	At first we just thought that there were no other charges. But I think we just didn't read the whole problem carefully. That was the major problem 'cause everything leads there. 'Cause

once we read that he only uses 3,000 cubic feet then we could figure out the sewer thing. But we just really have to read carefully. Right?

Charles: I think so. Are we supposed to mail this for rapid processing? Oh never mind. [students laugh]. I think we're done.

UNDERSTANDING IDEAS AND CONCEPTS IN PRACTICAL MATHEMATICS

Recently, Alvermann and Reinking, editors for *Reading Research Quarterly*, invited scholars of mathematics, social studies, English-language learning, and science education to write pieces to address their perceptions of the need for collaboration between their fields and literacy education (Alvermann & Reinking, 2004). In response, Cobb (2004) argued for a collaborative possibility between math and literacies, using literacies in the plural to define mathematics as not monolithic, but rather multiple in the sense that high school math teaching, and what students learn from their course work should not be divorced from aspects of their everyday lives. Thus, a possibility for collaborative efforts between math and literacy is within classrooms where lessons and activities "involve the analysis of both the students' development of a particular mathematical literacy and the means by which that process of development was supported and organized" (p. 333). Cobb suggested that such activities are multimodal and proposed teaching and learning opportunities that would include a variety of forms of text (Cobb, 2004).

One way to merge the gap between math and literacy teaching and learning is to develop collaborative design experiments to investigate the ways to support students' development of particular mathematical literacies (Cobb, 2004). This type of research would necessitate designing lessons and activities within a context that would emphasize meaning-making and thus mathematical literacy, which is the goal of instruction.

As indicated at the beginning of this chapter, Guiding Principle 4 states that "adolescents need opportunities to generate and express rich understandings of ideas and concepts." The vignette and transcripts presented illustrate that the teaching and learning of math concepts are enhanced by a context that includes teacher scaffolding and dialogue between a teacher and students. Mr. G. used his water bill to teach his ninth graders about real and practical math concepts and ideas. He walked them through the different costs of the bill (i.e., water, sewage, meter capacity charge) so they could use the numerical symbols to generate formulas. His careful scaffolding of details included his use of mathematical terms to clarify practical applications to the water bill to assist students in thinking about the formula they were charged to develop.

The dialogue that ensued among the group of students enabled them to generate a formula that they might use to figure the input and output for the water bill. The process by which the formula was accomplished involved everyday discourse and gesture as well as commentary involving mathematical terms and notations. This lesson and the processes students and teacher used provide an example of the merger of literacies valued by mathematics and literacy educators.

A SCHOLAR'S RESPONSE
Josephine Peyton Marsh,[1] Arizona State University

> Principle 4: Adolescents need opportunities to generate and express rich understandings of ideas and concepts.

This chapter focuses on the guiding principle, *adolescents need opportunities to generate and express rich understandings of ideas and concepts.* The principle implies an interactive form of learning that utilizes written and oral forms of literacy to construct and express understandings related to different academic content ideas and concepts. The chapter highlights one math teacher's ninth-grade class and how they used collaborative interaction to create a linear equation and understand how equations are relevant to real-life situations.

We read about how Mr. G. presented detailed explanations and then guided small-group discussions. He asked students questions, offered explanations, and supported their attempts to make mathematical sense out of the water bill. The transcript of the student-to-student talk and his interactions with them demonstrate the power of talk as a means of developing understandings and connecting content knowledge to real-life situations.

I applaud Mr. G.'s methods of math instruction and find his approach to teaching one that is supported by my varied research experiences (e.g., Alvermann, Commeyras, Young, Randall, & Hinson, 1987; Alvermann et al., 1996; Young, 2000). Through this research, I learned that adolescent students value discussion as a means to develop understandings, and that students make sense of what they read and develop new understandings of ideas and concepts through interaction with their peers and their teacher. They also make connections between their personal knowledge and diverse backgrounds and newly introduced ideas and concepts.

I wish more teachers of adolescents incorporated this principle into their regular curriculum. During the last decade or so, I have observed in many high school classrooms as a teacher, researcher, and consultant. I have learned that discussion is rare and when it does take place it is likely to follow an I–R–E (teacher initiates a question, the student answers, and then

---

[1]My name was formerly Josephine Peyton Young.

the teacher evaluates the answer giving either positive or negative feed-back) pattern of discussion. This type of discussion is more about transmitting or reciting information than it is about developing and expressing understandings of ideas and concepts.

Many teachers do not incorporate discussion and interactive learning into their daily curriculum because, they say: (a) it takes up too much class time and they are required to cover a large amount of content, (b) they lack control of what students learn during discussions, (c) students get off task during small-group discussions and the noise level is too high, (d) there is uneven participation among students, and (e) some students get heard, whereas others are silenced due to gender, race, or social status (Hinchman & Young, 2001).

The discussions highlighted in this chapter provided students with structured and supported opportunities to develop understandings of linear equations and how they are used in everyday life situations. Mr. G. provided what could be identified as supportive scaffolds (Wilkinson & Silliman, 2000). Supportive scaffolds are graduated assistance provided by the teacher so students can achieve higher competence and understandings than they otherwise would without support. Supportive scaffolds are based on Vygotsky's notion that learning is social and an active search for meaning. Further, that learning takes place within communities of learners and in student-centered environments (Wilkinson & Silliman, 2000). Supportive scaffolds provide the gradual transfer of responsibility for learning from the teacher to the students. The transcripts we read demonstrate four supportive scaffold sequences identified by Roehler and Cantlon (1997; cited in Wilkinson & Silliman, 2000) and offer a model for teachers to follow that may lessen their concerns about discussion as an interactive learning opportunity.

One scaffold demonstrated in this chapter was *explicit modeling*. Explicit modeling is when the teacher *thinks aloud* the process of understanding. For example, Mr. G. talked through the process of plotting a slope as he demonstrated on a white board and later as the students worked in small groups to model how he came to understand what the water bill problem was asking.

The second supportive scaffold identified was *direct explanations and reexplanations*. This means that the teacher makes explicit statements to help the students understand the concept or how to use the concept. Mr. G. made such statements throughout the chapter. For instance, prior to the students working to complete the water bill activity, he said, ". . . I'm calling it the starting point and that's my own terminology. . . . Now remember the output at the starting point does not have to be a 0. It can be negative or positive." In giving this explanation, he provided students information needed to complete the water bill activity.

Mr. G. used a third supportive scaffold—inviting students to participate in the conversation. By inviting students into the conversation, teachers are encouraging them to support their developing understandings and expand their thinking. Mr. G. regularly posed questions to the students as they worked in small groups and in whole-class discussion that facilitated this sort of thinking. Teachers can also respond to students using questions and statements such as, "What do you mean?" and "Tell me more" to expand student thinking and understandings.

The last scaffold—verifying and clarifying student understanding—happens when teachers provide explicit feedback to acknowledge students' growing understandings or ask questions to redirect misunderstandings. In Mr. G.'s classroom, this happened in whole-class and small-group discussion. For example, after Meloni defined the dependent variable, Mr. G. said, "Well, that's one of the things it's gonna be. . . ." In this way, Mr. G. gave positive feedback to Meloni while leaving the question open for other explanations.

Mr. G. used a combination of scaffolds to guide his students as they interacted to develop an understanding of linear equations within a real-life math problem. The scaffolding he provided not only helped students to develop this understanding, it helped them stay focused and ensured that students learned the content he had intended for them to learn. This chapter presents a model for teachers who are not comfortable facilitating discussion for reasons like the ones stated earlier. It is my hope that teachers will read this chapter and use it to model their instruction or as a springboard to finding their own ways of enacting the principle *adolescents need opportunities to generate and express rich understandings of ideas and concepts.*

Discussion Questions

As you reflect on the information presented in this chapter, consider the following questions as they relate to your own teaching and/or your experiences in schools:

- In your experience, to what extent do teachers encourage students to generate and express rich understandings of ideas and concepts? Is this easier in certain content subjects than in others? Why or why not?
- Do you think the instruction presented in this vignette is unusual? Why or why not?
- Compare and contrast the views of the expert responder to your own views.
- What dilemmas must teachers, schools, and others solve to implement Principle 4?

Chapter 7

Principle 5: Adolescents Need Opportunities to Demonstrate Enthusiasm for Reading and Learning

This principle emphasizes the value of instruction that involves students in their reading and learning. As noted in earlier chapters, students learn best when they are engaged and enthusiastic. Projects that encourage engagement also foster adolescents' motivation to continue their explorations and learning beyond the classroom after the initial project is completed. A wide variety of practices can encourage enthusiasm for reading and learning. Key elements include giving students choices, providing freedom but also adequate scaffolding, and encouraging students to link new learning to their prior knowledge and interests both within and outside of school.

Examples of types of instruction that exemplify this principle include a variety of long- and short-term assignments and projects. Younger adolescents might develop and perform poetry reflecting their inquiry into the growing-up experiences of senior citizens in their neighborhoods or engage in a read-a-thon to raise money for a local homeless shelter. High school students might complete a community action project, investigating and proposing solutions for an environmental problem in a nearby setting. Students also might engage in research projects, collecting data from family and friends about their memories about a particular time and era. Projects can also involve a whole school community, with leadership from students and their families. For example, a school might decide to put on a cultural fair, within which teens and their families mount exhibits and arrange performances reflecting the practices of the ethnic groups living in the community. Another school group might write a grant with a local public library to provide more Internet access for the community and its youth.

Educators face challenges when developing a curriculum that promotes student engagement and enthusiasm because this effort often requires teachers to become proactive in choosing what to teach and how to teach it. This can be complex, especially for courses that are subject to strict curriculum controls and high-stakes testing. External political pressures, in which teachers are held accountable for students' academic success as measured by high-stakes testing, may inhibit teachers from making pedagogical decisions that go beyond the narrow confines of teaching to enable students to pass a test.

In addition, teachers face the dilemma that adolescents' attention and enthusiasm are often hard to capture. Many teens are involved in numerous activities both in- and outside of school, and they may find it difficult to find the time to engage in extended reading and learning. However, when adolescents are given time and encouragement to do so, they can experience a joy of learning from a variety of activities that will serve them over a lifetime. Valuing such pursuits is easier for teens when they can see enthusiastic role models, such as teachers and family members, engaging in extended and purposeful reading and learning. In cases where adolescents find themselves struggling to identify their interests, sharing such indecision with others expands their repertoire of experiences, giving them insights about others' interests and enthusiasms.

It is also important for teachers and others who want to support adolescents' enthusiasm for reading and learning to develop an awareness of the popular culture and technology that entice this age group. These can change quickly, so careful observation and attention to student talk is important. Adults can also provide effective models by sharing examples of their own enthusiasms, such as texts related to their interests in music, sports, or subject-specific study. Adolescents often appreciate adults who invite them to share their enthusiasms and expertise; on the other hand, they may resent a teacher's misguided effort to use examples of teen popular culture as a bridge to required content in a way that ultimately sends the message that the required content is what is most important.

This principle is supported by an array of professional organizations. For example, Strand VIII of The National Council for the Social Studies (1994) is centered on science, technology, and society. Its premise is, "Social studies programs should include experiences that provide for the study of relationships among science, technology, and society" (p. 28). In addition, the Council recommends that teachers "participate as a partner in learning with students, modeling the joy of both discovering new knowledge and increasing understanding of familiar topics" (p. 168). Similarly, the National Science Education Standards state that students should engage in "active debate about the economics, politics, and ethics of various science- and technology-related challenges" (NRC, 1996, p. 199). From the Standards for the English Language Arts, Principle 8 states, "Students use a variety of technological and informational resources (e.g., libraries, databases, computer networks, video) to gather and synthesize information and to create and communicate knowledge" (p. 39).

Recently, Alvermann and Reinking (2004), editors for *Reading Research Quarterly*, invited researchers in mathematics education, the arts, history education, and science education to respond to several queries on their perceptions of collaborations between the literacy community and their disciplines that "transgresses traditional boundaries" (p. 332). In response, Van Sledright (2004), a scholar of social studies and history education, argued,

> . . . teaching history well involves immersing students in the extensive reading and study of primary and secondary source documents, using understandings gleaned from reading these sources as a means of building interpretations of what happened in the past. History teachers, therefore, would need to know something about how to effect a pedagogy that assists students in reading such texts and constructing ideas about the past from them. (p. 342)

The guiding principle of this chapter and the support of the professional standards across disciplines convey that situations need to be created to give adolescents the opportunities they deserve to develop and demonstrate an enthusiasm for reading and learning. Such pedagogical opportunities require more than minilectures and whole-class discussions. For students to develop and reveal enthusiasm, the curriculum must connect deeply to their points of view and their lives. Adolescents also need to know that their interests, including their teen culture, matter to the adults who mentor them. Although instruction that helps adolescents develop enthusiasm for reading and learning can be difficult to develop and sustain, the effort reaps many benefits for students' long-term personal and academic growth.

The following illustration is a description of an innovative unit for bridging literacy, history, and students' research skills. In this illustration, we focus on Ms. Ari Nicole Joseph's adaptation of a "birthday project" first developed by Tchudi and Huerta (1983). The first part of the illustration centers on a description of how Ari Joseph prepares her 12th-grade students to engage in research on the year they were born. The second part is a description of the results of several students' work.

VIGNETTE 1: THE BIRTHDAY PROJECT: INTEGRATING LITERACY, SOCIAL STUDIES, AND TECHNOLOGY

Ari Nicole Joseph is a novice history teacher. She is preparing her Grade 12 students to indulge in an interdisciplinary study that integrates literacy, historical research, and technology. Ari foregrounds her presentation of the unit by telling her students that often the study of history is perceived as acquiring information about federal and state governments, battles within various wars, national leaders, facts, and dates. Standing in close proximity to her students, Ms. Joseph adds, "While all of these topics are significant, historians learn much about history by studying the lives of everyday people as well as facts and dates. This is, in part, what you will be doing over the next four weeks." Ms. Joseph continues: "[the project will involve] . . . learning about the everyday experiences, traditions, and beliefs of ordinary people, and what society was like during your birth year. You will be engaging in a small scale research project to collect information about this very important year." She smiles as she takes a seat at her desk.

Ari has designed an innovative way to assist students in becoming enthusiastic about reading, research, history, and learning. Her pedagogical approach provides students with an essential understanding of the connections among content area literacy practices (i.e., reading, writing, social studies, the arts), as well as how to conduct research to develop their historical understandings using procedures analogous to those of historians. Ms. Joseph assists her students in understanding that history is an interpretive discipline, and that what they read in their history textbooks is someone's interpretations about events of the past.

One of the innovative assignments that Ms. Joseph developed is called *The Birthday Project* (Tchudi & Huerta, 1983). Designed to provide students with the chance to connect content subject matter (i.e., social studies, science, math, performing arts, technology) with literacy learning, Ms. Joseph's students engage in a research study to collect data from the year they were born. Beginning early in the 4-week unit, her seniors engage in collecting, thinking, conceptualizing, designing, and sharing information for The Birthday Project with their peers and teacher. They go to the library to read issues of news magazines such as *Time* and *U.S. News and World Report* that were published in their birth years, and they also consult archived editions of their local newspaper to collect data for their birth year. The seniors conduct informal interviews with adults who remember their birth year, such as parents, guardians, grandparents, family members, and friends. Through these interviews, they gain valuable information, which reinforces the concept that people are an excellent resource for gathering information about a particular time period.

Ms. Joseph also encourages students not to overlook documents they may have, such as baby books, pictures, birth certificates, and announcements. However, she does not require students to use personal documents because the project is focused on understanding a time period rather than students' own personal stories. Ms. Joseph is aware that some students, including those who were adopted after the age of 1, those in foster care, or those who immigrated to the United States from other countries during their childhood or youth, may have limited sources of personal history information available to them.

From these formal and informal data-collection procedures, as well as reading and talking with family and friends, Ari's students are scaffolded so that they work toward a possible foci and form for The Birthday Project. The form, and therefore the length the seniors choose to write, depends on the focus for the compendium and paper.

After Ms. Joseph's introduction, she gives her students a handout with detailed guidelines for The Birthday Project (see Fig. 7.1). The guidelines offer her students many format possibilities for their finished project, including, but not limited to, a: (a) written narrative, (b) radio script, (c) videotape, (d) *Time* magazine essay, (e) then-and-now electronic or paper scrapbook, or (f) PowerPoint presentation. Here the idea is to encourage knowledge representation using different forms of media (e.g., technology) collected from multiple points of view and to represent knowledge acquired in various text types.

Ms. Ari explains to the students:

> Early in the research of your birth year, you will decide to focus on a content area subject such as math, science, social studies, English language arts, music, art, etc., with the aim to reflect the one you most enjoy, so that the compendium can be a model for future discussions about historical understandings and representations. For example, if you like mathematics you may think about this project with a math focus.

Several students chuckle as Ms. Joseph uses the words *like* and *mathematics* together in the same sentence. "Likewise, if you like music you may conceptualize your birthday project with music or other performing arts, such as the movies as a content focus," she says. Jamaal, one of Ms. Joseph's seniors, says, "Music! Now that's more like it!" Part of Ms. Joseph's goal is to structure the assignment so that students narrow their topics to content that is manageable within the unit's imposed time limit. Students must choose an audience for their knowledge representation that is reflective of anyone and anything they choose. For example, they may choose their peers or parents as their audience. She explains to students: "On the final days of the research assignment . . . you will present, celebrate, and share your published work accompanied by a final paper." All across the classroom, a collective groan of displeasure is heard when Ms. Joseph mentions the final paper. But later, as students begin their work, there is the sound of chatter throughout the room. Seemingly, students are conversing among each other, minds ticking about what they will do for the special project that connects literacy learning and social studies.

There are several outcomes Ms. Joseph expects students to learn from The Birthday Project assignment, including: (a) research strategies and

Content objectives:

- To encourage students to engage in an interdisciplinary research project (e.g., literacy and history)
- To learn about literacy, life, and culture in an era other than the present
- To engage in interpretation of historical data
- To learn some historical fact about students' birth year
- To learn about historical facts from multiple perspectives
- To represent acquired knowledge in a variety of formats
- To write a historical text in forms removed from the research paper

For the next 4 weeks, you will engage in collecting, thinking, conceptualizing, designing, and sharing information for The Birthday Project. You will go to the Lockwood Library to read old issues of news magazines such as *Time* and *Life* as well as the local newspaper to collect data for the day/week/year you were born. You should also begin talking to your parents and others who may have valuable information to learn all you can about the day/week/year you were born. (Do not overlook baby books, pictures, siblings' versions, phone calls, birth certificates and announcements, etc.) From informal (and hopefully enjoyable) reading and talking, a possible focus and form for your project should emerge. The form (and therefore the length) you choose to write should depend on the focus you choose for your paper. Here are some possibilities . . . BUT feel free to invent your own!

—**A WRITTEN NARRATIVE** of the day/week/year you were born. Include historical details such as radio songs, historical facts, local tidbits of gossip, as well as information from your family and others.

—**RADIO SCRIPT** of the day/week/year you were born. Include appropriate music, sound effects, news items, D.J. Voice for the period, etc. For a local and/or national broadcast, present it as a tape. A written reflection and analysis about the process and procedures must accompany your tape.

—**VIDEOTAPE** of the day/week/year you were born. You might play the role of a journalist who reports the news for your specified year. News items might include world, national, and local news. Your report may include significant events in sports, the music industry, movies, television, politics in Washington, DC, state politics, local politics, the demise of famous people (and some not so famous), a report of Wall Street, etc. You might include commercials in your video that highlight new consumer products that were new on the market at the time or highlight a music group or movie. Have a friend(s) work on this with you so that s/he might make the announcements during the commercial or be a co-anchor person.

—*TIME* **MAGAZINE ESSAY** of the week/month/year that you were born. Include key pictures and come to some overall conclusions about the importance of the era.

—**THAT WAS THEN, THIS IS NOW SCRAPBOOK** of the week/month/year you were born. Compare your day in history to then and now. Consider fashions, sports, cartoons, technology, food, automobiles, etc. Include pictures and captions about changes you see. A written essay must accompany your scrapbook to pull it together for your audience.

—**POWERPOINT PRESENTATION** of the week/month/year you were born. Collect family artifacts to scan into the computer; conduct a search on the Internet; add the top hits (or any appropriate music) during the year you were born as background music to the PowerPoint slide show, etc.

FIG. 7.1. *(Continued)*

—**DVD MINIDOCUMENTARY** of the week/month/year you were born. Conduct and videotape interviews with family members and friends to collect data about local, state, national, and international politics in 1987; fashions and hairstyles; top 40 music hits; and best movies.

Your audience and purpose may be anyone and anything you choose, but please allow us to share it too. On the final days of this assignment, we'll celebrate and share our published works. In the meantime, you'll have lots of peer help in getting ideas and shaping them.

I have developed a list of criteria for class evaluation of this special project. If you've worked hard, you'll be richly rewarded—as will be your audience.

WRITING IDEAS: POSSIBLE FOCI

Early in your research of the day, week, month, or year you were born, you should decide to focus on a content area. Select the one you like most so that your project can be a model for future use. For example, if you like mathematics, you should think about this project with a math focus. Some ideas for ways to focus follow. Other ideas are possible, just check them out with me. The point is to *narrow the topic* to something you can manage during the time we have.

SOCIAL STUDIES: This assignment is a historical study (even for math and science majors). Therefore, everything fits! However, you may want to emphasize politics; lifestyles; state, national, or international events; etc. The point is not to try and cover everything.

GEOGRAPHY/HISTORY: Select a place in the world to report from such as Israel, the American south, Beijing, London, your hometown, an African country (i.e., Nigeria, Zimbabwe, South Africa, Zaire), or Vietnam. Trace an event in history over several months or the year such as civil rights, national independence, elections, legislation, battles, or a revolutionary leader.

HOME ECONOMICS: Focus on fashions, hairstyles, culinary interests, restaurant ads, food prices, fabrics available, child care and family advice. Seek out appropriate fashion and home magazines to supplement your findings.

SCIENCE: What was **HIGH TECH** in the year/month you were born? Consider one or several fields: music (stereo or compact disks?), industry, film, biology, chemistry, space exploration, etc. A good one to compare to today! Look for popular science magazines of the era too.

MATHEMATICS: What were the important numbers that month or year? You might research statistics on population, sports, election returns, distances, speeds, world records in everything (focus on *Guinness Book of World Records*), stock market, world monetary values, and the Top 10 in the music industry. Collect them all for then and now. Include tables, charts, and diagrams that you copy (quote source), or invent to present your data. Check out almanacs as well as news sources.

MUSIC: The Top 10, major concerts that year, popular artists, and musical styles that were new or outrageous or "outdated." Look for key people of that era in music from rock to classical from performers to conductors to composers. Cover all briefly or focus in on one area. Can you find any magazines specifically for musicians? What was Don Cornelius and Soul Train like during the month/year you were born? What about America's oldest teenager, Dick Clark? What was his show like during the year/month you were born? Who were the Emmy nominees and winners?

FIG. 7.1. *(Continued)*

ART: What styles are in and out? Who's new—and still around today? Who was new—and we never heard of again? What were classics? What prices did certain works or art attract? Where are the major museums and shows? Enjoy the magazines of the arts as well as the news.

PHYSICAL EDUCATION: Sports records and stars are easy to find, but can you go further to include the status of certain sports of the time? Did more people play/watch golf or tennis? Baseball or football? What sports were "new"? Check out Sports Illustrated (of course) and other sport magazines.

MINIMUM REFERENCES:

You must include a minimum of ten (10) references for your Birthday Project. Information collected from the Internet along with other references MUST be cited using the *American Psychological Association Publication Manual* (5th ed.).

CITING SOURCES:

Be sure you know from where every piece of information comes unless it would be common knowledge (i.e., Reagan was president in 1987). You may or may not cite these sources in the text of what you write. The form will determine that. (In an essay a reader may want to know; in a radio broadcast it would be stupid to interrupt to quote a source.) *However, every project must include a bibliography of all sources consulted!* Therefore, as you conduct the research, keep track of all relevant information as soon as you decide that a source is useful to design your Birthday Project.

I adapted this Birthday Project idea from:
Tchudi, S. N., & Huerta, M. C. (1983). Teaching Writing in the Content Areas: Middle School/Junior High. *Washington, DC: National Education Association Publication.*

Guidelines for Birthday Project Paper

Length

- 6–8 pages maximum (not including cover and reference pages)

Format

- Times New Roman—12-point font; double-spaced
- One-inch margins top; bottom; left; right
- Subheadings to easily identify various sections of paper

Content

- Process followed to design your Birthday Project—1 page max
- Significance of chosen focus and/or content—1 page max
- What was learned from conducting research to develop historical understanding and alternative forms of knowledge representation—1–2 pages max
- The nexus between theory and The Birthday Project—2 pages max
- Your thoughts about The Birthday Project—1 page max

NOTE: Please use subtitles to guide your audience when writing a lengthy paper.

FIG. 7.1. The Birthday Project guidelines.

skills, (b) an awareness of various way to represent knowledge via alternative media, and (c) the nexus between disciplines and literacy learning. Moreover, Ms. Joseph implicitly asserts her responsibility as a teacher to be a professional decision maker. Diversity of curriculum is acquired through the guidance, yet flexibility, afforded students in gathering information that is significant and relevant to their lives and that of ordinary people. Ms. Joseph is asserting her right to choose, create, appraise, and critique the materials, contexts, and artifacts for an interdisciplinary social studies curriculum in her classroom.

SETTING THE CONTEXT TO STUDY STUDENTS' BIRTH YEARS

After her initial introduction, Ms. Joseph begins The Birthday Project unit by scheduling an appointment with the school librarian so that he can introduce students to resources available to them while conducting historical research. In the library, the librarian stands between a huge podium and a projection screen, navigating the multiple databases available online. The podium houses one Macintosh and one PC computer, both connected to the Internet. The librarian can easily access databases and talk about the availability of resources so that students know where they might begin their research. A few of the databases introduced to Ari's seniors include: (a) the American Library Association—http://www.ala.org/, (b) The African American Registry—http://www.aaregistry.com/, and (c) The Library of Congress—http://www.loc.gov/. In addition, the librarian encourages students not to overlook government documents and archived local, regional, and international newspapers. Ms. Joseph chimes in with the librarian to let her students know that she would like them to begin their research by going through old newspapers on microfiche—a *historical* form of technology. She smiles as she leads students to the archived newspapers and microfiche machines. Several of the students who were born in nearby locations immediately go for the newspaper of the local community to search for their own birth announcements. Others search for the *New York Times* and the *Baltimore Sun* to read the headlines from the day they were born. The librarian reminds students that they can use the Internet to locate newspapers from around the United States and the world. He encourages students to print foreign articles of interest from their birth year, which may be written in a different language if they or a family member can translate it.

There are additional lessons about this research project that Ms. Joseph makes explicit to students while they collect data about their birth year. First, she explains the difference between a skill and a strategy. "It is important that you understand the differences between a strategy and a skill because you will be collecting much of the data for this project outside of class time," notes Ari. "Therefore, since this project requires that you fit it into your busy schedules, you cannot wait until the night before it is due to me to begin." She smiles. "I've been a student, too! So a strategy is a systematic plan for achieving a goal while a skill is the ability to perform, and often well. How will you consistently collect data for your birthday project over the next 2–3 weeks? This is a question you must entertain in order to develop strategic methods for doing so," continues Ms. Joseph. She continues by making it clear that the skills students use while collecting information are skills that they have acquired over the course of their schooling, including: (a) research, (b) critical thinking, (c) interpretation, (d) process writing, and (e) creativity. Given that this project expands over several weeks, Ms. Joseph explains to her students that the entire process occurs in phases before the final project, such as iMovie, will be completed. "First, you will gather information," she said.

Since their library visit as a class, many of Ari's students share that they have already begun using their research skills by accessing databases introduced to them by the librarian. After they gather information, students must begin organizing and sorting the data gathered. Next, after collecting and sorting, they must make decisions about how they will use the information to represent their knowledge, and then they will develop their final product. Along with the iMovie, videotape, or PowerPoint, for instance, students must write a paper to convey what they have learned from researching their birth year. The final phase includes a presentation where students will celebrate and share what they have learned with their peers.

What Students Learn and How They Represent Their Learning

Radio Show. Keith designed his project as a radio documentary highlighting some events that were current news at the time. He titled his radio show *History and Disco* because he culled the content of the era from audio clips. The audio clips document either a historical event or disco music. More specifically, Keith was very creative in designing his radio show because the audio clips were mostly news footage of historical events set to disco music selections off the Top 20 music charts for the month of February in his birth year. For instance, from the CNN audio archives, Keith collected footage from the assassination attempt on the life of President Ronald Reagan. His intent was to capture the chaos that ensued on the day that John Hinckley tried to shoot the president. Keith's creativity and imagination resulted in a bizarre juxtaposition to highlight some of the ironies and idiosyncrasies of history. Keith wrote in his paper, "No one time can be remembered as just one thing. . . . On the contrary it is many things—serious, light-hearted, irreverent, revolutionary, joyous, and sometimes tragic." Examples of additional audio clips Keith collected from CNN audio archives include: (a) the Bobby Sands hunger strike in Ireland, (b) the assassination of Egypt's Anwar Sadat, (c) the release of the American hostages in Iran, (d) the election of New York City's Mayor Ed Koch, and (e) the confirmation of Sandra Day O'Connor. As Keith went through the process, he saved each audio clip to his computer as a wave file (.wav) because he would be adding others as he put together his project. Keith included disco music from artists such as the Jackson's, Blondie, Prince, and Kool and the Gang. He wrote,

> Gathering the music selections was also a kind of history lesson for me, because it forced me to situate the context of what I [previously had] relegated to the realm of the "cheesy '80s funk." I'd be lying if I said I wasn't at least digging on the old Prince. I thought that the combination of history and disco music would be strange and quirky enough to keep my peers listening—but it was also a logical choice for such was the popular music of the time. And although they are seemingly incongruous . . . the coupling of assassination footage and falsetto-tinged fund . . . I believe that it [made] my project like a sort of post-modern sound collage—without getting into the haughtiness that all of that might entail.

Thus, Keith's postmodern sound collage moved back and forth between political historical events and disco music. Keith developed an index of the audio footage included in his CD. Following are examples of some audio footage for the first several minutes of Keith's CD:

Historical event:
CNN Report—Bernard Shaw reports Reagan's assassination attempt
NPR archive—Reagan assassination montage (with onsite audio feed)
Disco music:
Fantasy—"You're too Late"
Historical event:
History channel audio archive—Reagan neutron bomb defense
History channel audio archive—Anwar Sadat assassination (onsite audio feed)
CNN Report—Sadat assassination
Disco music:
Blondie—"Rapture"
Historical event:
CNN Report—Pope Pius II shot (onsite audio feed)
CNN Report—Iran hostages released

CNN Report—Jimmy Carter announces hostage release
Disco music:
Kool and the Gang—"Celebration"

Keith's learning during this process is just as much of a collage as the creativity represented in his Birthday Project research. He used audio media to form the basis of a historical radio documentary, which made history real and personal to him. Given that Keith was able to download actual audio footage from the Internet, he was able to "hear" what was going on during his birth year; for Keith, this was a different form of studying historical events. In his final paper, Keith stated,

> The tone of people's voices, the crowd's noise and cheering, the gunshots and explosions, the messages, the rhythms of the day's popular music all added up to give me an intuitive look into the past through sound. The experience for me at least, was something that was very different than simply reading about the past. Somehow this project was a lot of fun! The radio show approach I took was somewhat tedious at first (I was pessimistic of my ability to actually find audio) but soon revealed itself to be an infectious form of learning. I was incredibly engaged in the project. I am incredibly satisfied with the way it turned out.

iMovie Documentary.   Sabina centered her Birthday Project on popular culture. Entitled "The Electrifying 80s," she enables her audience to feel energized as if they are going to the movies to learn about the 1980s. Sabina begins her iMovie with a song, and spotlights make circular motions about the marquee. Sabina has catalogued her digital video so that one can either click on *play* to see the entire movie or on the selection button to go to specific categories. If one clicks *play*, the viewer enters the upbeat world of the 1980s. On a black screen, Sabina's audience learns that her iMovie is produced by Cash Productions. In the background, the song "The Glamorous Life" by Shelia E. plays as Sabina's first category of "Fashions" flashes in white against a black background. Models wearing tight-fitting jeans with denim jackets, cut-up jeans, jelly shoes, leg warmers, and multicolored pumps make quick flashes across the computer screen. Her next category is entitled "TV Shows." Still playing background music from the 1980s, pictures of characters in sitcoms such as "Alf," "Amen," and "Facts of Life" make their debut in Sabina's iMovie. Also, characters from "Hill Street Blues" briefly appear. Her remaining categories for the electrifying 1980s include cars, movies, cartoons, games, popular music groups (e.g., Kool and the Gang), and news events.

Sabina furthered her data-collection methods by interviewing six family members and friends who were 8 years old or older during her birth year.

Using videotape, she asked each person about their favorite songs, movies, TV shows, and styles of dress from the 1980s. Her rationale for interviewing people across age groups was that different age groups' memories would render different perspectives about the times. For instance, an 11-year-old's memories about 1987 would be very different from someone who was 29 or 36 years old during the same year. Sabina developed her interview questions for this project to parallel the categories she highlighted in the beginning of her movie, as well as information she wanted to know. In addition, her interview method enabled her interviewees' to talk about their fondest memories.

After the last interview is portrayed, Gladys Knight sings "Second Time Around" in the background, and Sabina ends her iMovie with a blackened screen as credits roll from the bottom to the top in white letters. The credits include the names of the interviewees in order of appearance, music titles, and special thanks to Tyrone Kimp, her resource for the music. Sabina includes the Web sites where she downloaded images from the Internet. Last, but not least, as the last credit rolls, the following text appears on the screen: "Anyone copying this DVD for personal use or unauthorized viewing without permission of Cash Productions will be fined $1,000,000 and or imprisonment. Persons interviewed were not paid for their services."

In her paper, Sabina discussed her enthusiasm for literacy learning through participation in The Birthday Project. She stated,

> At first I was reluctant to do this birthday project because I was not able to see the connections between what we've learned and why we were assigned the project. Now as I reflect on the long process of creating my project, I understand and have a greater appreciation for the year I was born. October 5th not only represents a day that I get to celebrate by myself. It reflects a date and a total year . . . the world was shaped by many influential people and events that identify the world as it is today. I enjoyed the creation of my birthday project. I hope the viewers get the same enjoyment and understanding I got from creating it.

A SCHOLAR'S RESPONSE
Richard T. Vacca, Kent State University, Emeritus

Principle 5: Adolescents need opportunities to demonstrate enthusiasm for reading and learning

The word *enthusiasm* is derived from the ancient Greek word *enthousiasmos*, which means quite literally "to be inspired by a god." Perhaps somewhere in the heavens there is a Greek god of reading who breathes into human beings an intense or eager interest in the act of reading. Perhaps not. Most teachers of adolescents, nevertheless, would be quick to suggest that many of their students, regardless of ability level, would rather have root canal surgery than engage enthusiastically in academic reading tasks. The passion to use reading to learn requires more than supernatural or divine inspiration. Enthusiastic readers in today's classrooms are made, not born with a fervor for reading and learning.

The so-called Birthday Project described in this chapter is an excellent example of how enthusiastic readers are made, not born. A novice history teacher breaks the textbook-only mold in her classroom to create an instructional environment in which her students approach literacy and learning tasks with enthusiasm. The teacher plans instruction to involve students actively in literacy and learning by allowing them to make personal connections with the concepts under study and to use a variety of texts (both print and electronic resources) in the study of historical and popular cultural events that occurred during their birth years. In doing so, the teacher skillfully integrates literacy, historical research, and technology into her instructional plans. She scaffolds instruction in a manner that provides structured choices by which students engage in research and the presentation of their findings. The enthusiasm for reading and learning exhibited by the students, as reflected in the scenarios highlighting the manner in which students present their research findings, did not occur by happenstance.

The teacher, who is a content specialist, knows enough about literacy use to know that it is situational. The National Assessment of Educational Progress (NAEP) for Reading conducted in 2003 indicates that the majority of today's adolescents have attained at least a basic level of competency as readers. Although competent in reading, many of today's adolescents may not be confident as readers, especially in academic situations.

Whenever adolescents engage in content literacy activities, some will feel confident in their ability to be successful with literacy tasks. Others will not. Those who are confident exhibit a high level of self-efficacy in content literacy situations, whereas those who are unsure about their ability to be successful exhibit a low level. If the history teacher directed students to read a single text, perhaps a textbook, to gather information for the projects, some students undoubtedly would believe they did not have a chance to be successful. They would have approached the material with a defeatist attitude. Self-efficacy, however, refers to an "I can" belief in self that leads to a sense of competence. Self-efficacy is not as concerned with the skills and strategies students bring to content literacy situations as with their judgments of what they can do with whatever skills and strategies they do bring to learning situations requiring literacy. This allows the teacher to focus on what she does best—teaching historical content and processes to her students. However, she scaffolds The Birthday Project in a way that allows students choice in the types of texts they will read and the type of discourse forms they will use to present their research findings to the class. Structuring the research project in this manner increases students' self-efficacy.

Self-efficacy and motivation are interrelated concepts. If students believe, for example, that they have a good chance to succeed at a reading task, they are likely to exhibit a willingness to engage in reading and complete the task. The Birthday Project puts a reading engagement model into play in the classroom (Guthrie & Wigfield, 2000). The reading engagement model underscores the importance of students' growth in content knowledge, as well as their use of comprehension strategies, social interaction in the classroom, and student motivation.

The history teacher wisely incorporates technology into The Birthday Project, thereby increasing the probability that students will approach reading and learning with enthusiasm. With continuously emerging information and communication technologies (ICT) a reality in today's world, many adolescents have developed "new literacies" to utilize ICT in ways that adults have not. Teachers who aim to engage students enthusiastically in reading and learning are continually rethinking how to use ICT and to fully exploit their potential for learning (Kist, 2005). The new literacies are grounded in students' ability to use reading and writing to learn, but require new strategic knowledge, skills, and insights to meet the conceptual and technological demands inherent in complexly networked environments. The Internet, for example, is one of the most powerful ICTs teachers can incorporate into academic learning situations. Using multiple media in The Birthday Project supports the use of new literacies and bridges the gap between academic literacy and the literacies that adolescents use outside of school.

Discussion Questions

As you reflect on the information presented in this chapter, consider the following questions as they relate to your own teaching and/or your experiences in schools:

- In your experience, to what extent do middle and high schools provide opportunities for students to demonstrate enthusiasm for reading and learning?
- Do you think the vignette presented here is unusual? Why or why not?
- Compare and contrast the views of the expert responder to your own views.
- What dilemmas must teachers, schools, and others solve to implement Principle 5?

Chapter 8

Principle 6: Adolescents Need Opportunities to Assess Their Own Literacy and Learning Competencies and Direct Their Future Growth

This principle focuses on assessment, with an emphasis on the value of students' self-assessment. Research on learning and cognition indicates that metacognition, or the "knowledge people have about their own thinking processes, and their ability to monitor their cognition" (Feldman, 1997, p. 386), grows during adolescence. For example, adolescents are more able than younger learners to decide how long they must study to learn material for a test or how they can adapt their written work so that it is understandable to various audiences. Although younger learners also benefit from learning to self-assess, adolescents are at a prime stage for participating with their teachers and families in supportive assessment processes that inform their own as well as their teachers' decision making.

Through the process of self-assessment, adolescents learn about their own strengths and limitations; with appropriate guidance, they can learn strategies for learning more effectively in the future. Self-assessment also can be powerful for helping adolescents develop motivation to read, write, and learn because it puts them in the "driver's seat." Numerous studies have found that personal choice and decision making are related to motivation to learn (Gambrell, Palmer, Codling, & Mazzoni, 1996; Ivey & Broaddus, 2001).

Assessments of adolescents' reading and learning should be ongoing, engaging, appropriate to learners' needs, and embedded within meaningful learning experiences. Thoughtful teachers can determine the most appropriate ways for students to demonstrate their knowledge and expertise; they can also develop ways to link required standardized assessments to those that are classroom-based. For example, although state-mandated tests may be sources of stress for both teachers and students, information gained from them can be helpful for students' self-assessment as long as the tests' purposes, construction, and results are explained in comparison to more situated measures of learning.

As students get older, they can take increasing ownership and gain a greater understanding of their own learning processes (Atwell, 1998). Classroom practices related to this principle will vary by discipline, age of the student, and goals of the course. Tools such as self-assessment rubrics, tape recordings of one's own reading or dramatic performance, or portfolios of written work can be used flexibly in a wide variety of circumstances. For example, when the focus of study is the development of students' basic literacy skills, such as in an English-language, academic literacy, or foreign-language class, students can engage in comparison of effective and not-so-effective patterns of oral reading and composition for particular audiences. Similarly, in science, social studies, mathematics, or other content areas, teachers can help students become strategic about their own literacy practices through a comparison of expectations of reading and writing across different assignments or in different content areas. For example, students might be asked to examine differences between reading a mathematics word problem and reading a novel, or writing a historical essay or a scientific report based on observations.

All students, including beginning English-language learners, students with exceptional needs, and those who struggle with reading and writing in academic settings, can benefit from the use of rubrics and scoring guides. These tools can help students and teachers evaluate the development of a student's literacies over time. In addition, they can help students gauge their progress in meeting standards set by districts or governmental agencies. Teachers may also provide minilessons and practice activities to teach students strategies for approaching different types of assessments. For example, if students are required to take multiple-choice tests, teachers can provide instruction in the types and formats of questions that might be asked.

Professional organizations in many disciplines support the concept that assessments should be multifaceted and adolescents should participate in their own assessment. For example, the Standards for the English Language Arts (1996) state, "The assessment process should involve multiple perspectives and sources of data" (p. 29). The National Standards in Science, even more specifically, note, "Assessment tasks must be set in a variety of contexts, be engaging to students with different interests and experiences, and must not assume the perspective or experience of a particular gender, racial, or ethnic group" (NRC, 1996, p. 86).

The National Council for Teachers of Mathematics (2000) makes particular note of the role of students:

Through the use of good tasks and the public discussion of criteria for good responses, teachers can cultivate in their students both the disposition and the capacity to engage in self-assessment and reflection on their own work and on ideas put forth by others. (pp. 22–23)

NCTM goes on to note, "Such a focus on self-assessment and peer assessment has been found to have a positive impact on students' learning" (pp. 22–23). The Council for Exceptional Children (2002) concurs, stating that effective special educators "shape environments to encourage the independence, self-motivation, self-direction, personal empowerment, and self-advocacy of individuals with ELN (Exceptional Learning Needs)" (Standard 5).

Overall, national standards documents encourage authentic assessments that enable both teachers and students to monitor progress on an ongoing basis to inform teaching as well as learning.

VIGNETTE 1: SELF-ASSESSMENT IN A SIXTH-GRADE READING CLASS

Theresa Parker works as a reading specialist in an elementary school of about 400 students located near Washington, DC. Her school is a diverse community that includes children from many cultural and language backgrounds. As the school's reading specialist, Theresa works extensively with other teachers to improve literacy instruction for all students. She also teaches two reading/writing groups a day, one of fifth graders and one of sixth graders. Most of the students in her reading groups have been identified as having difficulty in reading and/or writing.

One interesting aspect of Theresa's school is that it has been identified by the school district as an "Arts Integration" school whose "mission is to empower all students to be productive citizens and life long learners." Teachers have special opportunities to learn about arts integration—for example, many have attended workshops for teachers held at the Kennedy Center for Performing Arts in nearby Washington, DC. Theresa notes that a foremost school goal is to teach literacy and the arts in complementary ways. With this in mind, teachers often plan units and individual lessons that have both arts and literacy objectives.

Teachers in Theresa's school believe that self-assessment helps students become more self-directed and motivated. In fifth grade, students frequently assess their own writing using rubrics developed by teachers. In sixth grade, students build on their prior knowledge by learning to participate in creating rubrics, which they then use to assess their own written and oral communication.

This vignette is focused on Theresa's sixth-grade reading group, which used writing and oral presentation rubrics as part of a fantasy unit.

At noon on a Tuesday in October, seven students enter Ms. P's small reading classroom and sit at tables of two or three. Most take out folders containing drafts of Reader's Theatre scripts they have been creating for over a week in the school's computer lab. Lisa has a computer disk rather than a printout and explains that she was working on her script at home; she asks if Theresa can print it in the classroom. Theresa does so using the computer on her desk. Another student, Joseph, also lacking a printout, says he saved his script the day before in the school's computer lab, but did not use a disk. Theresa tells Joseph that after the class gets started, she can access his draft through her classroom computer if he saved it in her folder on the school's server.

After making a few announcements, Theresa gives a written schedule ("To Do List, October 15th") to each student. The schedule lists activities the class will work on during the 1½-hour class period as well as the home-work assignment due the next day. As indicated on the schedule, for the first 15 minutes, Theresa works with the students on activities related to an ongoing poetry project that includes an emphasis on vocabulary and oral expression. She then turns students' attention to the Readers' Theatre scripts they are writing.

At a break later in the day, Theresa explains that the Readers' Theatre project had begun several weeks earlier when she introduced a literature unit related to fantasy. This literature unit is based on the district's curriculum requirements for sixth grade. As part of the unit, Theresa taught students literary elements related to fantasy, and students evaluated different children's stories to see whether they contained evidence of these literary elements. They also read a variety of fantasy stories, in many cases revisiting stories they had heard when they were younger. Students then applied their knowledge to developing Readers' Theatre scripts. First they read and eval-uated published scripts, and then they practiced writing their own.

During this phase of the unit, Theresa printed several scripts from a Readers' Theatre Web site created by Aaron Shephard (www.aaronshep. com) for her class. According to information on the Web site, the Readers' Theatre scripts located there are "free and may be copied, shared, and per-formed for any noncommercial purpose, except they may not be posted on-line without permission" (Shephard, 2005, p. 1).

One of the scripts that students used was entitled *The Princess Mouse*, which was an adaptation of the story by the same title (Shephard, 2003). Theresa mentioned that earlier in the week she had asked students to read the script silently and then read it (taking parts) in a Readers' Theatre for-mat. After this reading, Theresa told students that they would be using other children's stories, such as *The BFG* (Dahl, 1998), to write Readers'

Theatre scripts, and they would later be using a rubric to evaluate their own scripts. Students also worked with partners to assess the professionally written script for *The Princess Mouse* using a simple rubric. Students had suggested several problems in the script. For example, Linda said that, according to the rubric, words to be emphasized orally should be written in italics, and the author had not done this. Theresa mentioned that when practicing a Readers' Theatre script they could "underline or highlight parts they wanted to emphasize."

On the Tuesday in October when the class was observed, students were learning to write their own scripts for a Readers' Theatre performance. After answering questions and making sure that everyone had a printout of their most recent script, Theresa asked students to take the script rubrics (Fig. 8.1) they had used earlier from their class folders. She also reminded students that they had a second rubric (Fig. 8.2) related to oral expression that they would use later in the week when performing the Readers' Theatre.

Students next worked for about 10 minutes with partners at their tables. Each pair evaluated each of the partner's scripts using the script rubric. First, the partners looked together at each of their scripts and listed each script's strengths and weaknesses. With the help of Theresa and a parent volunteer, each pair then made a short list of ways their scripts met the criteria on the rubric and ways that the scripts did not meet the criteria. For example, Tom and Joseph found that Tom's script identified who should read each part, and it also included a title, narrator, and one character. However, the script also had some misspelled words and did not include an introduction. When looking at Joseph's script, the boys found that Joseph spelled all words correctly and had an introduction, but did not identify who should say every line of dialogue.

After students had completed their analysis, Theresa reminded them again that the purpose of the self-evaluation activity in class was to help them decide how to revise their scripts, which was the homework assignment for the next day. At the end of class, she summarized for the students by saying, "Self-evaluation is a process [that] writers use—think about at least one thing you need to do or change in your script." She also asked every student to write an "Exit Slip" (Vacca & Vacca, 2004), noting any ways they thought the rubric should be modified.

Interestingly, when reading the Exit Slips later, Theresa found that a number of students suggested that the rubric should be changed to become more strict—that it should say (for a top score) that the author had *always* included various elements (such as title, author, etc.), rather than that the author had usually included these elements (as was stated in the original version of the rubric). Theresa decided to make this change on the rubric and printed copies to give to students the next day.

	4	3	2	1
Format	Always includes a title, author, and name of person who adapted the script. Always includes a narrator. Always includes dialogue for each character. Always identifies all of the roles. Includes an introduction with a story summary, author information, and description of how actors should sit.	Includes a title and author. Includes narrator. Includes dialogue for most characters. Identifies most of the roles. Includes an introduction with a story summary.	Includes a title. Includes a narrator. Includes dialogue for some of the characters. Identifies some of the roles. Includes an introduction.	Includes a narrator and one or two characters. Limited or no dialogue for each character. Does not identify any of the roles. Does not include an introduction.
Author's (Playwriter's) Purpose	Always identifies how each part should be read by writing adjectives and adverb descriptors in parenthesis. Words that should be read with expression are always emphasized with special font.	Usually identifies how each part should be read by writing adjectives and adverb descriptors in parenthesis. Usually emphasizes words that should be read with expression by using special font.	Sometimes identifies how each part should be read by writing adjectives and adverb descriptors in parenthesis. Sometimes emphasizes words that should be read with expression by using special font.	Never identifies how each part should be read by writing adjectives and adverb descriptors in parenthesis. Never emphasizes words that should be read with expression.
Mechanics	All words are spelled correctly. All punctuation including quotation marks are used correctly. All grammar is correct.	Most words are spelled correctly. Most punctuation is used correctly. Most grammar is correct.	Some words are spelled correctly. Some punctuation is used correctly. Some grammar is correct.	Many words are spelled incorrectly. Never uses punctuation. Never uses grammar correctly.

Self-Evaluation

Format: _____ Author's Purpose _____ Mechanics _____

Overall my script:

FIG. 8.1. Readers' Theatre script rubric. *Note.* The authors thank Thana Vance and Constance Monastra for the figures in this chapter.

	4	*3*	*2*	*1*
Oral Delivery: Volume	Always speaks loudly enough for audience to hear.	Usually speaks loudly enough for audience to hear.	Sometimes speaks loudly enough for audience to hear.	Speaks too softly.
Oral Delivery: Clarity	Words are always pronounced correctly and are easily understood.	Most words are pronounced correctly and are easily understood.	Some words are pronounced correctly; many words are misunderstood.	Many words are pronounced incorrectly; too fast or slow; mumbles.
Oral Delivery: Reads With Expression	Always reads with appropriate expression.	Usually reads with appropriate expression.	Sometimes reads with appropriate expression.	Reads with little or no expression.
Oral Delivery: Reads in Turn	Always takes turns accurately and appropriately.	Usually takes turns when appropriate.	Sometimes takes turns when appropriate.	Rarely takes turns on a consistent basis or doesn't participate at all.
Cooperation With Group	Always works well with others; always cooperative.	Usually works well with others.	Sometimes works well with others.	Difficulty in working with others; forgets part; not respectful; or tries to be the boss and take over.

FIG. 8.2.   Readers' Theatre presentation rubric.

When students entered the classroom on Wednesday, Theresa asked them to take out their revised scripts. She also passed out copies of the revised script rubric (Fig. 8.1) and asked students to silently read over their revised scripts and mark the score (1–4) they thought was appropriate for each of the three categories (Format, Author's Purpose, and Mechanics) on the rubric. She also showed students that they should mark the scores they had given themselves in the appropriate category at the bottom of the rubric. Most of the seven students seemed to struggle with the process, unsure how to rate themselves. One student insisted that Theresa should read her script before she self-evaluated and said, "I want to know if *you* like it!" Theresa replied that the point is not whether *she*, as a teacher, likes the script, but that as the author the student needs to decide whether the script tells the story the way *she* wants it told. Theresa turned the question back to the class, saying, "Why do you think I want you to self-evaluate?" Students suggested various answers. For example, David volunteered that it might help them get better grades. Joseph said, "You want to help us become better writers."

As they completed the rubric, several students were reluctant to give themselves scores of 4 (highest) in any category, but Theresa encouraged them to do so, if appropriate: "If you did what [the rubric] says, you get a 4." Others were worried that the scores they gave themselves would become a grade, but Theresa reassured them that she would base their grades for the project on a wide variety of factors, and that they were doing the self-evaluation to learn how to improve their writing, not to give themselves a grade for the project.

After all students completed the numerical scoring process, Theresa explained that at the bottom of the rubric there was a space for them to write a summary of their script's strengths and weaknesses. Students seemed unsure how to write this summary, so Theresa gave several models that demonstrated a format for stating strengths first and then weaknesses. For example, after speaking briefly to Joseph, she said, "Joseph might say, 'my strongest areas were in format and mechanics, but I gave myself a 2 in author's purpose because I forgot to use a special font to mark the words that should be read with expression.' "

At the end of class, Theresa explained to the group that the following week they would split into two smaller groups and practice and perform several Readers' Theatre scripts for students in other sixth-grade reading groups. She handed out copies of the Readers' Theatre Presentation Rubric (Fig. 8.2) and discussed the presentation criteria with students. She reminded students that in the scripts they created the student authors had already noted which words should be read with expression. She also reminded students that in their ongoing poetry unit they had recently practiced reading with expression. She pointed out that as part of this unit they used highlighters to mark words they wanted readers to emphasize when reading aloud. They also had listened to each other presenting poems orally and had informally self-evaluated their own and others' use of expression in reading the poetry.

When class ended, students gathered their papers and moved back to their homeroom classes. Later that week, they refined their Readers' Theatre scripts even further and practiced for their upcoming performances.

VIGNETTE 2: SELF-ASSESSMENT IN HIGH SCHOOL SPECIAL EDUCATION CLASSES

Claire Juliano teaches special education in a large high school about 30 miles from a major city on the east coast of the United States. All of her 9th- and 11th-grade students are identified as having learning disabilities. Some students also have other social and emotional difficulties that affect their adjustment and performance in high school. Claire has implemented two types of self-evaluation processes in her classes. Ninth graders self-evaluate their writing and their classroom behavior, whereas 11th graders self-evaluate their writing and their overall progress for their Individual Education Plan (IEP) meetings.

Grade 9

Claire notes that a major focus of the special education program for ninth grade is on helping her students transition from Grade 8 to ensure that students experience success in the high school environment. As is often the case, 9th grade in Claire's school is a year when students need to adapt to a larger school with teachers who may not collaborate as much as middle-school teachers. Middle schools often have teacher teams that share the same group of students and work with students and families to provide a supportive environment, but this team structure is much less common in high schools. Claire notes that her students are mainstreamed for several classes with teachers who may see each other rarely because they are in different locations within the large building.

For these young high schoolers, Claire has developed a simple yet powerful system in which all students assess their own class participation and work habits on a daily basis and receive feedback from Claire. The first component of the system is a simple questionnaire (see Fig. 8.3) that students complete with a "Yes" or "No" answer at the end of class each day. During the class, which is composed of eight students, Claire keeps anecdotal records about specific student behaviors. She later writes a daily message to each student that she discusses with him or her the next day, as needed.

Name _____   Date _____

Directions: Circle either "yes" or "no" for the following participation components:

I brought my binder	Yes	No
I brought paper/pencil	Yes	No
I brought other needed materials	Yes	No
I participated in class discussions	Yes	No
I required teacher prompts to remain on task	Yes	No
I worked without disrupting others	Yes	No

Student comments on participation:

FIG. 8.3. Self-evaluation participation checklist.

Date: _____   Name of student: _____

_____

_____

FIG. 8.4.   Teacher comments on participation.

This message includes Claire's evaluation of the student's self-management in class for the day, in comparison with the student's self-evaluation. For example, a student may write that "yes," he or she had all materials, but Claire might note in writing, "You said you had all materials, but I saw you asking someone for a pencil during class" (see Fig. 8.4). At the end of the week, students receive points for a participation grade. Claire finds that this system, although time consuming, has been beneficial in helping students reflect on and improve their behavior and class participation.

For writing instruction, students also self-evaluate in several ways. Claire notes that when they first enter her class, many of her ninth-grade students seem to resist all forms of writing assignments. She attributes this in part to a high use of worksheets with special education students in the earlier grade levels in her district. Claire requires students to write and works to help them develop an interest in writing and to see writing as nonthreatening. She begins the year by using a questionnaire she adapted from a book by Myers (1985). The questionnaire asks students to rate, on a scale from 1 to 5, their feelings about questions such as "I don't think I write as well as other people," "I avoid writing," and "I like to write my ideas down." This questionnaire gives Claire a sense of the students' attitudes toward writing at the beginning of the year and helps her plan effectively. She also uses some of the questions for class discussion.

All students keep journals, which they use to write about their own interests and concerns as well as for addressing prompts that Claire provides. Many prompts are designed to improve students' problem solving and critical thinking. For example, one prompt is: "Would you rather be a superhero or a famous athlete?" Claire notes that this question pushes students to compare and contrast the benefits of each and go beyond the surface-level memorization of facts they have been used to in the past. She instructs students on what should be included in a comparison/contrast essay, and then she asks them to self-assess and revise their work using a rubric (Fig. 8.5).

For Grade 11, the school curriculum requires that students learn to write papers that summarize information from a variety of sources and are documented appropriately. Claire explains that her students often have difficulty writing summaries. She teaches specific strategies for summarizing, explaining to students that they need to answer "who, what, where, when, why, and how" questions when they write. After writing a summary, students must self-assess using a checklist (Fig. 8.6). They also complete note cards

Did I tell what was being compared?	Yes	No
Did I state how they were alike?	Yes	No
Did I give details (related to similarity)?	Yes	No
Did I state how they were different?	Yes	No
Did I give details (related to difference)?	Yes	No
Did I use transition words?	Yes	No
Did I provide a concluding sentence?	Yes	No
Is my organization logical (Whole to whole? Point to point)?	Yes	No

These are the transition words that I used: _____

FIG. 8.5.　Self-evaluation for comparison/contrast essay.

My summary included the following components:

Who	Yes	No
What	Yes	No
When	Yes	No
Where	Yes	No
Why	Yes	No
How	Yes	No

I have written a concluding sentence: yes/no

Student comments:

Teacher comments:

FIG. 8.6.　Checklist used when writing a summary of a newspaper article.

for each of their sources, giving the appropriate citation on the back so they can later insert it into their paper. During the writing of the paper, Claire also uses a conference format (Burke, 2003) in which she meets with individuals and discusses a list of self-assessment questions such as "What are the writer's five questions about this paper?" and "What works, what doesn't work?" in the paper. Another strategy that Claire uses during the lengthy process of teaching students to write summaries and the research paper is an Admit Slip (Vacca & Vacca, 2004), which includes the prompt: "I am having difficulty writing a summary because. . . ." Claire indicates that students complete these when they enter class and use the completed form during class discussion about ways to overcome writing difficulties.

　　Eleventh-grade students in Claire's class are also taught self-advocacy strategies to use at their own IEP meetings so that they can participate in decisions about their own education. Claire expects students to review their IEPs each year and select work samples that illustrate their learning in relation to particular goals.

Although students are not required to attend their IEP meetings, Claire encourages all students to do so. She teaches them to read their IEPs and evaluate their own strengths and weaknesses so they can be ready to present their own opinion about what they believe they have accomplished in school. Before the IEP meetings occur, Claire also prepares students for communicating at the meeting through in-class role-plays. She explains to students that it is important to show by their verbal and nonverbal behavior that they realize the IEP is important and they want to take part in making decisions about it.

Overall, students in Claire's classes become more proficient in self-assessment of their attitudes, behavior, and written and oral communication during their time in high school. Claire finds that the self-assessment process is new for many of her students, and she believes it enables them to become increasingly aware of ways to improve their own learning and development.

Overall, both Theresa and Claire emphasize the importance of helping their students gain increased self-awareness of their own learning processes through a variety of types of self-assessment. They find that students develop these skills in a gradual way and that it is worth the effort.

A SCHOLAR'S RESPONSE
Patricia L. Anders, University of Arizona

> Principle 6: Adolescents need opportunities to assess their own literacy and learning competencies and direct their future growth.

Metacognition, a concept introduced to the field of reading theory by cognitive psychologists in the 1970s, is a *meta-idea*, so to speak. It encompasses the thinking about thinking that skilled readers and learners employ. It is a construct that involves all the active processes of comprehension—processes like predicting, purpose setting, selecting, organizing, elaborating, monitoring, planning, evaluating, and integrating—and it suggests that those who are in better control of these processes are the most successful comprehenders and learners. Because this is such an overarching big idea, educators are interested in supporting students' advancement as metacognitive learners and thinkers.

In practice, metacognitive instruction has been shown to be beneficial. Palinscar and Brown (1984) conducted numerous studies demonstrating the efficacy of "reciprocal teaching," an instructional plan that scaffolds students' development of metacognition. Jiménez (1997), however, noted that increased or more explicit instruction in metacognition is more likely to be needed for second-language learners. Another condition affecting students' abilities to be metacognitive has to do with how much background knowledge students have to bring to bear on a new learning situation (Alexander & Judy, 1988). Teachers who enact this principle share the goal of helping their students to self-assess and monitor their learning. These teachers are highly conscientious, strategic, and purposeful in their instruction as they carefully scaffold experiences that provide opportunities for students to engage in self-assessment.

The foregoing chapter highlights two points related to the value of developing adolescents' capacities to monitor their comprehension that bear repeating and elaboration. The first is that doing so is likely to increase motivation to read and learn. Time and time again, teachers report that students, especially those who are less successful, lack motivation (O'Flahavan et al., 1992). When given choices and opportunities to participate in making decisions about their own learning, students become much more engaged. Considerable evidence (Baker, Afflerbach, & Reinking, 1996) suggests that students who are more engaged are motivated, strategic, knowledgeable, and socially interactive. An agenda to promote students' self-assessment, then, is likely to be closely linked to their overall success.

The second point I want to underscore is the importance of students recognizing differing situations or settings and employing appropriate self-assessment processes. Across the subject areas and in different contexts, adolescents need to be able to shift gears and employ strategies appropriate for different purposes and audiences. This is a common problem in secondary school. Consider a student who is a creative writer in English class with a beautiful aesthetic sense of language, but in science appears to be incompetent when asked to write a clear description of methods employed in an experiment or a summary and interpretation of data.

A concern I have about the foregoing chapter is its emphasis on standards and the seemingly ever-increasing influences of a "culture of assessment and accountability" (Anders & Richardson, 1992). On the one hand, linking metacognition and student self-assessment to this seemingly cultural norm is probably a relief to many teachers. I can imagine teachers saying, with relief: "Ah, this idea of self-assessment doesn't have to be a goal that is in competition for instructional time; rather, it can be conjoined with what I am already doing to help my students do better on assessments." That may be true. On the other hand, however, integrating instruction that nurtures and supports students becoming capable of assessing their reading comprehension and learning is the very essence of helping students to become independent learners. It is the key that makes one a learner now and forevermore. It is not a capacity that is developed quickly or simply. Rather it needs to be taught over multiple situations and contexts for a long time.

A good example of how self-assessment is developed over time is the vignette about Theresa. In Grade 5, students use writing rubrics developed by teachers, but in Grade 6, students develop their own rubrics. The Grade 6 students were responsible for evaluating their own and their partner's behavior and learning. This is related to the idea that considerations of differing situations and settings are part and parcel of self-assessment: Students in this vignette are developing their self-assessment capacities within a social situation. This is important because performance norms and conventions for writing are agreed on among those who belong to the discourse community. A self-assessment does not exist outside of a social community.

Another lesson to be learned from this vignette is the scaffolded development of background knowledge that took place in this school—background knowledge related to both content knowledge and procedures. Grade 6 students used their procedural knowledge from Grade 5 to develop rubrics in Grade 6. Theresa was also very careful to scaffold students' content knowledge related to different genres of writing. This is important because metacognitive research suggests that students with more background knowledge are more likely to be able to monitor their own learning than students with less background knowledge (Alexander & Judy, 1988).

The discussion in the vignette about students struggling with being asked to score the rubric caused me to wonder whether the teacher and children needed more discussion/dialogue about both the reason for the rubric and how the scores on the rubric would be used. The students valued their teacher's judgment more than their own and were decidedly victims of the hegemony of grades. Grades—a judgment of performance made by an authority usually without consideration for student self-assessment—are a barrier to encouraging self-assessment. How many of us can remember situations when we thought we had done something well, only to suffer great embarrassment and shame when we discovered that we had somehow "missed the mark" and received a poor grade? Some students are likely to not want to risk making their self-assessment public if they know that a teacher's grade can contradict the self-assessment and make them appear foolish. Teachers need to have a deep understanding of *why* rubrics and self-assessments are important, and they need to communicate this to students.

The second vignette describes ways that self-assessment opportunities can support students for whom school is a struggle both academically and procedurally. Claire uses several strategies to help students understand themselves as learners and to understand the school as an institution with certain systemized procedures (i.e., the IEP) that are daunting to the uninitiated. I applaud Claire's use of various measures, such as Myers' writing questionnaire, to learn more about her students' feelings about writing. I think she is onto something: Self-assessment about one's experiences in school is no doubt fraught with emotional overlays. Every good teacher pays attention to the emotional and attitudinal subtexts of students. Questionnaires, such as the one Claire used, as well as one-on-one interviews and focus groups, are all effective methods to begin to uncover that subtext.

Educators who have taught students who have been less successful in school know that these students are often marginalized to such an extent that they have little voice or little to say about how well they do in school or how they might do better. The instructional opportunities described in this vignette can go a long way toward improving these students' learning and their time spent in school.

In summary, the principle of helping adolescents assess their own literacy and learning competencies is incredibly important for promoting literacy and learning. Students' abilities to self-assess their comprehension, composition, and learning is a requisite to becoming an independent learner who can shift situations, read the literacy performance that is called for, and engage in the process with a successful outcome. Development of metacognitive abilities is a theme that should run throughout the curriculum and instruction we offer adolescents throughout the upper elementary, middle, and high school grades and across the subject areas.

Discussion Questions

As you reflect on the information presented in this chapter, consider the following questions as they relate to your own teaching and/or your experiences in schools:

- In your experience, to what extent do middle and high schools provide opportunities for students to self-assess?
- Do you think the vignettes presented here describe instructional practices that are unusual? Why or why not?
- Compare and contrast the views of the expert responder to your own views.
- What dilemmas must teachers, schools, and others solve to implement Principle 6?

Chapter 9

Principle 7: Adolescents Need Opportunities to Connect Reading With Their Life and Their Learning Inside and Outside of School

High-achieving youth connect their daily classroom reading and learning with what they have accomplished other days, in other classes, and in their lives outside of school (Hull & Schultz, 2001). They link ideas and learning strategies across multiple situations, noting new ways to organize and apply knowledge (Phelps & Hanley-Maxwell, 1997). These learners build on all that has occurred in the past and look toward the future (Cushman, 1998). They weave their identities as students with other identities shaped by their family, community, friends, gender, immigrant status, and personal interests (Brozo, 2002b; Camitta, 1993; Finders, 1997; Mahiri, 1998; Noll, 1998; Norton Pierce, 1995). They evaluate the ways texts (print, visual, and oral) contribute to their identities (Alvermann, Moon, & Hagood, 1999). They might inquire into how a particular textbook relates to their aspirations, asking themselves, "Does it lead in the direction I see myself going?" When reading a popular magazine, they might ask, "Does this magazine reflect who I think I am and who I want to be or does it present a different model of adolescence?" Also, as high-achieving youth avail themselves of interactive communication technologies and multimedia outside of school, they often bring their proficiencies into school settings (Lankshear, 1997).

The ways in which teachers help students connect their out-of-school literacies with learning that goes on inside the school will vary according to immigration patterns, geographic locale, and families' understandings of the school culture (E. Garcia, 2001; Hinchman & Zalewski, 1996; Hull & Schultz, 2002; Jiménez & Gamez, 1999; Skilton-Sylvester, 2002). Newly arrived immigrants to the United States from Korea, for example, may possess knowledge of that country's political, social, and economic characteristics that can inform other students' understanding of life outside of North America. Geographic locale—whether it is suburban, urban, or rural—may influence the availability of and access to technological tools for connecting in- and out-of-school literacies (Schultz, 2002). For example, the small-town library with its bank of eight Internet-connected computers may support the needs of suburban and rural students, but would be insufficient to meet the needs of students in a large city school.

Central to this principle is that a teacher has to know his or her students well as individuals, not stereotyping or making assumptions across groups by age, race, ethnic background, neighborhood, socioeconomic level, or other label. Such a teacher converses with students between classes, asks them what they like to do outside of school, and notices out-of-school musical or athletic performances. Often such a teacher works on a team with other teachers of a cohort of students so they can learn how students express who they are in varied curricular settings, some of which may be more attentive to the personal while others focus more heavily on subject-specific knowing.

Teachers who base their practice on this principle employ genuine and interesting strategies for gathering information about students' interests and lives when they exit the school doors. They demonstrate the sincerity of their efforts to get to know students as individuals by encouraging and supporting connections between classroom and personal worlds. They nurture academic literacy achievement by making visible in school students' out-of-school identities and language competencies (Knobel, 1999).

Other practices that teachers of adolescents have engaged in that capitalize on this principle include bringing community members familiar to youth into the schoolroom for extended periods of time to share their knowledge and expertise (Moll, 1992); identifying discourse communities, such as African American hair salons, and using them to inform ways to conduct classroom discussions about text (Lee, 2000); generating language and critique in the classroom around common local literacy artifacts, such as parking tickets (Cushman, 1998); and teaching listening, writing and reading, math, and scientific and social skills through community-based arts programs (Heath, 1998).

The guiding principle of this chapter also enjoys solid support from several professional education organizations. Groups such as the International Reading Association and National Council of Teachers of English (1996) jointly endorse the idea that students be invited to "participate as knowledgeable, reflective, creative, and critical members of a *variety of literacy communities*" (p. 3; italics added). Similarly, the National Council of Teachers of Mathematics (1991) embraces "classrooms as mathematical communities" for the purpose of "empowering the student" (p. 3).

What follows are two vignettes of teachers and students that serve as enactments of the principle that literacy and learning in the personal and
community lives of youth has a critical role to play in school contexts.

VIGNETTE 1: STUDYING HISTORY
IN AN URBAN CLASSROOM

Manolo has been teaching history at Hawthorne, a large urban high school,
for over 20 years. He teaches mostly juniors and seniors in U.S. History.
Manolo teaches six classes per day, with students divided into sections designated as *regular, honors,* and *Advanced Placement* (AP). Hawthorne's school
community is culturally and ethnically diverse, and the district reports that
90% of the students are eligible for free or reduced lunch.

One of Manolo's highest goals is to make his curriculum meaningful to
his students and to help them increase their critical thinking and writing
abilities. One way he accomplishes these goals is by structuring lessons and
units to include a wide variety of print and nonprint resources. In addition
to their textbook, students read primary source documents, magazine articles, and Internet texts.

Another way that Manolo makes the study of history more meaningful is
by linking students' experiences to class topics. For example, when the
World Trade Center towers and the Pentagon were attacked, they were in
the middle of studying World War II. Manolo challenged his students to explore their feelings about the attack and how these might be similar to or
different from the feelings of Americans right after the bombing of Pearl
Harbor. Students recorded their responses in writing notebooks and ex-
changed them with other students or shared them aloud. He exploited the
learning lessons from the 9/11 experience much further.

Always eager to tie the study of history and current events to the heri-
tages of his students and the great variety of cultural perspectives they represent, Manolo asked them to think about how their lives might be forever
altered by 9/11. For many of his Muslim students and for those who were
very recent immigrants, the events of 9/11 left them and their families feeling particularly vulnerable to recently instituted laws and policies, such as
the Patriot Act. To explore this issue more critically, Manolo asked his
classes to consider:

- During World War II, the U.S. government rounded up Japanese
  Americans and placed them in concentration camps. What is the government doing today that is similar to what it did then? Who is being
  targeted? Why?

- How should the United States protect itself against terrorist attacks while protecting basic constitutional rights?
- Must Americans accept limits on some of these rights in the name of personal and national security?

Following a whole-class discussion of students' reactions and opinions to these questions, Manolo presented them with the following three controversial case studies (see Figs. 9.1, 9.2, and 9.3) and then gave them opportunities to discuss, debate, and write about civil liberties in a time of peril and war. To guide their thinking, Manolo distributed to his students copies of the sections of the U.S. Constitution relevant to each case, as well as a Web address to consult entitled "Civil Liberties and Terrorism."

Manolo organized his students into groups of three and requested they consider and discuss how the outcome of policies and practices described in the case studies would or could impact their own lives and freedoms. His guiding questions were:

- Which is more important: a potential terrorist threat or the privacy of your computer, your credit card, or your e-mail? Why?
- Which is more important: a potential terrorist threat or your right to be informed of any charges against you, your right to a lawyer, or your right to a fair and public trial? Why?
- How would you feel and behave if you knew the government was watching and recording everything you did in public?
- If you are against any of these new government policies and practices, how can you make your feelings known?

After 9/11, hundreds of immigrants without citizenship were rounded up. Courts held secret hearings about sending them back to their home countries because the government believed they might have some link with terrorism.

In a case involving Rabih Haddad, a Muslim clergyman who had overstayed his tourist visa, the courts were forced to rule on whether the hearing for him and others like him could be held in secret. A three-judge panel ruled that it could not. In their ruling, they said, "Democracies die behind closed doors. A government operating in the shadow of secrecy stands in complete opposition to the society envisioned by the framers of our Constitution."

But in another similar case involving Malek Zeidan, a Syrian citizen who had also overstayed his visa, a different three-judge panel ruled in favor of the government. The judges said, "At a time when our nation is faced with threats of such profound and unknown dimensions," deportation hearings should not be open.

It seems likely that the U.S. Supreme Court will at some point consider one of these cases and resolve the contradiction.

FIG. 9.1. Case Study 1.

Police in Washington, DC, are using TVs to keep an eye on as many of its residents as possible. When completed, the police department will have linked 1,000 cameras to watch streets, schools, buses and subways, federal buildings, and a business improvement district. It is the first of its kind in the nation. Video recordings from some of the cameras are already being logged by the police, Secret Service, FBI, and other agencies. When the entire system is finished, police will be able to read newsprint from hundreds of feet away, track cars, zoom in on individuals, and send these images to 1,000 patrol cars outfitted with laptops.

The American Civil Liberties Union (ACLU) is very concerned. The ACLU wants to know: Who will monitor the video? How long will the tapes be kept and by whom? What agencies will have access to them? What steps will be taken to prevent the misuse of the video information, such as racist and antihomeless profiling? Security cameras have been used on the streets in Washington, DC, before. They filmed thousands of anti-NATO demonstrators in 1999, protesters against the World Bank and International Monetary Fund meeting in 2000, and those protesting the presidential election dispute in 2001.

Attorneys with the ACLU and the Partnership for Civil Justice believe there is a very strong legal case for the elimination of these cameras. They argue that people have the right to walk on the streets and in the parks of DC without being watched by the police or the government. But recent opinion polls show over 60% of Americans like the idea of having our streets and public spaces monitored.

FIG. 9.2.   Case Study 2.

Yasser Esam Hamdi, 22 and an American citizen, was born in Louisiana, but brought up in Saudi Arabia. He may have joined a Taliban unit in July 2001 in Afghanistan. He was captured there and turned over to the American military. He has been in a Navy prison since April 2002 in Norfolk, Virginia. His family says that he went to Afghanistan to help the people and only accidentally became involved in the fighting. The government defines him as an "enemy combatant." It says it has the right to keep him in prison for as long as it likes without charging him with any specific crime.

Mr. Hamdi has a lawyer, but the government has not allowed him to meet or talk with Mr. Hamdi because it says that, although Mr. Hamdi is an American citizen, he is a threat to U.S. security. Mr. Hamdi's lawyer asked a federal court in Virginia to rule on whether the government was in the right. On January 8, 2003, the court agreed with the government. The court ruled that because we are fighting a war on terrorism and the war is not over, the government has the right to hold Mr. Hamdi in prison for as long as it feels necessary, under Article II, Section 2 of the Constitution.

The Lawyers Committee for Human Rights said that the court's ruling endangers basic protections guaranteed in the Constitution. Mr. Hamdi's lawyer will appeal to the Supreme Court, but there is no guarantee it will review the case.

FIG. 9.3.   Case Study 3.

Manolo's final classroom activity related to this topic was a believing game/doubting game activity. He discovered this strategy on an Internet site for high school teachers and has found it to be especially useful for stimulating critical thinking. The believing game asks students to find something about an issue, concept, or idea to accept or agree with, even if they are not predisposed to do so. In the doubting game, students are asked to consider the same issue, concept, or idea, but this time they have to find something disagreeable about it. Thoughtful disagreement involves asking probing questions, attacking faulty logic, pointing out inadequate evidence, and providing information that supports an alternative viewpoint. The last step in the believing/doubting game is to have students integrate the insights gained by experiencing an idea from the inside and scrutinizing it from the outside.

Manolo began the believing game/doubting game activity by projecting on the overhead the statement, *Personal and civil freedoms must be limited in times of war.* He then asked students to take out their notebooks and record their initial thinking about the assertion in a short paragraph. Next, he divided the class into small discussion groups of three students and told them to find as much about the statement they could believe in. Manolo urged students to ask themselves: What does the government see that I don't? How could this argument possibly be right? What can I agree with? During the believing game portion of the activity, they should try to suppress the inclination to disagree. Manolo reminds the class that this is not a role-playing or pretending exercise, but a process of finding some way to honestly connect with the assertion. Other questions that Manolo suggests his students ask themselves are: "What's interesting or helpful about the assertion? What would you notice if you believed in it? In what sense or under what conditions might this idea be true?"

After about 15 minutes, Manolo told students to record in their notebooks all the statements of agreement with the assertion their groups were able to generate. He then began the next phase of the activity—the doubting game. Just as Manolo asked his students to find authentic reasons to believe in the assertion about limiting freedoms during war no matter how difficult that may have been for some, the doubting game invites students to explore reasons to reject and critique that point of view. Now the same small discussion groups were asked to spend 15 minutes talking about problems with the assertion and were told to keep a record of them in their notebooks.

When group work concluded, Manolo encouraged sharing of ideas and points of view while writing them into a t-chart on the board. As expected, he received a range of responses. One student stated that no person is totally free in any society, and that sacrifices are necessary when we are at war. He gave the example of food rationing during World War II. Others, how-

ever, were equally firm in their belief that governments use war as an opportunity to restrict the behavior of undesirable people. One of Manolo's Muslim students said the treatment of people from the Middle East is similar to
how the American government treated the Japanese who were living here
during World War II.

Finally, Manolo had students revisit the statement of belief they had written in their notebooks before the believing game/doubting game activity
began. He asked them to reflect on the experience and comment in writing
about how it might have changed their point of view. For additional credit,
students were given the option of writing a letter to the president, a repre-
sentative, or a senator expressing an opinion on a civil liberties issue since
9/11.

VIGNETTE 2: SECONDARY SCHOOL ENGLISH
AND READING

Sylvia teaches English and Reading at Bayfront High School, a school on
the Gulf Coast comprised mostly of Hispanic Americans, with a much
smaller group of African American and Native American students. In the
2002–2003 school year, Sylvia was a member of a successful grant writing
team that brought resources to the school to enrich its overall literate culture and provide additional support for struggling readers. The grant process also helped build a stronger sense of community among administrators,
teachers, staff, and students. (For additional discussion of the grant-funded
initiatives at Bayfront, see chap. 11.)

Sylvia's second block is comprised entirely of freshmen who have low
reading scores on state achievement tests. Her focus in the class is on helping them develop literacy skills that will be useful in their other subject areas. Sylvia has forged close ties with science, history, and math teachers,
who also have her reading students in their classes. She collaborates with
these faculty members by creating activities and strategies in reading to support what they are teaching. For example, when the science teacher was
covering the topic of local marine ecology, Sylvia designed an activity in her
reading class in which students assumed the identities of various individuals, such as a scientist, a shrimp boat captain, a windsurfer, a land devel-
oper, and a political activist. The class simulated a town hall meeting after
reading about and discussing an actual proposal to build a resort hotel on
the beach. Based on the meeting, students composed e-mail letters to their
local representatives expressing their views.

At another time, Sylvia supported the history teacher's lessons related to
American immigration. In her class, after reading the picture book *Friends
From the Other Side* (Anzula, 1995), she gave students traveling bags to take

home that enlist family members in shared, culturally familiar experiences. The bags were comprised of a copy of the picture book and bilingual directions. One student read the book to his grandmother and then talked with her about her experiences immigrating to the United States from Guatemala. The student returned to the classroom to describe what he had learned from her. The traveling bag strategy not only created opportunities for students to enrich and personalize their understanding of the class topic in history, but also stimulated repeated readings of a familiar text, which helped build fluency and confidence.

Based on feedback from a student advisory council, formed to provide input on the types of literacy initiatives to go into the state-funded grant Sylvia and her colleagues obtained, she organized a mentoring program for the most seriously struggling readers. The program used high-achieving peers and community volunteers to read to and with low-ability students. The primary goal of the program was to find ways to motivate struggling readers to read more often and on a daily basis. Sylvia urged this goal on all of her volunteers, challenging them to be as resourceful as possible in creating motivating reading experiences. Once students become habitual readers, Sylvia believes, their skill level increases, improving overall academic achievement.

Tony had recently retired from his career as a Naval pilot and instructor. He had not given the idea of being a volunteer reading tutor much thought until he saw a piece about Sylvia's program in the local newspaper. When Tony contacted her to express an interest in the program, she was more than happy to have him participate. Here was a man who loved to read and had exciting and varied life experiences to bring to the tutorial experience. Because the overwhelming majority of the school's lowest readers were boys, Sylvia wanted to ensure the mentoring relationships she arranged for them would bring about attitude and achievement benefits she and her grant-team colleagues desired.

Sylvia teamed Tony with LaBron, a 15-year-old sophomore with a reading achievement level of fifth grade and a special education label. LaBron came from a particularly difficult home situation. For his entire freshman year, he and his four younger brothers and sisters lived with their mother in a motel room on a noisy commercial thoroughfare. The year before, LaBron spent the eighth grade in a juvenile detention facility after a conviction for auto theft. During the current school year, his mother was working closely with teachers and counselors to find ways of keeping this tall, soft-spoken boy in school and improving his reading skills.

Sylvia made arrangements to have LaBron excused from his first block study strategies class for 45 minutes 3 days per week so he could meet with Tony. Initially, they met in a small, private room adjacent to the library that was reserved for student club meetings. Before long, however, they began to search out comfortable spaces anywhere on campus to read and talk together, often finding themselves outside enjoying the mild coastal breezes.

Soon after they were introduced, LaBron wanted to learn more about Tony's flying career. They spent a couple of sessions looking through photos of airplanes Tony has flown and talking about the various places around the United States and world he has lived. This helped break the ice and allowed them to ease into the more structured, reading tutoring that would soon begin.

Although Sylvia gave Tony some general details about LaBron's academic and family background, Tony insisted she not tell him too much. He wanted to approach his relationship with LaBron as he would meeting any brand-new friend. So, it was by happenstance that Tony found out about LaBron's incarceration. Once when going through one of Tony's photo albums, he stopped to describe an incident he had in Kuwait during the first Gulf War, in which he and a couple of buddies were taken into custody by Kuwaiti officials on suspicion of spying. It was all a complete misunderstanding, but Tony said he had to spend a night in solitary confinement until his commander was able to clear up the matter. LaBron stared at the ground sheepishly, then shook his head up and down, "Yeah, I've spent time there." Thinking at first that LaBron was joking, Tony chuckled and asked what he knew about prison. So then the story came out.

As LaBron recounted his experience, he expressed a great deal of confusion and curiosity over his legal rights and the practices of officials in the juvenile justice system. Along the way, he asked Tony several personally important and even poignant questions that at that moment Tony simply could not answer, but promised to look into. Armed with this knowledge, Tony actively searched for reading materials and planned meaningful activities around the topic of juvenile crime, courts, and penal facilities. He reasoned that LaBron's inquisitiveness might motivate him to exert sustained effort to read about others with similar experiences to his own and explore related social policy and law in a critical way.

The next time they met, Tony spread several books and articles on the table and asked LaBron to select one to read together. LaBron took his time looking carefully at each one, then chose *The House That Crack Built* (Taylor, 1992). A somber redux of the house that Jack built, this is a tale with pictures of the depths to which one can sink when trafficking in and addicted to drugs. Tony read it aloud, while LaBron repeated the refrain, "This is the house that crack built." Eventually, after repeated readings, Tony was able to complete the entire book on his own.

The House That Crack Built was more than a useful text for developing reading fluency; it also instigated conversation about who and what is responsible for drug addiction and drug-related crimes. LaBron felt that kids who grow up in the 'hood without any money are tempted to sell drugs to make money. He also said to survive they have to be "tough." Tony challenged LaBron to think about whether individuals are responsible for their own behavior. Is it possible, he asked, for kids who grow up in poverty and without intact families to avoid crime and drugs? LaBron's reply was that anyone who thought so should go live that way and see for themselves. Tony's respect for this youth's ability to think critically was growing. He began his life as a farm worker's son. His father moved with the seasons every year from Texas to Minnesota, until an accident forced him out of the fields. Tony could only imagine what would have become of his life if it had not been for a cousin who joined the Navy and convinced him to do the same.

While researching why young people turn to delinquency, Tony found an excellent volume entitled *Juvenile Crime, Juvenile Justice*, edited by McCord, Spatz Widom, and Crowell (2001). Although the readability was somewhat more advanced than LaBron could handle, the book served as a valuable resource for current facts, trends, analysis of causes, and successful prevention and treatment programs. When a question came up in their conversation or reading that seemed to require an immediate answer, they consulted McCord et al.'s book. In it, for instance, they discovered youth crime has actually been on the decline since the mid-1990s, in contrast to a widespread public perception that it is ever on the increase. They also found statistical documentation that youth of color are processed in the juvenile justice system in numbers far out of proportion relative to their White peers. This issue came up when they were reading a newspaper article about a 14-year-old African American boy convicted of murdering his teacher in Florida.

The most rewarding mentoring experiences for LaBron and Tony occurred during the reading of W. Myers' (1999) *Monster*. Tony found the novel in Bayfront's library and realized shortly into it that virtually all the issues of juvenile crime and justice were embodied in the experiences of the main character and narrator, Steve Harmon. Steve, a teenager and aspiring script writer who is accused of complicity in a murder, tells the story of his experience from arrest through trial verdict in the form of a film score. This unique perspective draws the reader into the details of his life in a way that evokes empathy, disgust, suspicion, and finally vindication. LaBron was drawn in from the very first page.

As they read *Monster* together, Tony and LaBron kept a journal of their reactions to critical questions that arose during conversation and discussion. For example, Tony asked LaBron to compare and contrast how the American legal system is portrayed in the novel with his own experiences. To do this, LaBron devised a split-page approach, putting direct quotes and brief descriptions in one column and what he remembered about his treatment in juvenile court and detention in the other. At one point in the book, Steve says, "The best time to cry is at night, when the lights are out and someone is being beaten up and screaming for help." LaBron put this in his journal and then penned a memory of hearing new kids to the center crying at night because they realize for the first time they're in "something called a correctional center but it's prison."

Another interesting activity they tried while reading *Monster* was to assume the identities of different figures in the courtroom and argue the scenes of the trial and details of the case from those points of view. Tony chose to look at the events in one chapter from the perspective of Mr. Petrocelli, a witness for the prosecution, while LaBron pretended to be O'Brien, Steve's attorney. LaBron argued that most of the jurors saw a teenage Black kid and assumed he was guilty, even if they did not tell the lawyers that up front. Tony, responding as if he were Petrocelli, said all the kids involved in the fatal shooting were equally guilty, including the one who took the cigarettes; the one who wrestled the gun from the convenience-store owner; and Steve, the one who made sure the coast was clear.

At the conclusion of *Monster* and related readings on juvenile crime, LaBron felt so strongly about what he believed was the unfair treatment of minors in the criminal justice system that he urged Tony to help him express his feelings in some way that might influence lawmakers. This led to further research, taking them online to find information on their district's state representatives' policy positions related to youth crime. Their search uncovered some interesting facts. Although both representatives had cosponsored a youth advocacy task force, they also voted in favor of trying minors as adults, and one even supported legislation to make the death penalty an option for minors found guilty of capital murder. Tony suggested LaBron compose an e-mail letter to make his case to these legislators. The composition process necessitated discussion and work on form, punctuation, and grammar, as well as finding statistics and quotes from the various articles and books they had accumulated during their exploration of the topic. Tony observed a level of enthusiasm for this effort unlike any he had seen from LaBron before. Sylvia, too, could only marvel at LaBron's dedication to "wise them up," as he termed it, about what it was really like to be processed through the system as a teenager. Although his sense of empowerment was diluted once he received a perfunctory reply from the representatives, stating that they appreciated his input and asking him to continue to remain engaged in the political process, he remained proud of himself for doing it.

WHAT THESE PRACTICES TEACH US

In her book, *Beating the Odds: High Schools as Communities of Commitment*, Ancess (2003) said:

> . . . when personalization, powerful teaching, and intellectually demanding learning come together in a school . . . a compelling and impressive story unfolds about the achievements of conventionally marginalized students, about the daily, lived lives of students and teachers in their school, and about the idea and the possibility that public high schools can be humane, intellectually vital, caring, and personally responsive places. (p. 3)

The two scenes of teaching in this chapter paint a compelling and impressive story of responsive, principled teaching for youth in American high schools. Manolo, Sylvia, and Tony, sensitized by their own experiences as individuals of color, bring to their work as teachers and mentors a consciousness of caring, an attitude of respect for the diverse lifeworlds of adolescents. This disposition is reflected in the ways they structure learning around issues and concerns that matter to youth. Classroom walls are porous, allowing home, community, and cultural identities to serve as resonators of mainstream texts. History for Manolo and his students is not the ingestion of a series of facts and details, but a forum for expression and critical reworking of ideas to better understand their own place and possibilities within America's past and present.

Sylvia's push to establish long-term partnerships between adult mentors and youth has resulted in surprising levels of participation in reading and learning from reluctant and struggling students. Tony's informality and flexibility made possible a curriculum for LaBron based on personal interest and experience. Instead of slavishly following a prescribed set of instructional routines for teaching reading skills, Tony embedded skill development within an inquiry of a topic close to LaBron's life. In keeping to this course, he was able to leaven his reading motivation, abilities, and critical consciousness. Guided by the principle that students need the freedom to connect reading and learning in school with their outside-of-school interests, these teachers are able to engender engaged, sustained effort from adolescents who might otherwise invest little if the instruction were passionless, monotonous, and detached from personal experience.

A SCHOLAR'S RESPONSE
Elizabeth Birr Moje, University of Michigan

> Principle 7: Adolescents need opportunities to connect reading with their life and their learning inside and outside of school.

By focusing on the principle of providing students with opportunities to connect classroom reading to their own lives, this chapter puts forward a principle for adolescent literacy teaching and learning close to my work and heart—that of helping young people learn to traverse the many different discourse communities of their lives, both in and out of school. As indicated by the research reviewed in the chapter, the guiding principle that "adolescents need opportunities to connect reading with their life and their learning inside and outside of school" is important to the development of strategic, thoughtful, and engaged adolescent readers. It is also a principle that effective teachers have followed for years.

In many cases, teachers are well equipped to respond to students from mainstream backgrounds and experiences simply because many teachers are from such backgrounds, but they are less well equipped to respond to and connect texts to the lives of students whose backgrounds are different from their own. Indeed many recommended mainstream teaching practices *are* designed to be culturally responsive, but are enacted in ways that are responsive only to a segment of students (Moje & Hinchman, 2004). It is important to note that even high-achieving students may not be intellectually engaged in the texts they are asked to read in school; they may simply be more adept at what Judith Green called *studenting*, or complying with what the teacher asks one to do, without necessarily engaging in it (Kelly & Green, 1998). What this chapter highlights is the need to connect reading tasks to *all* students' lives and to connect in deep ways.

Specifically, the chapter suggests that effective teaching of literacy requires the awareness that, in fact, people's experiences differ—not only on an individual basis, but as a result of all sorts of differences, including ethnicity or race, age, religious belief, geographic location, sexual orientation, gender, and social class. Once teachers recognize how their own experiences are shaped by membership in many different networks or sets of relations, they can be open to seeing and working with difference. Furthermore, once we, as teachers, develop this awareness and appreciation for difference as a result of group membership—what we might label *culture*—then we can be open to multiple ways of making sense of various texts, and we are more likely to invite experiences outside our own into our classrooms. This chapter helps teachers think about all the different connections that could possibly be made to different texts in a variety of different textual practices.

The chapter is valuable in part because in providing examples the authors refuse to reduce this kind of teaching to the development of individualized curricula. Rather than casting the connecting task as something that must be tailored to the different experiences of each individual student, Vignette 1 provides a vision of what a good teacher could do to work with a whole class of students on a shared curriculum. Vignette 2 represents a more individualized rendering of the principle, probably more suited to a clinical setting, as illustrated in the case. But the inclusion of two different enactments helps to make clear that this principle is not a call for individualization. In fact one key to connecting readings across lives and space lies in building a community of learners who share the connections they experience. It is important to note that building a *community* does not suggest making the space an always happy and uncontested space. Students and teachers should bring different experiences, beliefs, and values—or subjectivities—to bear on their readings, and they should share their subjective readings with one another as a way to expand their knowledge.

Just as it is useful to engage students from different backgrounds in conversations about the materials they read and the experiences they bring to their reading, it is also important for teachers and students to learn from one another. In other words, it is not necessary that teachers have the *same* experiences as their students to support students in making connections. It certainly helps to have similar experiences, but it is clear from my ethnographic work with young people whose experiences are quite different from mine that the most important ingredient to connecting is not shared skin color, socioeconomic status (SES), or some other demographic quality, but is rather the willingness to listen and the ability to communicate to others that one wants to know something about them.

Despite my enthusiasm for this principle, a few words of caution are necessary. In our attempts to connect adolescents' out-of-school literacies to their in-school literacy learning, it is important that we do not essentialize adolescents' experiences on the basis of their racial and ethnic backgrounds, gender, SES, age, or other qualities of difference (Moje & Hinchman, 2004). In other words, we should not assume that all young people are the same by virtue of their age, and we should not assume that all young people of a certain race are the same by virtue of their age and race. For example, a popular myth is that all young people engage in Instant Messaging (IM). To the contrary, a significant portion of young people do not have the economic resources to purchase the computer hardware necessary to IM. In fact many young people do engage in some sort of electronic communication, but the methods and practices vary for a host of reasons. By the same token, not all Black youth listen to rap, not all urban youth are gang members, not all boys are struggling readers, and not all girls read relationship novels.

The list could go on and on; the important point here is that there is a fine line between understanding that some sets of experiences, some cultural practices, and some language practices may be common to racial and ethnic, social class, or gender groups, but that people within those groups cannot be reduced to common practices of those groups. Individual difference is a complex intersection of all of those qualities of difference, so that a third-generation Latina living in Detroit may be more like an African American girl living in Detroit than she is like a Latino living in New Mexico. We cannot assume that all youth who exhibit particular demographic characteristics will enjoy the same texts. The Latino/a youth I worked with in Salt Lake City, Utah, for example, hated reading what they labeled *Chicano* literature (Moje, Young et al., 2000), whereas many of the Latino/a youth I work with in Detroit hunger for texts that represent Mexicans, Mexican Americans, and Chicano/as.

In summary, connecting adolescents' out-of-school literacies to their in-school lives is important, but must be carefully done. It is incredibly challenging work, as my colleagues and I are learning through our attempts to write science texts that may be both age and culturally responsive to young people in Detroit. We continually grapple with how to represent characters without drawing on stereotypes and with what to do about the fact that the school population, although predominantly African American, is not completely homogeneous, and that the African American, Latino/a, and White students in Detroit come from many different sets of cultural experiences. We also struggle with how to integrate information drawn from everyday experiences with information related to abstract scientific concepts. None of these challenges goes away with the admonition to *connect* to students' lives. Yet like the authors of this volume, we work from the principle that, without connections to their lives, adolescent students will not be intellectually engaged in the subject matter we wish to teach, and they will be less likely to develop sophisticated literacy skills and strategies that allow them to bring their experiences to bear on unfamiliar texts in the service of learning content in deep and meaningful ways.

Discussion Questions

As you reflect on the information presented in this chapter, consider the following questions as they relate to your own teaching and/or your experiences in schools:

- In your experience, to what extent do middle and high schools provide opportunities for adolescents to connect reading with their life and their learning inside and outside of school?
- Do you think the vignettes presented here describe instructional practices that are unusual? Why or why not?
- Compare and contrast the views of the expert responder to your own views.
- What dilemmas must teachers, schools, and others solve to implement Principle 7?

Principle 8: Adolescents Need Opportunities to Develop Critical Perspectives Toward What They Read, View, and Hear

In chapter 9, the vignettes we shared demonstrated how enlightened teachers can enmesh students' life worlds with curricular concerns in the classroom. Valuing adolescents' outside-of-school lives by foregrounding their interests and experiences in school offers students a chance to find something meaningful in what might otherwise be detached and irrelevant curricula. The guiding principle of this chapter calls on those responsible for schooling youth not only to honor students' everyday literate practices, but to support critical multiliteracies. Advocates of this view of education (Gee, 2002; Luke, 1999; New London Group, 1996) stress the need to infuse school curricula with literacies that promote critical, participatory citizenship (Buckingham, 1997; King & Brozo, 1992; Muspratt, Luke, & Freebody, 1997). Because young people today dwell in a *mediasphere* (O'Brien, 2001), a world saturated by inescapable, ever-evolving, and competing media that both flow through them and are altered and created by them, their efforts to understand, critique, and manipulate media need to find a nurturing context in schools (Alvermann, 1998, 2002; Alvermann et al., 1999; Tyner, 1998). This does not imply that the teaching of print literacy should be suspended. We are well aware that control over the written word is vital to becoming critically literate, as has been demonstrated throughout this book. What we are advocating, however, is that middle and secondary schools offer responsive curricula for adolescents who are engaged participants in the mediasphere, who are literate in and create forms of discourse that are visual and oral as well as print-based (Greene, 2003), and who need to become critical consumers and users of the various media at their disposal.

This principle informs practices that will help students learn that texts are perspective, and that what is written, viewed, or heard represents the point of view of an author, auteur, speaker, or composer and her or his way of seeing the world. They learn to recognize that various stances may be used to compose written work, paintings, or music, or to orchestrate and conduct hypothesis testing or mathematical problem solving.

The implications of this principle will vary, although the common goal of a curriculum of critical literacy is to impel students to confront, question, and rework text. Some students may be motivated to explore the assumptions that authors, video artists, Web page designers, cartoonists, and so on may have been operating under when constructing their messages. Other students may be interested in thinking about the decisions that chat room participants make when it comes to choice of words, content, topics included or excluded, and interests served. Still others may use media to rethink and reshape critical work futures. Students may benefit from instruction that encourages them to do multiple readings, viewings, and hearings of the same topic from different perspectives (e.g., an ecology text, documentary, and speech on water resources read, heard, and seen from the perspectives of a scientist, a swimmer, a shrimp boat captain, a beachfront homeowner, a Green Peace activist, and a politician).

Professional organizations in many disciplines support this principle. For example, the Curriculum Standards for the Social Studies (1994) state that students should "explain and apply concepts such as power, role, status, justice, and influence to the examination of persistent issues and social problems" (p. 41), while the National Science Education Standards (1996) state that students "formulate and revise scientific explanations and models using logic and evidence" and "recognize and analyze alternative explanations and models" (p. 175).

Middle and secondary schools that make it a priority to educate adolescents to make choices and think critically about what they read, view, and hear can help students develop the confidence and conviction that they can make a difference in the world (Brozo & Simpson, 2003; Hull, 2000). The two vignettes in this chapter tell the stories of youth who learned to manipulate traditional print and electronic media to communicate personally meaningful messages. Both come from a single setting where the inspiration and energy of the school's literacy coach helped turn what had been for at least two students an educational experience devoid of meaning into one marked by growing skills in critical literacy and multimedia and pride in academic and workplace accomplishment.

VIGNETTE 1: CROSS-AGE TUTORING
AT MOORE HIGH SCHOOL

Tremayn had been talking about quitting school since the start of 10th grade. His two older brothers had dropped out, and his 17-year-old sister was receiving homebound instruction after having a baby. Brenda, the literacy coach working in Moore High School, Tremayn's school, saw another possible future for this young teen. She took particular notice of him while observing his English class one mid-October afternoon.

The English teacher had assigned the class the task of locating a short article from the newspaper and writing a summary of it. First, students gathered around the two long tables in the back of the room, rummaging through various local papers, until they found a piece of interest and of suitable length; then they gradually made their way back to their desks to read and craft their summaries. Tremayn took more time than the others with his newspaper selection and seemed engrossed in the content. Brenda, who though early in the school year was no stranger to the class, moved slowly around the room, eventually stopping to visit with Tremayn. She was curious to find out what had captured his attention. He greeted her and then immediately began explaining how the article was about a new mayoral task force designed to eliminate graffiti by linking graffiti artists with gangs. Tremayn became animated on this point, telling Brenda how he thought this tactic was unfair because he personally knew many graffiti artists and none of them were in gangs. Brenda was impressed with Tremayn's passion for the topic and his sensitive, critical reading of the article. By digging beneath the surface level of the article, Tremayn had uncovered the fallacy of one of its central assumptions. Tremayn had not had time that period to write his summary, but was given the opportunity to provide an oral encapsulation of his article for the class, and he did so with the same level of enthusiasm he had exhibited when sharing his reactions with Brenda.

Brenda was on the lookout for young men and women like Tremayn—students at risk of dropping out due to poor academic performance, low ability levels, or difficult home circumstances. She was hoping to recruit them for a cross-age tutoring program as part of an overall plan to improve reading skills for struggling students and keep them in school. She had made arrangements with the neighborhood elementary school to host tutorial sessions twice weekly involving second and third graders and high school reading buddies. Although the elementary school was only five short blocks away, Brenda received permission from the high school principal to use a school van to save transportation time.

Brenda spoke with Tremayn and several other students individually about participating in the program. When she had commitments from 10 of them, she began preparing them for their roles. The students were all members of the same third-block English class, so Brenda was able to use that time for group training sessions. More important, the English teacher agreed to allow the tutoring activity to count toward students' grades. This would be an important recruitment incentive for Brenda. Moore High tutors learned techniques for finding out the children's interests. They were taught simple read-aloud and vocabulary strategies. They learned how to facilitate writing in response to reading and how to make books. Reinforced throughout was the expectation that the high schoolers would be encouraging of their younger buddies' reading and writing efforts and would help them see that these activities can be enjoyable. Above all, Brenda hoped that by developing literacy strategies for helping younger, less able readers than themselves, these adolescents would, in fact, expand their own reading and writing skills. The literature, at least, left open this expectation (Boyd, 2000; Brozo & Hargis, 2003b; Fisher, 2001).

Tremayn was matched with Marcus, a second grader who was already experiencing difficulties with grade-appropriate reading materials. He discovered in their first meeting that Marcus lived in an apartment complex just a couple of streets away from Tremayn's building. He learned that Marcus "loved" football and, because his father lived in Chicago, wanted to play for the Chicago Bears when he grew up. Marcus also told Tremayn what he wanted most was a computer so he could play "cool games." Tremayn made sure to tell Marcus about his interests, too, such as "roundball" and dancing. After talking and getting to know one another, Tremayn read some pages he had practiced from a short biography about Michael Jordan. Before long it was time to board the van for the quick drive back to the high school. Marcus asked Tremayn if he was coming back, and Tremayn reassured him he would return in a couple of days. It was a humble start of what was to become an important experience for the two of them.

Over the next few months, some of the Moore High School students decided tutoring was not for them. They became impatient or did not want to plan reading and writing activities for their elementary partners—or, in the case of 2 of the original 10 students, eventually dropped out. But Tremayn seemed to have what it takes and came to enjoy his newfound status as a role model and "expert" reader for his young buddy, Marcus.

Much of what Tremayn and Marcus read and wrote about had to do with football. With Brenda's help in finding appropriately difficult, high-interest books, they enjoyed biographies of great Bears players from the past, such as Walter Peyton, Jim McMahon, and the "Fridge" Perry. They kept a scrapbook of the Bears' performance that season, reading newspaper stories and cutting out pictures of their favorite players. Along with these, they wrote captions, statistics, and bits of trivia from players' records.

While cutting out a magazine photo of the Bears' premier running back, Anthony Thomas, better known as the *A-Train*, Marcus commented about his powerful physique, wondering out loud how he got so big. Tremayn thought they could find information on that topic using the Internet. Because the cross-age tutoring sessions were held in the elementary school's media center, computers were available throughout the large open room. Brenda helped get their search started using descriptors such as *football players' training*, and they found pages of sites concerned with body building and fitness. What caught Tremayn's eye, however, were references to performance-enhancement drugs. Brenda helped them locate sites with straightforward, objective information about these supplements, which they printed for reading later.

Brenda talked with Tremayn about how he might share this information with Marcus, cautioning him not to present it in a way that might inadvertently glorify drug use. Tremayn assured her he was going to "set him straight about that junk." Under Brenda's watchful eye, Tremayn planned ways he would read, write, and talk about performance-enhancement drugs in the next few sessions. Her own research yielded a book on the topic for young adolescents entitled *Steroid Drug Dangers* (Monroe, 1999), which she found in the high school's library. The information in Monroe's book is presented in a colorful, easy-to-understand format, with many illustrative photographs. She helped Tremayn develop strategies for sharing selected content from the book that would help Marcus begin to appreciate the drug-free ways of building muscle and stamina for athletic competition.

It was Tremayn, however, who came up with the idea of a digital activity related to the topic. Aware of Marcus' keen interest in computers, he developed a plan for taking a closer look at the characters from popular computer games. His plan was inspired by reading that one of the most common pastimes among many American football players when on the road or during the off season was playing such games as *True Crime: Streets of LA* (Activision) and *WWF Wrestlemania* (THQ). Typically, the heroes and villains in these games are exaggeratedly muscled in ways that football players and body builders must envy and, perhaps, strive to resemble.

Demonstrating once again for Brenda his ability to reason critically, Tremayn saw how these images might influence certain athletes to do whatever it takes, including using drugs, to achieve unusual physiques. With Brenda's help and assistance from the elementary school media specialist, Tremayn and Marcus used the Internet to find pictures of popular computer game figures from *Take No Prisoners* (Red Orb), *The Hulk* (Vivendi-Universal), *Army Men: Sarge's Heroes* (3DO), and *X-Men: Mutant Academy* (Activision). These pictures were then downloaded into *Adobe Photoshop* so they could be altered. Tremayn and Marcus learned how to rework the main characters' physiques, reshaping them in ways that were more proportional to normal muscle development. They displayed their work in a PowerPoint presentation with before slides, accompanied by captions warning of the dangers of steroids and other illegal substances for building muscle, and after slides with statements about good health, diet, and fitness. Proud of the brief PowerPoint show they had created, Tremayn and Marcus were given special opportunities to share the slides with other students in the cross-age tutoring program. The elementary school's principal was so impressed she made sure the slides were shown to the children during drug awareness events that year.

VIGNETTE 2: A SCHOOL-TO-WORK GED PROGRAM

Brenda's initiatives with Tremayn and other struggling readers at Moore High School comprised only one of the facets of an overall program to reverse the upward trend in dropouts. Recommendations for these initiatives resulted from the efforts of a student retention study group she had formed. The group, comprised of teachers, parents, counselors, students, members of the business community, and clergy, made several suggestions for finding ways to retain potential and soon-to-be dropouts. One of those suggestions was to establish an in-school GED program while also sponsoring workplace experiences for GED students.

Moore High School's principal was persuaded by compelling information the study group acquired about successful GED programs across the state, demonstrating that the best ones kept potential dropouts attending high school for half of the day and gaining valuable work experiences the other half. The most effective of these GED programs also provided special support for students' literacy development. The principal was also assured by the state commissioner of education that students who attended the GED classes at Moore could remain on the average daily attendance rolls, which would provide recoverable funds to help pay for the costs of the program.

Brenda knew even for those students who pursued an alternative path to a high school diploma, sound reading skills were essential for success. She also reasoned that students in a GED program who were anxious to find gainful employment needed to develop a kind of literacy that was functional for the new demands placed on modern workers, such as flexible problem solving and critical thinking. Brenda hoped that by developing literacy skills within the context of workplace realities and possibilities, GED students, who often come to view traditional education as detached from their lives and interests, would see a connection between school-based learning and work-based activities.

Loy, Moore High's vocational-education teacher, and Roxanne, the counselor, both members of the student retention committee who endorsed the establishment of a GED program, agreed to coordinate and teach the GED class. Brenda already had an excellent working relationship with them, which made early planning and implementation of curriculum an enjoyable collaborative experience. Loy concentrated on establishing partnerships with local businesses and industry to ensure apprenticeship and internship opportunities would be available to students, while Roxanne and Brenda focused on designing contextualized literacy learning strategies. They visited each worksite, interviewing employees, managers, foremen, supervisors, and human resource personnel about the reading and/or writing required to fulfill job duties. They brought back brochures, copies of manuals, and other literacy artifacts around which strategies for learning were constructed.

At the same time, the three of them were determining the best candidates for the inaugural GED class. One invitee, Hermalinda, failed the state's high school graduation test each of the three times she took it. By her senior year, she had lost the will to try again. She, her three sisters, and her own 2-year-old son were living with her mother in public housing. Hermalinda was 18 and wanted a place of her own, but needed a job that paid enough to make that possible. When she came to Roxanne's office to tell her she had decided to drop out, she was not prepared for the option the counselor offered: remain in school, earn a GED, and earn money and job skills at the same time. Roxanne explained that as her teacher she would do everything she could to help her get through the year-long program. She also impressed on Hermalinda the importance of a high school diploma for keeping life and career options open for both herself and her child. Roxanne hoped Hermalinda's motivation to improve living conditions for her son would help her persevere through graduation.

Loy was able to find a work placement for Hermalinda in a private doctor's office. Although for several years the office had been serving mostly Anglo patients from the surrounding suburban neighborhood, the number of Latinos/as settling in the suburb and availing themselves of the conveniently located medical facility had been steadily increasing. Mindful of the slowly shifting demographics of their clientele, the two doctors who ran the office thought Hermalinda, with her bilingual skills, could be a particularly helpful addition to their all-White staff. When Roxanne and Loy interviewed her at the start of the class, she expressed an interest in nursing, so she was excited to learn she would be working in a medical office. As prearranged, her first experiences were shadowing different members of the staff, such as nurse practitioners, lab technicians, secretaries, and custodian.

Hermalinda's mornings were spent at Moore—not in the general curriculum, but pursuing an alternative track toward graduation. In this way, Moore counted Hermalinda and her classmates in the GED program in its daily enrollment, while the state, a strong supporter of creative plans for student retention, continued to provide a per-pupil expenditure for each them. The program's success would mean a win–win outcome for all stakeholders.

With Brenda's support, Roxanne created learning experiences for the 14 students in the initial GED class that included multiple strands of instruction. For example, every day she engaged students in activities involving writing as meaningful communication, using information and communications technologies (ICTs) for research and production, reading for working, and developing test-taking strategies. The GED classroom resembled a lab, so students did not sit in desks and rows and listen to theoretical lectures, but were given plenty of freedom of movement especially when pursuing assignments tailored to their unique interests and workplace experiences. This freedom also made it possible for Loy and Roxanne to provide individual attention to students in the class.

Hermalinda's assignments were applied to the content and texts of her work placement in the doctor's clinic. For example, when learning how to organize ideas and specific information from text, she was provided guided practice with content from brochures and manuals actually used by employees in the clinic. Thus, Hermalinda practiced the split-page technique for taking notes by separating the major concepts from the significant details and recording them in a two-column format using manual pages describing emergency labor and delivery procedures. In another example, when discovering routines for self-questioning before reading, Hermalinda used the titles of various brochures, such as "Counter Effects of Aspirin with Other Drugs," "Life Expectancy Is Going Up," and "Preoperative Precautions," to practice constructing appropriate prequestions as guides to reading.

The approach of tying literacy strategies to workplace content created a highly engaged atmosphere of learning in the GED classroom. By being led to recognize the immediate functionality of strategies to competence and success in their work settings, Hermalinda and her classmates became more interested participatory learners than they had been as students in the general high school curriculum. In no instance was this more apparent than when the GED students were asked to develop a work-based project as one of the major assignments of the class. The goal of the project was to help students think critically about their work settings and how to better inform and serve the intended clientele or consumer. An actual product was to be created that could be constructed and/or presented using ICTs. The product would be made available to employers as a demonstration of the meaningful and creative contributions the student-employee might make to his or her business.

As soon as the assignment was explained, Hermalinda had a good idea what she wanted to do to make the office waiting room a more consumer-friendly environment. After the first month, she had already had some invaluable experiences, reinforcing her conviction to seek a career in the health field. She learned how to pull patient files and cue them for the triage nurses. Shadowing the custodian, she discovered the proper way to dispose of hazardous biowaste. She observed simple medical procedures, such as taking blood, checking blood pressure, and inspecting eyes, ears, and throat. She was called on to visit with and help relax unaccompanied seniors in the waiting room and patient rooms. With her fluent Spanish, she facilitated the nurse practitioners and the two office doctors when communicating with the growing number of Latino/a patients.

It was in the role of translator that Hermalinda began to realize a better system of sharing important health information with non-native English speakers was needed in the office. It was also in this role that she began to hear horror stories from Spanish-speaking patients about navigating the medical insurance bureaucracy when seeking needed care. Actually, Hermalinda knew about this firsthand when she developed complications during her pregnancy: waiting in lines and sitting in emergency rooms for hours, filling out endless forms, facing the humiliation of being turned away due to lack of insurance or the wrong insurance. She wondered whether, at some level, her interest in a career in the health professions did not emerge out of those desultory experiences.

When Roxanne was told of Hermalinda's desire to learn more about health care in America for individuals with limited or no private health insurance, she was eager to help. Taking advantage of the flexible nature of the GED curriculum, Roxanne allowed Hermalinda to research this topic and apply reading and learning strategies to the texts she found. Hermalinda's Internet research uncovered a wealth of information about America's health care system, including facts and statistics on Medicaid and Medicare, political action and grassroots groups, the powerful medical insurance lobby, and the so-called Patients' Bill of Rights. Roxanne worked with Hermalinda to understand and organize the information she was finding and plan critical ways it might be used.

Among the staggering volume of information available, one finding that shocked and saddened Hermalinda the most was that infant mortality rates in some U.S. cities rivals those of developing countries. As she explored these statistics further, she learned that a health care safety net for all American citizens was a myth because nearly 14 million low-income adults are uninsured and ineligible for public health insurance programs. She felt lucky to be receiving Medicaid and at least some public assistance for her child, but wondered how other poor families could survive without these benefits.

While working with Roxanne to critically read texts on America's health care problems, Hermalinda was also working on developing her ideas for an ICT project. Loy's knowledge of and facility with computer technology were often called on by the GED students as they prepared their projects. His skills were vital in helping Hermalinda realize her plan to create an interactive CD for Spanish-speaking clients that would answer basic questions for them about checking in, payments and copayments, government and privately funded medical insurance, preventative health, and more. Using information on these topics from brochures and forms, along with Flash-

Player technology, Hermalinda and Loy created a colorful, interactive computer screen in Spanish accompanied by photos and clip art. One could read or, for those with reading or vision problems, listen to directions and information by pointing and clicking the mouse. There was even a button for frequently asked questions and answers.

Roxanne encouraged Hermalinda to incorporate some aspect of what she was learning through her research into problems with the health care system into her ICT project. She liked the idea and decided to create links to Web sites on health care insurance issues; positions and voting records of local, state, and national representatives on health care policy; and resources for low-income individuals and families. Loy suggested they attach the links to the existing interactive Q&A area on medical insurance.

A special evening reception was held at Moore to showcase student work. Invited were the employers and staff of the workplace partners, high school teachers and administrators, parents, and student retention committee members. At this event, Hermalinda and her classmates unveiled for the first time their various technology-mediated projects to a much appreciative audience. Hermalinda's coworkers in attendance were quick to try out the interactive CD she and Loy developed, and they felt certain it would improve information dissemination for Spanish-speaking clients and help them feel more welcomed.

The next step was to put the ideas to the test in the students' actual workplace settings. The office doctors were more than willing to try out Hermalinda's interactive CD for Latino/a patients. Two computers were set up in the waiting room, and bright flyers in Spanish invited users to give it a try. On the table next to the computers were response forms, also written in Spanish, to gather feedback from users on problems with the system and suggestions for improving it. When Latino/a patients arrived, Hermalinda guided them to the computers to make certain they felt comfortable using the program.

Mrs. Pantoja, whom Hermalinda had never seen in the office before, came in one afternoon complaining of intense leg and knee pain. As the woman shuffled to a seat in the crowded waiting room, leaning on her cane, Hermalinda greeted her warmly and helped her fill out new patient forms. In brief conversation, the friendly older woman told Hermalinda that she was in her 70s, lived alone, and was finding it more and more difficult to walk to the grocery store and bus stop. Hermalinda invited her to use the computer, helping her get settled in front of the machine. She showed Mrs. Pantoja how to manipulate the mouse to click on buttons for information about the clinic's services as well as insurance and methods of payment. Mrs. Pantoja caught on quickly and seemed to be maneuvering through the interactive program with confidence when she was finally called to be seen. Hermalinda asked whether she could accompany her to facilitate conversation with the nurse and doctor, and she eagerly accepted the younger woman's offer.

A diagnosis of arthritis was easy enough to understand, but the doctor's concern for possible thrombophlebitis in the legs left Mrs. Pantoja shaken, especially when he made a referral to a vascular specialist. With a hint of fear in her voice, she asked Hermalinda for help finding more information about the disorder. Although the doctor had explained, with Hermalinda's help, the nature of phlebitis and its possible consequences, the word was difficult to pronounce and fully understand. Hermalinda agreed to find out more information for Mrs. Pantoja and asked Roxanne for help.

Roxanne was more than happy to assist Hermalinda in her search for information on thrombophlebitis because it would provide the opportunity to reinforce links between workplace needs and literacy skills. That was an overriding goal of the GED program. They began with an Internet search that yielded numerous pages of technical as well as easy-to-read material on the topic. Content within Hermalinda's independent reading range, around the sixth grade, was read on her own or was used to support fluency. With more challenging material, Roxanne modeled reading strategies such as previewing, self-questioning, determining word meanings from context, gisting, organizing information into graphic displays, and checking for understanding. As each of these literacy processes was modeled, Roxanne would immediately elicit similar behaviors from Hermalinda. For example, with a passage about deep vein thrombophlebitis, they worked side by side moving through the text in a model-elicit process, thinking aloud about content and processes for organizing and understanding it. When they came on the word *anticoagulant*, Roxanne drew attention to the other words in the sentence that referred to treatments involving thinning the blood, which helped Hermalinda understand it. Later, when Hermalinda encountered the word *vascular*, she was able to use the words and sentences around it to determine that it was related to the veins.

One Internet site that very much engaged Hermalinda was concerned with the use of folk remedies for blood clots and improved circulation. From that site she linked to a passage written about a famous *curandera* (a woman, particularly in Mexican cultures, who practices healing rituals and has extensive knowledge of medicinal plants and herbs) who used green medicines to cure patients of numerous ailments, including arthritis and phlebitis. As she read this text, she was reminded of her own grandmother's stories and confirmed with her mother that when her grandmother fell ill as a child she had to drink specially brewed teas or eat foods mixed with particular herbs. These natural curatives for children's everyday ailments substituted for doctor-prescribed medicines, which were often impossible to obtain in rural Mexico at that time or too expensive. Realizing that traditional healing was largely unknown to her generation and even rarely practiced by her parents' generation, Hermalinda wondered whether Mrs. Pantoja and others her age might still benefit from trying simple folk remedies.

Acquiring critical facts about and gaining a deeper understanding of thrombophlebitis was only part of Hermalinda's goal; she also wanted to provide Mrs. Pantoja with useful information. For this she turned once again to her other GED teacher with expertise in computer technology. Loy taught Hermalinda how to use the desktop publishing software Publish It! to create her own Spanish-language pamphlet. She organized information around Causes, Signs/Symptoms, Risk Factors, Dos/Don'ts, Care, and Risks. Under the Care heading, she decided to include information about herbal curatives still recommended by Latino/a specialists in green medicines. The colorful brochure was written at a level and in a tone that would make it accessible to Latino/a patients with basic reading abilities.

With the completed brochure in hand, Hermalinda sought the doctors' approval to place copies in the stand in the clinic waiting room. He listened as she read the text of the brochure aloud to him in English. He was pleased with everything except the section on herbal remedies. He worried that such advice might be taken over prescribed medicines and that the clinic would be liable for any serious health conditions that might result. This put Hermalinda in a quandary. She discussed the situation with Loy and Roxanne, who wondered whether the brochure could not include a disclaimer about folk treatments—something to the effect that these approaches to treating sickness and disease should never be regarded as a substitute for the therapies prescribed by a trained medical professional. Put in this way, green medicines and traditional folk remedies could go hand in hand with standard medical practices, one approach complementing the other in the elimination of illnesses.

When she presented the revised brochure to the director a few days later, he was more agreeable and, after changing the wording of the disclaimer, gave Hermalinda permission to make copies and add them to the others. He even suggested she affix the label, "En Español," to the rack because additional pamphlets in Spanish would need to be developed eventually.

The next day, Hermalinda dropped off a brochure at Mrs. Pantoja's house, which was just a few blocks from work. The older woman was overjoyed to see her and invited her in. Hermalinda told her what she had learned in her research on phlebitis and showed her pertinent information in the brochure. She urged Mrs. Pantoja to continue to follow the clinic doctor's recommendations that she keep her legs elevated when sitting and try to walk around every couple of hours to maintain good blood circulation. She also told her to expect that the vascular specialist may prescribe medicine to thin her blood, and the brochure had cautionary advice about that, too.

Hermalinda realized after saying goodbye to Mrs. Pantoja and beginning the short trek to the office that she had never felt pride like this before. She was going to earn a high school equivalency diploma after all. Her life's work was becoming increasingly clear.

WHAT THESE PRACTICES TEACH US

It is worthwhile to imagine the present and future lives of Tremayn and Hermalinda without the opportunities afforded them at Moore High School, without instructional experiences predicated on the idea that alternatives to common remedial practices and traditional curriculum for students at risk of dropping out can make a difference (Polakow & Brozo, 1993).

When given the chance to become a role model for a younger, less-able reader, Tremayn discovered a new sense of control over literacy as well as a purpose for becoming increasingly critical as a reader and thinker. Just as important, he was free within the cross-age tutoring context to explore with his younger reading buddy other media in a discursive process not unlike what Knobel and Lankshear (2002) called *culture jamming*—that is, using digital technologies to alter and spoof dominant or popular culture.

Instead of dismissing Hermalinda as another curriculum casualty (Hargis, 1997), Brenda, the literacy coach, instituted proactive measures to keep her in school and better prepare her for the future. Again because of the freedom attendant to a GED curriculum centered on learners' needs, in this case in the real world of work, Hermalinda's teachers, Loy and Roxanne, could focus on supporting her efforts to redefine herself as a valued employee in the medical office. Hermalinda's sensitivity and critical understanding of the information needs of Latino/a patients led to the development of user-friendly digital media. Furthermore, her Internet research into topics important to her, because of her own experiences in the public health care system and the needs of a Latina patient in the clinic, resulted in reading multiple texts from various points of view, creating links to critical health care information in a functional ICT project, and producing through electronic means a useful pamphlet. This invaluable experience in "shape shifting" (Gee, 2002), or using digital technologies to create identities of influence, will likely serve Hermalinda throughout her community and work life.

The teachers in these vignettes designed supportive contexts for learning that allowed teens to think critically about information and messages in print and digital form and to express themselves through those same media. These practices were guided by the principle that the omnipresence of information and media in the lives of youth is enough to warrant the need for developing in them critical literacy (Goodman, 2003). This would seem to be especially necessary for those students who are marginalized and do not have easy access to ICT tools (Brozo, 2004/2005). Tremayn, by jamming popular culture, and Hermalinda, by imagining for herself a new possible future, demonstrated that when given the chance they, like most adolescents, can put their literacies to functional and critical uses.

A SCHOLAR'S RESPONSE
Thomas W. Bean, University of Nevada, Las Vegas

> Principle 8: Adolescents need opportunities to develop critical perspectives toward what they read, view, and hear.

There is now a well-documented chasm between students' in- and out-of-school literacies (Bean & Harper, 2004; Hinchman et al., 2004; Moje, 2002). This divide, coupled with a vast array of media texts and traditional print-based reading material, all compete for students' limited time and attention. There is a critical need for developing adolescents' dispositions and skills in critical literacy and critical citizenship, and this principle clearly states that curriculum goal. The vignettes offered in this chapter point to productive and engaging curricula changes that integrate students' in- and out-of-school literacies. Nevertheless, there are a number of issues that still need to be addressed, particularly with respect to our understanding of citizenship as a curriculum construct and its relation to critical literacy and critical citizenship.

Definitions of *citizenship* and recent theoretical discussions of this construct suggest that there are a number of ways to envision curriculum aimed at developing adolescents' critical citizenship (Westheimer & Kahne, 2004). Specifically, Westheimer and Kahne (2004) offered three conceptions of the good citizen taken up in various curriculum designs in schools, most often within social studies classrooms. These include: (a) the personally responsible citizen, (b) the participatory citizen, and (c) the justice-oriented citizen. These authors and others (Hebert & Wilkinson, 2002) noted that notions of citizenship will undoubtedly be debated for some time to come. The central question in these discussions, and one that is addressed in this chapter, is: What kind of citizen do we need to support an effective democratic society? (Westheimer & Kahne, 2004). These authors argued that each of the three forms of citizenship differ in terms of their impact on the status quo and systemic amelioration of injustices in society. For example, a personally responsible citizen takes individual action to volunteer in times of crisis, perhaps contributing to a food drive. This action helps the hungry, but fails to alter the root causes of hunger. It is fundamentally an individual act of kindness. At a more advanced level, participatory citizenship involves active leadership to mobilize a collective effort—for example, organizing a food drive. Finally, the justice-oriented citizen seeks to alter the status quo—in this instance, exploring why people are hungry and trying to change societal structures that produce hunger. Westheimer and Kahne (2004) argued that we should interrogate curriculum, asking: "Do programs that support civic participation necessarily promote students' capacities for critical analysis and social change?" They see community activism at the heart of true, participatory, and justice-oriented citizenship.

Applying these criteria to the two vignettes in this chapter reveals that both scenarios embodied changes in material practices that, while taken up initially as individual actions, resulted in a broader impact on school and community practices. For example, Tremayn was involved in a school-based cross-age tutoring experience with Marcus, a second grader interested in football. Tremayn used his own knowledge of football and the Internet to develop a PowerPoint presentation on the dangers of performance-enhancing drugs like steroids. Tremayn's slide show used Photoshop to morph the overly developed, muscular photos of star players into more realistic, normal body types. As a result of this effort, Tremayn's slide show became part of the school's drug awareness week, impacting a broader segment of the school population. Nevertheless, his action remains the work of one individual. Without serious discussion among student athletes about the pros and cons of performance-enhancing drugs, this positive act of citizenship, growing out of a form of service learning (i.e., tutoring Marcus), remains at the level of the personally responsible citizen.

Similarly, but within a larger community context, Hermalinda, a GED student interning in a workforce medical setting, used her bilingual skills and recognition of a social injustice to create a CD-ROM for Spanish-speaking patients to explain copays and other medical administrative jargon. Like Tremayn, Hermalinda was able to individually create a solution to a problem of social injustice impacting members of her community, but her act remained at the level of the personally responsible citizen.

Both these students made a difference in their respective settings, but they did so as individuals. Westheimer and Kahne (2003) argued that, although this sort of contribution is important, "Democracy requires more than community service; it requires citizen participation in affairs of the state" (p. 12). Recent data suggest that adolescent participation in affairs of the state, despite many school and university-based service learning requirements, is declining (Galston, 2003). Indeed in a longitudinal study of UCLA freshman, every indicator of political engagement dropped by about half, with only 33% of students regarding politics as important versus 60% in the 1960s (Galston, 2003). Rather, youth now see volunteering as an alternative to official, collective politics. According to Galston, individual choice and action "has emerged as our central value" (p. 31). In a fairly cynical view of postmodern society, Galston noted: "When the chips are down, we prefer exit to voice, and any sense of loyalty to something larger than ourselves has all but disappeared" (p. 31).

Yet students like Tremayn and Hermalinda, and their respective teachers, offer a glimmer of hope and a counterpoint to Galston's grim view. Both of these students saw social problems with fresh eyes, and they acted enthusiastically, albeit individually, on their concerns. It would seem to me that taking to heart the recent critiques of citizenship education advanced by Westheimer and Kahne (2003, 2004) and others, we could reconceptualize curriculum to increase students' involvement in participatory and justice-oriented debate, critique, and transformative action. How might this look?

In my own work, I have recently been interested in how notions of freedom and democracy play out in internationally based young adult novels and related discussions rooted in critical literacy (Bean, 2004). Reading and responding to the present chapter made me realize that many of these contemporary novels reproduce the rugged individualist form of personally responsible citizenship critiqued by Westheimer and Kahne. For example, in Naidoo's (2000) award-winning novel, *The Other Side of Truth*, Sade, the main character, is exiled from her homeland of Nigeria to London, England, as an illegal refugee. She saves her imprisoned journalist father by contacting the local TV media to publicize his plight. In essence, this is the heroic act of a young girl, rather than a collective protest of concerned Nigerian expatriates living in England. The classical narrative hero reproduces the success of the rugged individual in countless young adult novels where collective political action is largely absent.

What the present chapter and analysis suggests to me is that we need to create curriculum spaces to discuss and critique how adolescents are represented when it comes to critical citizenship, in light of current models of participatory and justice-oriented options. We need to consider media and pop culture representations, along with young adult novels, graphic novels, consumer ads, political ads, and a host of other texts that position people as good and productive citizens, but often with the individual at the forefront. By posing and considering questions from a critical literacy standpoint, we can expose gaps and limitations in the material ways that critical citizenship curriculum is enacted. With respect to school curricula, Greene (1988) noted:

> Little, if anything, is done to render problematic a reality that includes homelessness, hunger, pollution, crime, censorship, arms build-ups, and threats of war, even as it includes the amassing of fortunes, consumer goods of unprece-

dented appeal, world travel opportunities, and the flickering faces of the rich and famous on all sides. (p. 12)

Maxine Greene's long-standing belief in the kind of collective participatory and justice-oriented citizenship described by Westheimer and Kahne (2003, 2004) is embodied in a small, but important, way by the individual actions of Tremayn and Hermalinda profiled in this chapter. If students like Tremayn and Hermalinda have opportunities to collaborate in solving societal ills, there is indeed hope for a curriculum of critical citizenship.

Discussion Questions

As you reflect on the information presented in this chapter, consider the following questions as they relate to your own teaching and/or your experiences in schools:

- In your experience, to what extent do middle and high schools provide opportunities for adolescents to develop critical perspectives?
- Do you think the vignettes presented here describe instructional practices that are unusual? Why or why not?
- Compare and contrast the views of the expert responder to your own views.
- What dilemmas must teachers, schools, and others solve to implement Principle 8?

Supporting Principled Practices

Principled practices such as connecting students with print, promoting active learning, and developing critical perspectives are complex undertakings that require considerable support. This chapter sheds light on typical supports for the practices described earlier in this book. It clarifies conditions that permit educators and students to engage in principled literacy practices.

To focus this chapter, we concentrated on one question: What supports principled practices for adolescent literacy? To answer this question, we reviewed the secondary-school literacy-reform research literature published between 1990 and 2005, and we linked findings from this review with the situations described in the vignettes.

At least four elements seem to commonly support teachers' and students' principled practices: leadership, belief, opportunity, and partnership. Although these elements no doubt interact, shaping and being shaped by one another, we present them one at a time for purposes of clarity.

LEADERSHIP

Teachers take on countless classroom roles, serving as subject-matter experts, counselors, and mediators; disciplinarians, facilitators, and gate keepers. Serving as a classroom leader is a significant role many teachers assume when working toward principled practices. Acting as the person in charge, they share their visions for their classroom and guide students' efforts toward the vision. They do what is needed to lead students toward classroom goals. They assert themselves when arranging the classroom to promote desired interactions, establishing an appropriate classroom climate and set of routines, obtaining funds for literacy projects, bringing along recalcitrant youth, and so on.

Along with teachers serving as leaders in their classrooms, school leaders provide the guidance that is needed to initiate and sustain certain practices throughout schools (Ogle & Hunter, 2001). Indeed practically every effective upper grade literacy program includes a well-respected district-level coordinator, building principal, or school literacy coach supporting teachers' and students' efforts (Langer, 2002, 2004).

Literacy leaders maintain collective attention to what is important. They communicate regularly with others, engaging in activities such as developing their staff's capabilities, designing curriculum, and updating stakeholders on program results. They often publish newsletters, develop professional libraries, and personally meet with teachers, administrators, and community members about literacy programs. They interpret and report test scores.

Literacy leaders play a major role in supporting literacy commitments (Davidson & Koppenhaver, 1993). Commitments to literacy are seen in the norms of behavior enacted throughout the day that are dedicated to promoting literacy. Educators adhere to a plan, assuming individual and collective responsibility for enacting principled practices in their classrooms. Teachers regularly examine indicators of students' principled practices and modify efforts when appropriate. They systematically involve students in these efforts. They interact with literacy advocates, read the professional literature, and talk with each other about practice on a regular basis.

Visitors to a school with a commitment to literacy first might sense it without even realizing it exists. They might see unusual numbers of students carrying library books and paperbacks, overhear teachers planning literacy-related lessons, and notice posters promoting an author in residence. The visitors might be unable to immediately point to this commitment, but they eventually realize that it circulates throughout the school.

Three specific types of school-level leadership are associated with middle- and high school literacy programs that aspire to principled practices. The three are literacy coaches, literacy advisory councils, and students as authorized members of reform communities.

Literacy Coaches

No single leader is more important to school-wide reading programs than a literacy coach or specialist. A literacy coach is a master teacher who is highly knowledgeable of current literacy theory, research, and practice (International Reading Association, 2003). He or she typically is the primary source of support for a school's overall literacy program. Literacy coaches are seen as such vital personnel for teachers of adolescents that in 2003, U.S. Senator Patty Murray (D–WA) introduced the Pathways for All Students to Succeed (P.A.S.S.) Act, a plan to set aside $1 billion for hiring coaches at a ratio of at least one for every 20 secondary-school teachers (NASSP, n.d.). As of this writing, the National Governors Association is holding an education summit addressing the need to provide leadership support for high school students to achieve high standards (*Bill Gates to join nation's governors, education and business leaders*, 2005). While spending part of each day directly teaching students face to face, literacy coaches generally spend their remaining time advancing principled practices through professional development.

To support principled literacy practices in secondary schools, literacy coaches take prominent leadership roles in staff development (Sturtevant, 2003; Symonds, n.d.). Several models of professional development are available (Guskey, 2003; Hirsh, 2005). Our review of the school change record shows that admonitions such as "every teacher should be a teacher of reading" will not lead to curricular changes in science, math, and history unless teachers (a) are adequately prepared in content-area literacy strategies, (b) can directly observe the benefits of such strategies, (c) can support one another in their attempts to implement new literacy strategies, and (d) are able to reflect on and refine strategy instruction over time. Coaches lead teaching staff through these actions.

Coaches train teachers in content literacy strategies through large- and small-group workshops and classroom demonstrations. They organize teacher teams to observe and debrief with one another as they try out strategies. Coaches establish teacher study groups and professional learning communities to pose and solve problems related to adolescent literacy.

Those involved in school restructuring have always known that teachers make or break educational innovation. As Brozo and Simpson (2003) asserted: "Policy makers can enact the laws, administrators can supply the pressure, staff developers can present the innovative strategies, but teachers make the decision to change or not to change the ways they teach" (p. 459). As experienced professionals, literacy coaches recognize that change can be difficult for secondary teachers unless they are able to claim ownership of the processes involved in restructuring curriculum and instruction (Putman & Borko, 2000; Tichenor & Heins, 2000). To build this sense of ownership, the literacy coach can create formal opportunities for teachers to work together in professional learning communities that support the risk taking and struggle entailed in transforming practice. To support broad-based change in literacy teaching and learning, the literacy coach can help a school's staff form purposeful teams known as *study groups* (Murphy & Lick, 1998) or *learning communities* (Dufour & Eaker, 1998).

Chapter 10 portrayed a literacy coach supporting principled practices through study groups. Teachers and administrators wanted to stem the ever-increasing dropout rate among high-poverty minority students. The school's dropout statistics made the problem self-evident; however, solutions were not as clear. To gain a better appreciation for the causes and to explore the effectiveness of potential solutions, the literacy coach obtained a small grant from the foundation of a large corporation with a manufacturing plant in the community and brought together all vested stakeholders, including parents and students, to form a student retention study group. Working after school and on weekends, the literacy coach and teachers researched the phenomenon by conducting literature searches, phone interviews, and even site visits. Teachers were given a stipend for their efforts through the grant. After a month of study, the group recommended six key initiatives:

- Assign faculty mentors to students at risk of dropping out.
- Provide one-to-one and small-group intensive reading assistance.
- Institute an in-house GED program.
- Form ties with local businesses to provide part-time employment to students in the GED program.
- Establish a reading program for teen parents and their babies.
- Maintain a student retention study group for receiving regular parental and student input, support, and feedback.

With the administration's commitment to addressing the dropout problem, the literacy coach was able to move proactively on at least four of the study group's recommendations. Knowing how critical positive role models can be in the academic and personal lives of youth (Zirkel, 2002), she spoke at faculty meetings and met with staff individually to identify teacher mentors. She immediately began tutoring students among the high-risk group who had the lowest reading achievement scores, arranging with teachers to meet with these students during the 20-minute homeroom period and for part of their 90-minute class blocks. She enlisted the help of the school and public librarians, who created a special book program for teen parents and their infants based on a successful model program the literacy coach had discovered in her research (Tichenor, Bock, & Sumner, 1999). Finally, the literacy coach gladly and appreciatively authorized the formative role of the student retention study group, arranging for regular monthly meetings throughout the school year.

In addition to the various roles played by the literacy coach in the setting just described, another common, although critical, responsibility is to work collaboratively with subject-area teachers in support of language-based strategy teaching. Teachers at the secondary level have a proclivity to think of themselves as content specialists only (Moje, 1996). Consequently, penetrating their classrooms with literacy-rich methods for engaging students in content learning has never been easy (O'Brien, Stewart, & Moje, 1995). With a designated literacy professional on hand to serve as teacher mentor and strategy demonstrator, this challenge becomes less daunting. Unlike outside consultants, who might interact with faculty at one or two staff development workshops per year, literacy coaches are members of the faculty, available to their colleagues on a daily basis to provide sustained support in facilitating content literacy instruction. A literacy coach will not only explain to teachers how to conduct content-area literacy lessons, but also conduct the lessons in classrooms for teachers to observe, debrief afterward with teachers, and guide teachers in the implementation and personalization of the strategies as they attempt to incorporate them into their instructional repertoires. Through a process of building collegial relationships, providing frequent modeling of literacy innovations, and supporting teachers' own efforts to improve practice over the course of the school year and perhaps multiple years, literacy coaches are well positioned to bring about principled literacy practices.

Literacy Advisory Councils

Literacy advisory councils consist of stakeholders such as community members, parents, students, teachers, district and school administrators, department chairs and team leaders, curriculum coordinators, and media specialists. They play a major role supporting literacy efforts (Vogt & Shearer, 2003).

Direction is the primary support that literacy advisory councils provide. For instance, council members consult surveys, test scores, and the professional literature to prioritize efforts. They customize and finalize program visions, often specifying goals and action plans. They align curriculum with standards and monitor results through ongoing assessments that include self-study as well as independent outside evaluators.

Literacy advisory councils also direct specific program initiatives. They might decide to focus program efforts on struggling readers who are not served well in remedial classes. They might concentrate on developing partnerships with the business community. They might address the specifics of recreational reading across the curriculum. They might procure grants and enlist school media specialists in acquiring appropriate computer software.

Students As Authorized Members of Reform Communities

For many years and for good reasons, literacy educators such as Harste (1988) have advocated that teachers draw on students as curricular informants and providers of educational information. These educators believe that individuals for whom reform activity is undertaken should be involved directly in planning and implementing the change. They view the relative success or failure of literacy reform efforts transactionally, seeing both students and teachers as critical negotiators rather than compliant functionaries.

Accepting only teachers' perspectives on classroom practice results in a limited view (Brophy & Good, 1985), failing to account for students' roles as active negotiators of school knowledge and purposeful shapers of classroom life (Bloome & Green, 1984; Dillon, 1989; Erickson & Shultz, 1981). Those who believe that innovative practice need be embraced only by teachers without accounting for students' reactions and perceptions may be hard pressed to explain the failure of reform initiatives (Moje, Brozo, & Haas, 1994). Consequently, the likelihood of principled literacy practices increases as student input is sought and genuinely regarded.

School change is mediated by students' purposeful decisions to be compliant or resistant. However, students' perspectives on educational policy, practice, and reform are the ones least often consulted (Cook-Sather, 2002a). Nearly all reform efforts in American schools have been based on adults' conceptions of what education should be for children and youth. To invite students into a democratic dialog about what counts as education and worthwhile literacy practice requires a complex process of reconfiguring power dynamics and discourse patterns and authorizing students' knowledge and positions as legitimate members of a community (Cohen, Christman, & Gold, 1998). Many educators have claimed that authorizing students' perspectives can directly improve educational practice by helping teachers better appreciate the lifeworlds of youth and make their teaching more responsive to the experiences and perspectives of students (Cook-Sather, 2002b, 2002c, 2003; Lee, 1999; Wasley, Hampel, & Clark, 1997). In addition, when students are taken seriously as knowledgeable members of a reform community, they are more likely to participate constructively in their education (Shultz & Cook-Sather, 2001).

All students can be informants to help bring about curricular reforms that support principled literacy practices. For example, low-achieving struggling readers in high school can be quite capable of articulating the nature of their learning problems and offering legitimate recommendations for instructional modifications (Lee, 1999). Academically able students are often mindful of how they are discounted by administrators and teachers in reform negotiations and may feel little compunction to contribute to the success of new school-wide literacy initiatives (Brozo, 2002a).

One way that secondary students can participate in district- and school-wide conversations about reform is through school board membership. A growing national trend involves placing students on boards to ensure their voices are heard on important curricular and policy issues. Over 20 states have laws providing for student board members, although most serve without voting rights. These students can act as adults' reality checks relative to being an adolescent in the 21st century (Luna, 2003). Student school board members can liaise with peers and adults, review district programs, offer feedback on proposed initiatives, and make suggestions for continued improvement from their vantage point as adolescent learners. This process makes for better-informed board members who can enact curricular policies with the input and feelings of the intended recipients of the policies.

At the school and classroom levels, administrators and teachers can formalize structures for ensuring students' voices are heard and continuous input gathered concerning literacy reform. In chapter 9 of this book, for instance, Bayfront High School educators regarded students as partners in initiating and sustaining a new school-wide literacy effort. Staff and teachers at Bayfront High formed a student advisory council to assist them in planning the project. The council was comprised of students at all ability levels and from the school's various ethnic and cultural groups to guarantee representation of diverse viewpoints. At the beginning of the school year, right after the student advisory council was formed, the school's grant-writing team invited student representatives from the council to participate in formulating literacy objectives and programs. The advisory council was asked to generate a list of prioritized ideas and strategies the grant could support to help all students enjoy reading and learning and improve their abilities. The council offered the following recommendations, which are strikingly consistent with the supports for principled practices presented in this chapter:

- a reading mentor for struggling readers
- time every day for recreational reading
- the library and classrooms well stocked with various types of reading material
- book drops and exchanges
- fun reading in science, math, and history
- more group work
- more interesting, upbeat lectures and discussions
- time taken to get to know students personally
- more culturally relevant reading material
- more communication, discussion, and freedom of expression

- greater student voice in deciding classroom topics
- more interest-based activities and projects

When the grant was funded, Bayfront High administrators and teachers made every effort to meet the requests of students—not solely because the recommendations were legitimate, but to demonstrate sincerity in partnering with students in the literacy reform. Literacy reforms consistent with students' suggestions and put in place at Bayfront included: (a) a reading mentor system for struggling readers using high-ability students and community volunteers; (b) daily sustained silent reading (SSR) time; (c) stocking the library and classrooms with hundreds of books, magazines, and other print material at various difficulty levels and relevant to various cultural groups; (d) teacher professional development opportunities for learning how to incorporate more student-centered and participatory experiences into their instruction; and (e) purchasing novels and various other print sources and providing training for teachers in using these materials to support learning across subject areas.

In summary, leadership is a key support for principled literacy practices. Leaders provide guidance, maintain attention to what is important, and promote commitment. Literacy coaches, literacy advisory councils, and students as authorized members of reform communities comprise three forms of leadership that fit middle- and high school programs devoted to principled practices.

BELIEF

Teachers' beliefs about schooling and literacy support their classroom practices (Readence, Kile, & Mallette, 1998). Diverse classroom practices such as freewheeling discussions about text, close readings followed by analytical writing, and theatrical representations of print are associated with teachers' beliefs about their values. Adolescents' deep-seated beliefs affect the ways they take up these practices (Moje, Dillon, & O'Brien, 2000). As a result, convictions about topics such as schooling, adolescence, reading, and writing deserve considerable attention as supports for principled literacy practices.

The beliefs that people bring to bear on literacy are associated with understandings and values derived from their life experiences. For instance, Moje (1996) connected one teacher's instructional emphases on organization with her preferred learning style, aspirations for students, and even religion. This educator emphasized her personal responsibility to help students organize subject matter, a duty shaped according to her personal belief system more than doctrinaire adherence to a curriculum guide or an authority's philosophy of education.

Two aspects of instructional beliefs are presented here. Beliefs about adolescence and connecting youths' sociocultural worlds with their academic worlds are associated with principled literacy practices.

Adolescence

Lewis and Finders (2002) asserted that an "implied adolescent" (p. 101) dominates traditional thinking about education, downplaying individuality and diversity and shortchanging youth. Believing that youth enact predetermined biological roles and are imperfect adults evolving to more advanced life forms supports conventional controlling school practices. Viewing adolescence as something constructed socially, in the context of everyday face-to-face interactions, frees educators to look at youth in a more responsible and sensitive manner. Consequently, rethinking beliefs about adolescence might be needed before rethinking beliefs about principled literacy practices.

The concept of time as it relates to adolescence is a belief especially worth rethinking. As Lesko (2000) pointed out, many people view the past, present, and future as discrete segments of life, slices that are separate, unconnected, and unidirectional. Such a linear and incremental view of time positions adolescents in a certain stage of development, somewhere above childhood yet below adulthood. In contrast, Lesko suggests thinking of time as something that contains disparate dimensions simultaneously. This way of thinking leads to a view of adolescents as simultaneously immature and mature, dependent and independent, young and old. Such a multidimensional and dynamic interpretation of adolescence leads to a rich view of possibilities, one that emphasizes meaningful work in the here and now rather than in simply training for the future (Serafini, Bean, & Readence, 2004).

Sociocultural Connections

The perceived value of connecting youths' sociocultural worlds with their academic worlds is another belief worth examining. Youths' sociocultural worlds are shaped by conditions such as their home language; ethnic, religious, and family heritage; employment and career trajectory; and peer group membership. Gender, immigrant status, socioeconomic class, and sexual preference also shape youths' worlds. These worlds influence the degrees to which youth see themselves as readers and writers and help determine their participation in school literacy practices.

Middle- and secondary-school educators who believe that connecting youths' sociocultural worlds with their academic worlds support principled literacy practices in many ways. Teachers look to and invest in the real-world interests and experiences of adolescents as contexts for school-based learning (Hinchman, Alvermann, Boyd, Brozo, & Vacca, 2003/2004; Hull & Schultz, 2001). They compare media targeted directly at youth with media focused elsewhere. Informally, teachers and staff ask questions about students' outside-of-school experiences during everyday conversations. Equipped with this information, they present actual materials or recommend books, articles, Web sites, and other sources.

Another way that secondary teachers and staff support principled practices via youths' sociocultural worlds is by stocking classrooms and libraries with reading materials in multiple languages and from diverse viewpoints. Principals find and provide funding for these materials while helping teachers create structured opportunities for students to access them. Resources abound for helping educators create inclusive and responsive supports for diverse learners. Books and Web sites we have found to be especially helpful are listed in Fig. 11.1.

Books

Brown, J., Stephens, E., & Salvner, G. (1998). *United in diversity: Using multicultural young adult literature in the classroom.* Urbana, IL: National Council of Teachers of English.

Kuipers, B. (1995). *American Indian reference and resource books for children and young adults* (2nd ed.). Greenwood Village, CO: Libraries Unlimited.

McCaffrey, L. (1998). *Building an ESL collection for young adults.* Westport, CT: Greenwood.

Reed, A. (1999). *Multicultural literature anthology.* Reading, MA: Addison-Wesley.

Rochman, H. (1993). *Against borders: Promoting books for a multicultural world.* Chicago, IL: American Library Association.

Roscow, L. (1996). *Light 'n lively reads for ESL, adult and teen readers: A thematic biography.* Greenwood Village, CO: Libraries Unlimited.

Totten, H., Brown, R., & Garner, C. (1996). *Culturally diverse library collections for youth.* New York: Neal-Schuman.

Valdez, A. (1998). *Using literature to incorporate multicultural education in the intermediate grade school level.* Upper Saddle River, NJ: Prentice-Hall.

Willis, A. I. (1998). *Teaching multicultural literature in grades 9–12: Moving beyond the canon.* Norwood, MA: Christopher Gordon.

Web Sites

http://www.pampetty.com/multiadolescent.htm
http://bullpup.lib.unca.edu/multconf/multcultlit.html
http://www.literacymatters.org/adlit/selecting/multicultural.htm
http://www.indiana.edu/~reading/ieo/bibs/adol-lit.html
http://homepages.wmich.edu/~tarboxg/Book_Review_List_on_Adolescence_and_Adolescent_Lit.html
http://www.lib.msu.edu/corby/education/multicultural.htm
http://brtom.org/litlinksus.html
http://www.ric.edu/astal/multicultural/
http://www.scils.rutgers.edu/~kvander/ChildrenLit/bookssen.html

FIG. 11.1.   Multicultural adolescent literature resources and Web links.

Along with supplying ample diverse reading material, educators who believe sociocultural worlds should connect with academic ones address discussion strategies. For instance, teachers might honor the custom of recounting a narrative individually, one student at a time, as well as collectively, several students at a time. Teachers can respect both customs, explicitly engaging students in each throughout the school year. Further, in response to home languages that differ from English, schools can hire teachers and aides with dual language or English as a second-language competence. Social studies teachers who connect readings of current events with the past respond to students' sociocultural worlds. Linking the September 11, 2001 terrorist attacks on New York and Washington, DC, with the December 7, 1941 military attack on Pearl Harbor provides space for youth to examine what is happening in their worlds. Sanctioning literacy and talk about current events is one way to support the practice of "Connecting reading with youths' lives and their learning inside and outside of school."

To conclude, convictions about adolescence, schooling, and literacy shape what occurs in middle and high schools. Reflecting on one's views about adolescence and about connecting adolescents' sociocultural worlds with their academic worlds deserves attention when addressing principled practices for adolescent literacy.

OPPORTUNITY

Some educational circumstances provide a better opportunity than others for principled practices to occur. For instance, students of extreme poverty often have little chance of experiencing principled practices over time (Ancess, 2003; Barton, 2003; Strickland & Alvermann, 2004). Their opportunities are limited because adolescents of poverty are often entrusted to beginning teachers who have developed few plans for instruction or classroom management. They frequently meet in overcrowded dilapidated classrooms. The classrooms often contain few teaching materials, and the equipment is in ill-repair. Parental and community expectations for first-rate academic work are often low.

However, students of privilege often have ample opportunities for principled practices. These opportunities include highly qualified teachers with clear plans for instruction, clean classrooms with more than enough equipment in working order, reasonable numbers of students in class (about 20 per teacher), classroom stability, and access to plentiful print in and out of school. Other opportunities include coursework requirements for graduation that call for high levels of reading and writing as well as arrangements that enable administrators, teachers, youth, and family members to get to know each other.

The vignettes offered earlier in this book vividly portray how combinations of favorable circumstances link with principled literacy practices. For example, the vignette in chapter 3 shows that two teachers, Susan Fleener (Science) and Sam Berger (Art), are able to collaborate on a unit that enables students to use reading, writing, and oral communication in a wide variety of interesting ways. Susan and Sam are able to implement this project in part because they have administrative support for their efforts as well as funding that includes money for print materials, a digital camera, a field trip to a nature museum, and a variety of other resources. They also benefit from a team structure in their middle school as well as a reasonable number of students (125) per team.

The chance of principled literacy practices occurring increases as opportunities like the ones presented earlier increase. With such arrangements, youth have good prospects of taking the next step and enacting literacy practices such as, "Engaging with print and nonprint texts for a variety of purposes" and "Connecting reading with their life and learning inside and outside of school."

Two especially important opportunities for principled literacy practices involve materials (Hargis, 1997; McQuillan & Au, 2001) and time (Fielding & Pearson, 1994). Frequently, teachers are forced to lecture students on topics instead of having them read related information and ideas because available texts are either too difficult for struggling readers or too simple for advanced readers to use in a principled manner. The chances of principled literacy practices occurring are dismal when the only medium of instruction is teacher lecture. Furthermore, a wide range of reading abilities always exists in secondary-school classrooms (Stanovich, 1986), so abundant texts at multiple levels of difficulty are needed. Locating appropriate texts at various levels of difficulty on specific class topics certainly is not easy (Brozo & Hargis, 2003a). Nevertheless, material is available and can be created, if necessary, to accommodate virtually any reader.

Technology eases the task of providing appropriate texts at various levels. Numerous Internet sites have readings both simple and difficult on nearly every topic covered in a typical secondary-school curriculum. For low-achieving students, Web-based readings can be copied into word processing documents, making it possible to enlarge the print, reformat the overall layout, and even give the texts attractive, eye-catching covers. Most word processors have built-in readability checks, so texts can be modified to very low levels of difficulty for those few but inevitable students with reading ability well below their actual grade placement.

The research literature is clear that severe reading difficulties become especially complex in secondary schools (Capella & Weinstein, 2001), and the amount of time adolescents engage in reading relates to their reading achievement (Donahue, Voelkl, Campbell, & Mazzeo, 1999). Hence, secondary educators should make every effort to provide students the opportunity to spend extended time reading. Programs of this nature may be particularly critical for the substantial numbers of urban minority youth who typically do not spend outside-of-school time reading or writing extended texts (Larson, Richards, Sims, & Dworkin, 2001). To increase opportunities for principled literacy practices, many educators have rearranged school conditions. They have extended the school day and/or year, offered weekend and summer academies, and met students before and after the school day. Many secondary schools provide extramural academic activities to extend students' learning opportunities beyond regular school hours. Academic Decathlon, Science Olympiad, We the People, Reading Is Fundamental, and various service learning clubs exemplify these opportunities.

To recapitulate, opportunity is a vital support for principled adolescent literacy practices. Teachers and learners require conditions such as positive expectations for learning, purposeful direction to classroom events, and stability. Appropriate materials and time to read are imperative.

PARTNERSHIP

Partnerships occur when people join with others and work together toward common purposes. Partnerships are based on the idea that collective efforts are more productive than individual ones. Partnerships can be considered a particular type of opportunity; they are collaborative supports for principled practices. This section distinguishes five types of partners especially pertinent to literacy practices: library-media centers, cross-grade, school–home, school–community, and external change agents.

Library-Media Centers

Librarians and media specialists provide valuable support for principled literacy practices (Krashen, 2004). They are especially useful in providing access to materials youth can and want to read during self-selected reading and inquiry projects. When teachers initiate new units, library-media specialists often visit the classrooms and let the youth know about pertinent materials.

Many of these specialists also intervene directly in individuals' efforts with reading. They engage adolescents with literacy-related CDs, videos, and computer software that fit individuals' work paces and offer privacy to protect youth from peers' sometimes hurtful comments. Specialists help students use electronic networks and search engines to access and compile information. They frequently lead schools through district, state, and national literacy incentive programs. Teachers rely regularly on library and media specialists to support their literacy practices.

Cross-Grade

Students who partner with each other provide another base for principled practices. One way to accomplish this is to have youth act as mentors or tutors for younger readers. The most powerful benefit of these cross-age partnerships comes with older low-achieving readers gaining a sense of responsibility for the reading growth of others while gaining a purpose for improving their own competence (Avery & Avery, 2001; Brozo & Hargis, 2003b; Giesecke, 1993). Youth who have a sense of belonging and membership in the social structure of the school through personal relationships with faculty, staff, and other students are more likely to stay the course academically (Riehl, 2000) and are less likely to have behavior and delinquency problems (Johnson, Crosnoe, & Elder, 2001). Furthermore, cross-age tutoring offers teachers and students a viable alternative to remedial classes and other segregated placements that might not improve youths' reading (Kennedy & Fisher, 2001; Vaughn, Moody, & Schumm, 1998).

In the vignette presented in chapter 10, Tremayn, a 10th grader whose skill level was several years below his grade placement, becomes a reading buddy to second grader, Marcus. Tremayn's preparation for the weekly reading sessions with Marcus gave him desperately needed practice developing fluency with simple text. At the same time, Marcus benefited from his relationship with an older boy who cared enough to share positive book experiences with him. This example of cross-age tutoring presents a viable approach to principled practices.

Reading coaches, general and special education teachers, and school administrators often build cross-age tutoring programs into the reading curriculum for struggling adolescent readers. Arrangements are made with elementary schools to participate with middle and high schools to bring together reading buddies in regular structured tutoring sessions. Successful tutoring programs involving one older struggling reader and one younger novice reader tend to include components such as the following (Fisher, 2001; Thorpe & Wood, 2000):

- Developing fluency with high-interest instructional materials for the younger student to be tutored.
- Crafting teaching activities around words with common spellings that are high frequency and decodable.
- Reading and re-reading age- and difficulty-appropriate books.
- Guiding comprehension with story structure and prediction questions.

- Writing journal entries in response to readings.
- Creating co-authored books that have been edited for spelling, grammar, and punctuation.

Cross-age partnerships are especially valuable for youth who may be at risk of academic failure. Students of color and recent immigrants are especially vulnerable to reading problems (Donahue et al., 1999), and disproportionate numbers of minority students are placed in remedial reading and learning disabilities programs (Duncan, 2000; Ogbu, 1994). Reading problems are particularly acute for adolescent males of color (Brozo, 2002b). In efforts to promote principled literacy practices with these youth, many secondary school faculty and staff bring together academically talented students from cultural and ethnic groups and partner them with academically challenged students from the same groups. Partnerships of this kind are important because adolescents with race- and gender-matched role models often demonstrate greater interest in school-related activities and greater academic performance than students without similarly matched role models (Zirkel, 2002).

One example of a cross-age partnership occurred recently in a small community in East Tennessee with a thriving mushroom factory nearby. The children of a steadily increasing number of factory workers from Mexico and Central America were entering local schools and necessitating innovative approaches to meet their instructional and language needs. The curriculum specialist along with the middle-school reading and ESL teachers instituted a peer-support program for these new students. Hispanic eighth graders, who have become fluently bilingual and academically successful, were paired with newly arrived, culturally similar sixth and seventh graders. The student pairs were provided time during the school day to meet so the older ones could provide tutoring and converse with the younger students about personal and academic issues in both Spanish and English. Such one-to-one arrangements enabled the youth to engage in practices often inaccessible to teachers who are responsible for 25 students or more at a time.

School–Home

Another type of partnership that supports principled literacy practices involves youths' homes. Teachers, students, and family members working together toward common literacy goals can be quite productive. Such arrangements typically contain multiple efforts to tie together the school and home. For instance, students, family members, and teachers often sign educational compacts indicating that they agree to perform certain actions. Some actions typically included in a literacy compact are as follows:

- Student will read a self-selected book for at least one hour each week outside of school.
- Student will talk at least once a week about what they are reading or writing in school.
- Student will complete homework prior to the day it is due.
- Student will submit one piece of writing to the class literary journal.
- Student will accomplish state standards for Reading with a Purpose.
- Student will attend or participate in at least one school artistic production such as a play, music, or dance performance.
- Student will read aloud to young family members at least once a week. (Moore & Hinchman, 2004, p. 134)

Along with compacts, family book talks and interviews exemplify school–home partnerships that support principled practices. The following summarizes these arrangements.

Family Book Talks.   Family book talks involve youth and family members conversing about something they all have read. The family members consist of whoever is at home and is willing and able to participate. Teachers inform participants of the reasons for book talks, explain how they function, specify schedules, and often have participants sign informal contracts agreeing to participate. Teachers typically prepare a list of no more than 15 books suggested for family book talks, and they introduce the books during class. Youth rank their top five selections and then receive books according to their orders of preference.

Once the family members begin reading, they might record their thoughts and then have their partners react to what they wrote. This can be done in a letter format, or partners might write simultaneously and then talk about what each wrote. The partners might simply have a conversation about what they read with no written prompts. As a follow-up reflection on the experience, students might write their partners a letter commenting on it, sharing what became clear, and expressing appreciation for participating. Students also might write up a report for their teacher's analysis, possibly attaching audio- or videotaped records of their book talks.

Family Interviews.   Interviews are question–answer interactions. Adolescents can interview family members about countless topics. Interviewers typically obtain background on a topic before conducting the session; some kind of report typically culminates it.

Family stories are quite appropriate for interviewing. Adolescents might construct a scrapbook reporting family members' experiences with the following:

- athletics/sports
- favorites
- first encounters
- holidays
- homecomings
- house moves
- illnesses
- jobs/occupations
- leaving home
- military
- music
- outdoor experiences
- pets
- pranks
- purchases
- schooling
- vacations/car trips
- winning (Moore & Hinchman, 2004, p. 133)

During subject-matter study, students might be instructed to interview family members about the following:

- What is the most important invention?
- Who has affected history the most?
- What are our biggest social problems?
- In which decade were people better off?
- What toxic agents are in our house?
- What do we do—and what might we do—to reduce, reuse, and recycle?
- How do you use mathematics on your job and in your personal life?
- Who are your favorite authors? What are your favorite things to read?

- How might the media be improved? (Moore & Hinchman, 2004, pp. 133–134)

Literacy compacts, family book talks, and family interviews are specific techniques for linking schools with homes. They are meant to build partnerships that support youths' literacies.

School–Community

School–community partnerships connect youth with senior citizens, local business personnel, religious leaders, governmental leaders, and service group members like Rotarians and Optimists (Epstein, 2002). Such arrangements can set the stage for many principled literacy practices, as was seen in chapter 9 in the description of the interactions between Tony, a community volunteer, and LaBron, a struggling high school reader. Completing reading and writing activities jointly is meant to promote adolescents' confidence, pleasure, and competence with literacy.

Community volunteers acting on their own and as representatives of local groups can promote literacy in much the same way as the cross-age and family member partnerships just described. Community members might perform the following:

- assist with special projects
- describe career-related or personal experiences, including literacy-related activities
- participate in book talks
- respond to interviews
- serve as an external audience or evaluator for student exhibitions
- tutor adolescents

School–community partnerships occur in numerous ways. They often occur in the name of service learning efforts. Youth who volunteer their services in child-care centers, hospitals, senior homes, food banks, and recreational programs often read and write about issues related to their experiences. Partnerships also happen in the workplace. Youth might visit people at their work sites to observe out-of-school norms of behavior. Job shadowing, internships, and mentoring arrangements are common school–community partnerships of this type that support literacy. Business and community groups at the local level and beyond often grant money for educational purposes. Many teachers fund technological resources as well as book sets through these partnerships. Finally, many four-plus-four programs (high school plus college) help students navigate their futures by offering guidance, identifying favorable openings, and facilitating applications.

Professional Organizations

The final partnership described in this section involves professional organizations that offer specific school interventions. These organizations include commercial (albeit not-for-profit) educational services, higher education institutions, successful schools, and philanthropic groups. Schools partner with these organizations to obtain technical expertise and materials, consultants, research support, and other resources for school-wide or categorical programs. Many organizations address comprehensive school reform—a focus on reorganizing and revitalizing entire schools (Borman, Hewes, Overman, & Brown, 2003).

The educational marketplace comprises numerous organizations that focus on adolescent literacy. Examples include enterprises such as Project CRISS (Creating Independence through Student-owned Strategies; www.projectcriss.org), which trains subject-matter teachers in strategies like note taking and graphic organizing. Advancement Via Individual Determination (AVID; www.avidonline.org) presents a combination of approaches to literacy and subject-matter learning. The Alliance for Excellent Education (www.all4ed.org/), a group consisting of business and political leaders, is pursuing an adolescent literacy initiative as part of its mission of enabling America's six million at-risk middle- and high school students to achieve high standards and graduate prepared for college and success in life. The Strategic Literacy Initiative (SLI; www.wested.org/stratlit) emphasizes academic literacy classes that focus on metacognitive conversations. The International Reading Association (www.reading.org) offers numerous publications and services relative to adolescent literacy. To be sure, numerous other external change agents exist. Entering *adolescent literacy service* in an Internet search engine provides many examples, and consulting advertisements at conferences and in the mail reveals others.

As can be seen, people come together in numerous ways to partner for adolescent literacy. Working collaboratively provides opportunities that are not available when working alone. Educators who look outside their classrooms to other school services, families, communities, and professional organizations go far in promoting principled literacy practices.

A CLOSING WORD

The professional knowledge base regarding secondary school reform is clear that instructional change comes slowly (Darling-Hammond, Ancess, & Ort, 2002; Fullan, 2001; Sunderman, Amoa, & Meyers, 2001). For active print-rich practices to occur, teachers benefit from active leadership, productive beliefs, ample opportunities, and meaningful partners. We encourage educators wanting to initiate and sustain the principled practices described earlier to consider ways of capitalizing on these supports.

Discussion Questions

As you reflect on the information presented in this chapter, consider the following questions as they relate to your own teaching and/or experiences in schools:

- In this chapter, four main types of support for principled practice were presented: leadership, belief, opportunity, and partnership. Reflect on a time as either a student, teacher, some other school professional, or parent when you experienced firsthand the presence or absence of these supports. How was student learning affected? Which supports made the biggest difference?
- We propose that adolescents be viewed as important partners in curricular reforms that support principled literacy practices. How can middle and secondary schools take fuller advantage of youth as a resource for principled literacy?
- Many believe that teachers who connect youths' real-world interests and experiences with their academic worlds are supporting principled literacy practices. What is your belief? What experiences have you had that have helped shape your belief?
- Among the various partnerships described in chapter 11, which partnerships do you think are most crucial for ensuring support for principled teaching and learning practices? What other partnerships might be helpful to principled adolescent literacy?

References

Abi-Nader, L. (1993). Meeting the needs of multicultural classrooms: Family values and the motivation of minority students. In M. J. O'Hair & S. J. Odell (Eds.), *Diversity in teaching: Teacher education yearbook I* (pp. 212–236). Fort Worth, TX: Harcourt Brace Jovanovich.

Alexander, P., & Jetton, T. L. (2000). Learning from text: A multidimensional and developmental perspective. In M. L. Kamil, P. B. Mosenthal, P. D. Pearson, & R. Barr (Eds.), *Handbook of reading research* (Vol. 3, pp. 285–310). Mahwah, NJ: Lawrence Erlbaum Associates.

Alexander, P., & Judy, J. E. (1988). The interaction of domain-specific and strategic knowledge in academic performance. *Review of Educational Research, 58*(4), 375–404.

Allington, R. L. (2002). You can't learn much from books you can't read. *Educational Leadership, 60,* 16–19.

Alvermann, D. E. (1998). Imagining the possibilities. In D. E. Alvermann, K. A. Hinchman, D. W. Moore, S. F. Phelps, & D. R. Waff (Eds.), *Reconceptualizing the literacies in adolescents' lives* (pp. 353–372). Mahwah, NJ: Lawrence Erlbaum Associates.

Alvermann, D. E. (2001a). *Effective literacy for adolescents: Executive summary and paper commissioned by the National Reading Conference (NRC White Paper on effective Literacy Instruction).* Retrieved June 2, 2002, from http://nrc.oakland.edu

Alvermann, D. E. (2001b). Reading adolescents' reading identities: Looking back to see ahead. *Journal of Adolescent & Adult Literacy, 44,* 676–690.

Alvermann, D. E. (2002). *Adolescents and literacies in a digital world.* New York: Peter Lang.

Alvermann, D. E., Commeyras, M., Young, J. P., Randall, S., & Hinson, D. (1987). Interrupting gendered discursive practices in classroom talk about texts: Easy to think about, difficult to do. *Journal of Literacy Research, 2,* 73–104.

Alvermann, D. E., & Hagood, M. C. (2000). Fandom and critical media literacy. *Journal of Adolescent & Adult Literacy, 43,* 436–446.

Alvermann, D. E., Hinchman, K. A., Moore, D. W., Phelps, L. A., & Waff, D. (Eds.). (1998). *Reconceptualizing the literacies in adolescents' lives.* Mahwah, NJ: Lawrence Erlbaum Associates.

Alvermann, D. E., Moon, J., & Hagood, M. (1999). *Popular culture in the classroom: Teaching and researching critical media literacy.* Newark, DE: International Reading Association.

Alvermann, D. E., & Phelps, S. F. (2002). *Content reading and literacy: Succeeding in today's diverse classrooms.* Boston: Allyn & Bacon.

Alvermann, D. E., & Reinking, D. (2004). Cross-disciplinary collaborations. *Reading Research Quarterly, 39,* 332.

Alvermann, D. E., Young, J. P., Weaver, D., Hinchman, K. A., Moore, D. W., Phelps, S. F., Thrash, E. C., & Zalewski, P. (1996). Middle and high school students' perceptions of how they experience text-based discussions: A multicase study. *Reading Research Quarterly, 3,* 244–267.

Ancess, J. (2003). *Beating the odds: High schools as communities of commitment.* New York: Teachers College Press.

Anders, P. L., & Richardson, V. (1992). Teacher as game-show host, bookkeeper, or judge? Challenges, contradictions, and consequences of accountability. *Teachers College Record, 94*(2), 382–396.

Anzula, G. (1995). *Friends from the other side.* San Francisco: Children's Book Press.

Applebee, A., Langer, J., & Nystrand, M. (2003). Discussion-based approaches to developing understanding: Classroom instruction and student performance in middle and high school English. *American Educational Research Journal, 40,* 685–730.

Atwell, N. (1998). *In the middle: New understanding about writing, reading and learning.* Portsmouth, NH: Boynton/Cook-Heinemann.

Avery, C., & Avery, K. (2001). Kids teaching kids. *Journal of Adolescent & Adult Literacy, 44,* 434–435.

Baker, L., Afflerbach, P., & Reinking, D. (1996). Developing engaged readers in school and home communities: An overview. In L. Baker, P. Afflerbach, & D. Reinking (Eds.), *Developing engaged readers in school and home communities* (pp. xiii–xxvvii). Mahwah, NJ: Lawrence Erlbaum Associates.

Barr, R., Kamil, M. L., Mosenthal, P. B., & Pearson, P. D. (Eds.). (1991). *Handbook of reading research* (Vol. 2). White Plains: Longman.

Barton, P. E. (2003). *Parsing the achievement gap: Baselines for tracking progress.* Retrieved November 8, 2003, from http://www.ETS.org/research/pic

Beals, M. P. (1994). *Warriors don't cry: Searing memoir of the battle to integrate Little Rock.* New York: Simon & Schuster.

Bean, T. W. (2000). Reading in the content areas: Social constructivist dimensions. In M. L. Kamil, P. B. Mosenthal, P. D. Pearson, & R. Barr (Eds.), *Handbook of reading research* (Vol. 3, pp. 631–644). Mahwah, NJ: Lawrence Erlbaum Associates.

Bean, T. W. (2004). *Notions of freedom in multicultural young adult novels.* Paper presented at the 48th annual conference of the Comparative and International Education Society, Salt Lake City, UT.

Bean, T. W., & Harper, H. J. (2004). Teacher education and adolescent literacy. In T. L. Jetton & J. A. Dole (Eds.), *Adolescent literacy research and practice* (pp. 392–411). New York: Guilford.

Biancarosa, G., & Snow, C. (2004). *Reading next: A vision for action and research in middle and high school literacy.* Retrieved January 23, 2005, from www.all4ed.org

Bill Gates to join nation's governors, education and business leaders to focus on better preparing young people for college and work. (2005). Retrieved February 10, 2005, from http://www.nga.org/nga/newsRoom/1,1169,C_PRESS_RELEASE^D_7822,00.html

Birken, B. (Ed.). (1989). *Using writing to assist learning in college mathematics classes.* New York: Teachers College Press.

Blackburn, M. (2003). Exploring literacy performances and power dynamics at The Loft: Queer youth reading the world and the word. *Research in the Teaching of English, 37,* 467–490.

Bloome, D., & Green, J. (Eds.). (1984). *Directions in the sociolinguistic study of reading* (Vol. 1). New York: Longman.

Bolter, J. D. (1998). Hypertext and the question of visual literacy. In D. Reinking, M. C. McKenna, L. D. Labbo, & R. D. Kieffer (Eds.), *Handbook of literacy and technology* (pp. 3–14). Mahwah, NJ: Lawrence Erlbaum Associates.

Borman, G. D., Hewes, G. M., Overman, L. T., & Brown, S. (2003). Comprehensive school reform and achievement: A meta-analysis. *Review of Education Research, 73*, 125–230.

Boyd, F. G. (2000). The cross-aged literacy program: Developing mediational activity to assist ninth-grade African-American students who struggle with literacy and schooling. *Reading and Writing Quarterly, 15*, 381–398.

Brophy, J., & Good, T. (1985). Teacher behavior and student achievement. In M. Wittrock (Ed.), *Handbook of research on teaching* (3rd ed., pp. 328–375). New York: Macmillan.

Brozo, W. G. (2002a). *Tales out of school: Accounting for adolescents in a literacy reform community*. Paper presented at the National Reading Conference, Miami, FL.

Brozo, W. G. (2002b). *To be a boy, to be a teacher: Engaging teen and preteen boys in active literacy*. Newark, DE: International Reading Association.

Brozo, W. G. (2004/2005). Book review: Adolescents and literacies in a digital world: Teaching youth media: A critical guide to literacy, video production, and social change. *Journal of Literacy Research, 36*, 533–538.

Brozo, W. G., & Hargis, C. H. (2003a). Use it or lose it: Three strategies to increase time spent reading. *Principal Leadership, 4*, 36–40.

Brozo, W. G., & Hargis, C. H. (2003b). Taking seriously the idea of reform: One high school's efforts to make reading more responsive to all students. *Adolescent & Adult Literacy, 47*, 14–23.

Brozo, W. G., & Simpson, M. L. (2003). *Readers, teachers, learners: Expanding literacy across the content areas* (4th ed.). Upper Saddle River, NJ: Pearson Education.

Buckingham, D. (1997). News media, political socialization and popular citizenship: Towards a new agenda. *Critical Studies in Mass Communication, 14*, 344–366.

Burke, J. (2003). *Writing reminders*. Portsmouth, NH: Heinemann.

Camitta, M. (1993). Vernacular writing: Varieties of literacy among Philadelphia high school students. In B. V. Street (Ed.), *Cross-cultural approaches to literacy* (pp. 228–246). Cambridge, UK: Cambridge University Press.

Capella, E., & Weinstein, R. S. (2001). Turning around reading achievement: Predictors of high school students' academic resilience. *Journal of Educational Psychology, 93*, 758–771.

Cazden, C. (1988). *Classroom discourse: The language of teaching and learning*. Portsmouth, NH: Heinemann.

Chandler-Olcott, K., & Mahar, D. (2003). "Tech-savviness" meets multiliteracies: Exploring adolescent girls' technology-mediated literacy practices. *Reading Research Quarterly, 38*, 356–385.

Chapman, K. P. (1996). Journals: Pathways to thinking in second-year algebra. *The Mathematics Teacher*, pp. 588–590.

Cobb, P. (2000). Constructivism in social context. In L. P. Steffe & P. W. Thompson (Eds.), *Radical constructivism in action: Building on the pioneering work of Ernst von Glaserfeld* (pp. 152–178). London: Routledge Falmer.

Cobb, P. (2004). Mathematics, literacies, and identity. *Reading Research Quarterly, 39*, 333–337.

Cohen, J., Christman, J. B., & Gold, E. (1998). Critical literacy and school reform: So much to do in so little time. In D. E. Alvermann, K. A. Hinchman, D. W. Moore, S. F. Phelps, & D. R. Waff (Eds.), *Reconceptualizing the literacies in adolescents' lives* (pp. 303–324). Mahwah, NJ: Lawrence Erlbaum Associates.

Cook-Sather, A. (2002a). Authorizing students' perspectives: Toward trust, dialogue, and change in education. *Educational Researcher, 31*, 3–14.

Cook-Sather, A. (2002b). Re(in)forming the conversations: Student position, power and voice in teacher education. *Radical Teacher, 64*, 21–28.

Cook-Sather, A. (2002c). A teacher should be . . . When the answer is the question. *Knowledge Quest, 30*, 12–15.

Cook-Sather, A. (2003). Listening to students about learning differences. *Exceptional Children, 35*, 22–26.

Counts, W. (1999). *A life is more than a moment: The desegregation of Little Rock's Central High.* Bloomington, IN: The Indiana University Press.

Cushman, E. (1998). *The struggle and the tools: Oral and literate strategies in an inner city community.* Albany, NY: SUNY Press.

Dahl, R. (1998). *The BFG.* New York: Puffin.

Darling-Hammond, L., Ancess, J., & Falk, B. (1995). *Authentic assessment in action: Studies of schools and students at work.* New York: Teachers College Press.

Darling-Hammond, L., Ancess, J., & Ort, S. W. (2002). Reinventing high school: Outcomes of the Coalition Campus Schools Project. *American Educational Research Journal, 39,* 639–673.

Davidson, J., & Koppenhaver, D. (1993). *Adolescent literacy: What works and why* (2nd ed.). New York: Garland.

Davis, S. J., & Gerber, R. (1994). Content area strategies in secondary mathematics classrooms. *Journal of Reading, 38,* 55–57.

Dillon, D. R. (1989). Showing them that I want them to learn and that I care about who they are: A microethnography of the social organization of a secondary low-track English-reading classroom. *American Educational Research Journal, 26,* 227–259.

Donahue, P., Voelkl, K., Campbell, J. R., & Mazzeo, J. (1999). *NAEP 1998 reading report card for the nation.* Washington, DC: National Center for Education Statistics.

Dufour, R., & Eaker, R. (1998). *Professional learning communities at work.* Bloomington, IN: National Educational Service.

Duncan, G. A. (2000). Urban pedagogies and the ceiling of adolescents of color. *Social Justice, 27,* 29–42.

Eccles, J. S., Wigfield, A., & Schiefele, U. (1998). Motivation to succeed. In N. Eisenberg (Ed.), *Handbook of child psychology: Vol. 3. Social, emotional and personality development* (5th ed., pp. 1017–1095). New York: Wiley.

Echevarria, M. (2003). Anomalies as a catalyst for middle school students' knowledge construction and scientific reasoning during science inquiry. *Journal of Educational Psychology, 95,* 357–374.

Eken, A. N. (2002). The third eye. *Journal of Adolescent & Adult Literacy, 46,* 220–230.

Epstein, J. (2002). *School, family, and community partnerships: Your handbook for action.* Thousand Oaks, CA: Corwin.

Erickson, F., & Shultz, J. (1981). When is a context? Some issues and methods in the analysis of social competence. In J. Green & C. Wallat (Eds.), *Ethnography and language in educational settings* (pp. 147–160). Norwood, NJ: Ablex.

Feldman, R. S. (1997). *Development across the life span.* Upper Saddle River, NJ: Prentice-Hall.

Fielding, L. G., & Pearson, P. D. (1994). Reading comprehension: What works. *Educational Leadership, 51,* 62–68.

Finders, M. J. (1997). *Just girls: Hidden literacies and life in junior high.* New York: Teachers College Press.

Finn, P. J. (1999). *Literacy with an attitude: Educating working class children in their own self-interest.* Albany: State University of New York Press.

Fisher, D. (2001). Cross age tutoring: Alternatives to the reading resource room for struggling adolescent readers. *Journal of Instructional Psychology, 28,* 234–240.

Fowler, A. (1998). *Life in a wetland.* New York: Children's Press.

Freebody, P., & Luke, A. (1990). Literacies programs: Debates and demands in cultural context. *Australian Journal of TESOL, 5*(7), 7–16.

Freedman, S. W., Simons, E. R., Kalnin, J. S., Casareno, A., & Teams, T. M.-C. (1999). *Inside city schools: Investigating literacy in multicultural classrooms.* New York: Teachers College Press.

Freire, P. (1970). The importance of the act of reading. In B. M. Power & R. Hubbard (Eds.), *Literacy in process.* Portsmouth, NH: Heinemann.

Fullan, M. (2001). *The new meaning of educational change.* New York: Teachers College Press.

Fullan, M., & Miles, M. B. (1992). Getting reform right: What works and what doesn't. *Phi Delta Kappan, 73,* 744–752.

Galston, W. A. (2003). Civic education and political participation. *Phi Delta Kappan, 85*(1), 29–33.

Gambrell, L. B., Palmer, B. M., Codling, R. M., & Mazzoni, A. A. (1996). Assessing motivation to read. *The Reading Teacher, 49*(7).

Ganguli, A. B. (1994). Writing to learn mathematics: Enhancement of mathematical understanding. *AMATYC Review,* pp. 45–51.

Garcia, E. (2001). *Project THEME: Collaboration for school improvement at the middle school for language minority students.* Retrieved June 30, 2001, from http://www.ncbe.gwu.edu/ncbepubs/symposia/third/garcia.htm

Garcia, G. E. (2000). Bilingual children's reading. In M. L. Kamil, P. B. Mosenthal, P. D. Pearson, & R. Barr (Eds.), *Handbook of reading research* (Vol. 3, pp. 813–834). Mahwah, NJ: Lawrence Erlbaum Associates.

Gavelek, J., & Raphael, T. (1996). Changing talk about text: New roles for teachers and students. *Language Arts, 73,* 182–192.

Gee, J. P. (2002). Millennials and bobos, Blue's Clues and Sesame Street: A story of our times. In D. E. Alvermann (Ed.), *Adolescents and literacies in a digital world* (pp. 51–67). New York: Peter Lang.

Ghaith, G. (2003). Effect of think alouds on literal and higher-order reading comprehension. *Educational Research Quarterly, 26*(4), 13–21.

Giesecke, D. (1993). Low-achieving students as successful cross-age tutors. *Preventing School Failure, 37,* 34–43.

Goodman, S. (2003). *Teaching youth media: A critical guide to literacy, video production, and social change.* New York: Teachers College Press.

Greene, M. (1988). *The dialectic of freedom.* New York: Teachers College Press.

Greene, M. (2003). Foreword. In S. Goodman (Ed.), *Teaching youth media: A critical guide to literacy, video production, and social change* (pp. ix–x). New York: Teachers College Press.

Guskey, T. R. (2003). Analyzing lists of the characteristics of effective professional development to promote visionary leadership. *NASSP Bulletin, 87*(637), 4–20.

Guthrie, J. (1996). Educational contexts for engagement in literacy. *The Reading Teacher, 49,* 432–445.

Guthrie, J., & Humenick, N. (2004). Motivating students to read: Evidence for classroom practices that increase reading motivation and achievement. In P. McCardle & V. Chhabra (Eds.), *The voice of evidence in reading research* (pp. 329–354). Baltimore, MD: Brookes.

Guthrie, J., & Wigfield, A. (2000). Engagement and motivation in reading. In M. L. Kamil, P. B. Mosenthal, P. D. Pearson, & R. Barr (Eds.), *Handbook of reading research* (Vol. 3, pp. 403–422). Mahwah, NJ: Lawrence Erlbaum Associates.

Hagood, M. C. (2000). New times, new millennium, new times. *Reading Research and Instruction, 39,* 311–328.

Hargis, C. H. (1997). *Teaching low achieving and disadvantaged students* (2nd ed.). Springfield, IL: Charles C. Thomas.

Harp, D., & Horton, T. (2002). *The Great Marsh: An intimate journey into a Chesapeake wetland.* Baltimore: Johns Hopkins University Press.

Harste, J. (1988). Tomorrow's readers today: Becoming a profession of collaborative learners. In J. E. Readence & R. S. Baldwin (Eds.), *Dialogues in literacy research (37th Yearbook of the National Reading Conference)* (Vol. 37, pp. 3–13). Chicago: National Reading Conference.

Harvey, S. (1998). *Nonfiction matters: Reading, writing, and researching in grades 3–8.* Portland, ME: Stenhouse.

Heath, S. B. (1998). Living the arts through language plus learning: A report on community-based youth organizations. *Americans for the Arts Monographs, 2,* 1–19.

Hebert, Y. M., & Wilkinson, L. (2002). The citizenship debates: Conceptual, policy, experiential, and educational issues. In Y. M. Hebert (Ed.), *Citizenship in transformation in Canada* (pp. 3–36). Toronto, Canada: University of Toronto Press.

Hinchman, K. A., Alvermann, D. E., Boyd, F., Brozo, W. G., & Vacca, R. T. (2003/2004). Supporting older students' in- and out-of-school literacies. *Journal of Adolescent & Adult Literacy, 47*(4), 304–311.

Hinchman, K. A., Alvermann, D. E., Boyd, F., Brozo, W. G., & Vacca, R. T. (2004). Supporting older students' in-and out-of-school literacies. *Journal of Adolescent & Adult Literacy, 47*(4), 304–311.

Hinchman, K. A., & Young, J. P. (2001). Speaking out but not being heard: Two adolescents grow silent during classroom talk about text. *Journal of Literacy Research, 33*(2), 243–268.

Hinchman, K. A., & Zalewski, P. (1996). Reading for success in a tenth-grade global-studies class: A qualitative study. *Journal of Literacy Research, 28*(1), 91–106.

Hirsh, S. (2005). Professional development and closing the achievement gap. *Theory into Practice, 44*(1), 38–44.

Hull, G. (2000). The changing world of work. *Journal of Adolescent & Adult Literacy, 42,* 26–29.

Hull, G., & Schultz, K. (2001). Literacy and learning out of school: A review of theory and research. *Review of Educational Research, 71,* 575–611.

Hull, G., & Schultz, K. (2002). *School's out! Bridging out-of-school literacies with classroom practice.* New York: Teachers College Press.

Hynd, C. (1999). Instructional considerations for literacy in middle and secondary schools. In J. T. Guthrie & D. E. Alvermann (Eds.), *Toward an integrated model of instruction. In Engaged reading: Processes, practices, and policy implications* (pp. 81–104). New York: Teachers College Press.

International Reading Association. (2002). *What is evidence-based reading instruction?* Retrieved March 15, 2005, from http://www.reading.org/resources/issues/positions_evidence_based.html

International Reading Association. (2003). *The role and qualifications of the reading coach in the United States: A position statement of the International Reading Association.* Retrieved October 25, 2004, from http://www.reading.org/positions/reading_coach.html

International Reading Association & National Council of Teachers of English. (1996). *Standards for the English language arts.* Newark, DE: Author.

Ivey, G. (2002). Getting started: Manageable literacy practices. *Educational Leadership, 60*(3), 20–23.

Ivey, G. (2004). Content counts with urban struggling readers. In D. Lapp, C. C. Block, E. J. Cooper, J. Flood, N. Roser, & J. V. Tinajero (Eds.), *Teaching all the children: Strategies for developing literacy in an urban setting* (pp. 316–326). New York: Guilford.

Ivey, G., & Broaddus, K. (2001). Just plain reading: A survey of what makes students want to read in middle school classrooms. *Reading Research Quarterly, 36,* 350–377.

Jetton, T. L., & Dole, J. A. E. (2004). *Adolescent literacy research and practice.* New York: Guilford.

Jiménez, R. T. (1997). The strategic reading abilities and potential of five low-literacy Latina/o readers in middle school. *Reading Research Quarterly, 32,* 224–243.

Jiménez, R. T. (2004). Reconceptualizing the literacy learning of Latino students. In D. S. Strickland & D. E. Alvermann (Eds.), *Bridging the literacy achievement gap, grades 4–12* (pp. 17–29). New York: Teachers College Press.

Jiménez, R. T., & Gamez, A. (1999). Lessons and dilemmas derived from the literacy instruction of two Latina/o teachers. *American Educational Research Journal, 36,* 265–301.

Johnson, M. K., Crosnoe, R., & Elder, G. (2001). Students' attachment and academic engagement: The role of race and ethnicity. *Sociology of Education, 74,* 318–340.

Kamil, M. L., Intrator, S. M., & Kim, H. S. (2000). The effects of other technologies on literacy and literacy learning. In M. L. Kamil, P. B. Mosenthal, P. D. Pearson, & R. Barr (Eds.),

Handbook of reading research (Vol. 3, pp. 771–788). Mahwah, NJ: Lawrence Erlbaum Associates.

Kamil, M. L., Mosenthal, P. B., Pearson, P. D., & Barr, R. (Eds.). (2000). *Handbook of reading research* (Vol. 3). Mahwah, NJ: Lawrence Erlbaum Associates.

Kelly, G. J., & Green, J. (1998). The social nature of knowing: Toward a sociocultural perspective on conceptual change and knowledge construction. In B. Guzzetti & C. E. Hynd (Eds.), *Perspectives on conceptual change: Multiple ways to understand knowing and learning in a complex world* (pp. 145–181). Mahwah, NJ: Lawrence Erlbaum Associates.

Kennedy, C. H., & Fisher, D. (2001). *Inclusive middle schools.* Baltimore: Paul H. Brookes.

King, J. R., & Brozo, W. G. (1992). Critical literacy and the pedagogies of empowerment. In A. Frager & J. Miller (Eds.), *Using inquiry in reading education* (pp. 33–40). Oxford, OH: College Reading Association.

Kist, W. (2005). *New literacies in action: Teaching and learning in multiple media.* New York: Teachers College Press.

Knobel, M. (1998). *Everyday literacies: Students, discourse, and social practice.* New York: Peter Lang.

Knobel, M. (1999). *Everyday literacies: Students, discourse, and social practice.* New York: Peter Lang.

Knobel, M., & Lankshear, C. (2002). Cut, paste, publish: The production and consumption of zines. In D. E. Alvermann (Ed.), *Adolescents and literacies in a digital world* (pp. 164–185). New York: Peter Lang.

Kos, R. (1991). Persistence of reading disabilities: The voices of four middle school students. *American Educational Research Journal, 28,* 875–895.

Krashen, S. D. (2004). *The power of reading: Insights from the research* (2nd ed.). Portsmouth, NH: Heinemann.

Kuncan, L., & Beck, I. (1997). Thinking aloud and reading comprehension research: Inquiry, instruction, and social interaction. *Review of Educational Research, 67*(3), 271–299.

Ladson-Billings, G. (1994). *The dream keepers: Successful teachers of African American children.* San Francisco: Jossey-Bass.

Langer, J. A. (2002). *Effective literacy instruction: Building successful reading and writing programs.* Urbana, IL: National Council of Teachers of English.

Langer, J. A. (2004). *Getting to excellent: How to create better schools.* New York: Teachers College Press.

Lankshear, C. (1997). *Changing literacies.* Buckingham, UK: Open University Press.

Lapp, M., Grigg, W. S., & Tay-Lim, B. (2002). *The nation's report card: U.S. history 2001* (No. NCES-2002-483). Washington, DC: National Center for Education Statistics Publication.

Larson, R., Richards, M., & Moneta, G. (1996). Changes in adolescents' daily interactions with their families from ages 10 to 18: Disengagement and transformation. *Developmental Psychology, 32,* 744–754.

Larson, R., Richards, M., Sims, B., & Dworkin, J. (2001). How urban African-American young adolescents spend their time: Time budgets for location, activities, and companionship. *American Journal of Community Psychology, 29,* 565–597.

Leander, K. (2002). Locating Latanya: The situated production of identity artifacts in classroom interaction. *Research in the Teaching of English, 37,* 198–250.

Lee, C. D. (1995). A culturally based cognitive apprenticeship: Teaching African American high school students skills in literary interpretation. *Reading Research Quarterly, 30,* 608–630.

Lee, C. D. (1997). Bridging home and school literacies: Models for culturally responsive teaching, a case for African American English. In J. Flood, S. B. Heath, & D. Lapp (Eds.), *Handbook of research on teaching literacy through the communicative and visual arts* (pp. 334–345). New York: Macmillan.

Lee, C. D. (2000). *The cultural modeling project's multimedia records of practice: Analyzing guided participation across time.* New Orleans: American Education Research Association.

Lee, P. W. (1999). In their own voices: An ethnographic study of low-achieving students within the context of school reform. *Urban Education, 34,* 214–244.

Lesko, N. (2000). *Act your age: A cultural construction of adolescence.* New York: Routledge/Falmer.

Lewis, C., & Finders, M. J. (2002). Implied adolescents and implied teachers: A generation gap for new times. In D. Alvermann (Ed.), *Adolescents and literacies in a digital world* (pp. 101–113). New York: Peter Lang.

Li, G. (2006). *Culturally contested pedagogy: Battles of literacy and schooling between mainstream teachers and Asian immigrant parents.* Albany: SUNY Press.

Lipsitz, J. (1983). *Successful schools for young adolescents.* New Brunswick, NJ: Transaction.

Lisowski, M., & Williams, R. (1997). *Wetlands: Exploring ecosystems.* New York: Grolier.

Luke, A. (1999). Media and cultural studies in Australia. *Journal of Adolescent & Adult Literacy, 42,* 622–626.

Luna, C. (2003, December 10). In the classroom: Students offer school boards a special perspective: While seniors' votes don't always count, their opinions offer a dose of reality in debates. *Los Angeles Times,* p. B2.

Mahiri, J. (1998). *Shooting for excellence: African American and youth culture in new century schools.* Urbana, IL: National Council of Teachers of English.

McCord, J., Spatz Widom, C., & Crowell, N. (Eds.). (2001). *Juvenile crime, Juvenile justice.* Washington, DC: National Academy Press.

McCray, A. D., Vaughn, S., & Neal, L. I. (2001). Not all students learn to read by third grade: Middle school students speak out about their reading disabilities. *Journal of Special Education, 35,* 17–30.

McQuillan, D., & Au, J. (2001). The effect of print access on reading frequency. *Reading Psychology, 22,* 225–248.

Meier, D. (1995). *The power of their ideas: Lessons for America from a small school in Harlem.* Boston: Beacon.

Moje, E. B. (1996). "I teach students, not subjects": Teacher–student relationships as contexts for secondary literacy. *Reading Research Quarterly, 31*(2), 172–195.

Moje, E. B. (2002). Re-framing adolescent literacy research for new times: Studying youth as a resource. *Reading Research and Instruction, 41,* 211–228.

Moje, E. B., Brozo, W. G., & Haas, J. (1994). Portfolios in a high school classroom: Challenges to change. *Reading Research and Instruction, 33,* 275–292.

Moje, E. B., Dillon, D. R., & O'Brien, D. G. (2000). Reexamining the roles of learner, text, and context in secondary literacy. *Journal of Education Research, 93,* 165–180.

Moje, E. B., & Hinchman, K. A. (2004). Culturally responsive practices for youth literacy learning. In T. L. Jetton & J. A. Dole (Eds.), *Adolescent literacy research and practice* (pp. 321–350). New York: Guilford.

Moje, E. B., Young, J. P., Readence, J. E., & Moore, D. W. (2000). Reinventing adolescent literacy for new times: Perennial and millennial issues. *Journal of Adolescent & Adult Literacy, 43,* 400–410.

Moll, L. C. (1992). Bilingual classroom studies and community analysis: Some recent trends. *Educational Researcher, 21,* 20–24.

Monroe, J. (1999). *Steroid drug dangers.* Berkeley Heights, NJ: Enslow.

Moore, D. W. (1996). Contexts for literacy in secondary school. In D. J. Leu, C. K. Kinzer, & K. A. Hinchman (Eds.), *Literacies for the 21st century: Research and practice: Forty-fifth yearbook of The National Reading Conference* (pp. 15–46). Chicago: The National Reading Conference.

Moore, D. W., Bean, T., Birdyshaw, D., & Rycik, J. (1999). Adolescent literacy: A position statement. *Journal of Adolescent & Adult Literacy, 43*(1), 97–112.

Moore, D. W., & Hinchman, K. A. (2004). *Starting out: A guide to teaching adolescents who struggle with reading.* Boston: Allyn & Bacon.

Moore, D. W., Readence, J. E., & Rickelman, R. J. (1983). An historical exploration of content area reading instruction. *Reading Research Quarterly, 18,* 419–438.

Mowat, F. (1963). *Never cry wolf: The amazing true story of life among arctic wolves.* Back Bay Books.

Murphy, C., & Lick, D. (1998). *Whole-faculty study groups: A powerful way to change schools and enhance learning.* Thousand Oaks, CA: Corwin.

Muspratt, S., Luke, A., & Freebody, P. (Eds.). (1997). *Constructing critical literacies: Teaching and learning textual practice.* Cresskill, NJ: Hampton.

Myers, M. (1985). *The teacher researcher: How to study writing in the classroom.* Urbana, IL: ERIC/NCTE.

Myers, W. D. (1999). *Monster.* New York: HarperCollins.

Naidoo, B. (2000). *The other side of truth.* New York: HarperCollins.

NASSP. (n.d.). *Advocacy: Legislation and issues.* Retrieved February 10, 2005, from http://capwiz.com/nassp/issues/bills/?bill=3057156

National Council for the Social Studies. (1994). *Curriculum standards for social studies.* Silver Spring, MD: Author.

National Council for Teachers of Mathematics. (1991). *Professional standards for teaching mathematics.* Reston, VA: Author.

New London Group. (1996). *A pedagogy of multiliteracies: Designing social futures* (Vol. 66, pp. 60–92). Cambridge, MA: Harvard Educational Review.

Nieto, S. (1999). *The light in their eyes: Creating multicultural learning communities.* New York: Teachers College Press.

Noddings, N. (1992). *The challenge to care in schools: An alternative approach to education.* New York: Teachers College Press.

Noll, E. (1998). Experiencing literacy in and out of school: Case studies of two American Indian youths. *Journal of Literacy Research, 30,* 205–232.

Norton Pierce, B. (1995). Social identity, investment, and language learning. *Review of Educational Research, 67,* 197–226.

National Reading Conference. (1996). *National Science Education Standards.* Washington, DC: National Academy Press.

National Reading Panel. (2000). *Report of the National Reading Panel: Teaching children how to read.* Washington, DC: National Institute of Child Health and Human Development.

O'Brien, D. G. (2001). "At risk" adolescents: Redefining competence through the multiliteracies of intermediality, visual arts, and representation. *Reading Online, 4*(11).

O'Brien, D. G., Stewart, R. A., & Moje, E. B. (1995). Why content literacy is difficult to infuse into the secondary school: Complexities of curriculum, pedagogy, and school culture. *Reading Research Quarterly, 30*(3), 442–463.

O'Flahavan, J., Gambrell, L. B., Guthrie, J., Stahl, S., Baumann, J. F., & Alvermann, D. E. (1992). Poll results guide activities of research center. *Reading Today,* p. 12.

Ogbu, J. (1994). Racial stratification and education in the United States: Why inequalities persist. *Teachers College Record, 96,* 264–298.

Ogle, D. M. (1986). K-W-L: A teaching model that develops active reading of expository text. *The Reading Teacher, 39*(6), 564–570.

Ogle, D. M., & Hunter, K. (2001). Developing leadership in literacy at Amundsen High School: A case study of change. In M. Bizar & R. Barr (Eds.), *School leadership in times of urban reform* (pp. 179–194). Mahwah, NJ: Lawrence Erlbaum Associates.

Pajares, F. (1996). Self-efficacy beliefs in academic settings. *Review of Educational Research, 66,* 543–578.

Palinscar, A. S., & Brown, A. L. (1984). Reciprocal teaching of comprehension-fostering and monitoring activities. *Cognition and Instruction, 1,* 117–175.

Pang, V. O., & Sablan, V. A. (1998). Teacher efficacy: How do teachers feel about their abilities to teach African American students? In M. E. Dilworth (Ed.), *Being responsive to cultural differences* (pp. 39–54). Thousand Oaks, CA: Corwin.

Payne-Bourcy, L., & Chandler-Olcott, K. (2003). Spotlighting social class: An exploration of one adolescent's language and literacy practices. *Journal of Literacy Research, 35*, 551–590.

Phelps, L. A., & Hanley-Maxwell, C. (1997). School-to-work transitions for youth with disabilities: A review of outcomes and practices. *Review of Educational Research, 67*, 197–226.

Polakow, V., & Brozo, W. G. (1993). Deconstructing the "at-risk" discourse: Power, pedagogy, and the politics of inequity. *The Review of Education, 15*, 217–221.

Purves, A. (1998). Files in the web of hypertext. In D. Reinking, M. C. McKenna, L. D. Labbo, & R. D. Kieffer (Eds.), *Handbook of literacy and technology* (pp. 235–251). Mahwah, NJ: Lawrence Erlbaum Associates.

Putman, R., & Borko, H. (2000). What do new views of knowledge and thinking have to say about research on teacher learning? *Educational Researcher, 29*, 4–15.

Readence, J. E., Kile, R. S., & Mallette, M. H. (1998). Secondary teachers' beliefs about literacy: Emerging voices. In D. E. Alverman, K. A. Hinchman, D. W. Moore, L. A. Phelps, & D. R. Waff (Eds.), *Reconceptualizing the literacies in adolescents' lives* (pp. 129–148). Mahwah, NJ: Lawrence Erlbaum Associates.

Rex, L. A. (2001). The remaking of a high school reader. *Reading Research Quarterly, 36*, 288–314.

Ridgeway, V. G., Peters, C. L., & Tracy, T. S. (2002). Out of this world: Cyberspace, literacy, and learning. In C. C. Block, L. B. Gambrell, & M. Pressley (Eds.), *Improving comprehension instruction: Rethinking research, theory, and classroom practice*. San Francisco, CA: Jossey-Bass.

Riehl, C. (2000). The principal's role in creating inclusive schools for diverse students: A review of normative, empirical, and critical literature on the practice of educational administration. *Review of Education Research, 29*, 4–15.

Rush, L. S. (2004). Full steps toward a full and flexible literacy: Case studies of the four resources model. *Reading Research and Instruction, 43*, 37–55.

Schultz, K. (2002). Looking across space and time: Reconceptualizing literacy learning in and out of school. *Research in the Teaching of English, 36*, 356–390.

Schunk, D. H., & Rice, J. M. (1993). Strategy fading and progress feedback: Effects on self-efficacy and comprehension among students receiving remedial reading services. *Journal of Special Education, 27*, 257–276.

Seidman, I. (1998). *Interviewing as qualitative research* (2nd ed.). New York: Teachers College Press.

Serafini, F., Bean, T. W., & Readence, J. E. (2004). Reconceptualizing adolescent identity [Review of Act your age!; Conversational borderlands, and School kids/street kids]. *Reading Research Quarterly, 4*, 482–489.

Shephard, A. (2003). *The princess mouse*. New York: Simon & Schuster (Trade Division).

Shephard, A. (2005). Reader's theater editions. http://www.aaronshep.com/rt/RTE.html. Accessed October 30, 2005.

Shultz, J., & Cook-Sather, A. (2001). *In our own words: Students' perspectives on school*. Lanham, MD: Rowman & Littlefield.

Sizer, T. (1996). *Horace's hope: What works for the American high school*. Boston: Houghton-Mifflin.

Skilton-Sylvester, E. (2002). Literate at home but not at school: A Cambodian girl's journey from playwright to struggling writer. In G. Hull & K. Schultz (Eds.), *School's out! Bridging out-of-school literacies with classroom practice*. New York: Teachers College Press.

Smagorinsky, P. (2002). *Teaching English through principled practice*. Upper Saddle River, NJ: Merrill/Prentice-Hall.

Smith, M., & Wilhelm, J. D. (2004). I just like being good at it: The importance of competence in the literate lives of young men. *Journal of Adolescent & Adult Literacy, 47*, 454–461.

Snow, C. (2002). *Reading for understanding: Toward an R&D program in reading comprehension*. Santa Monica, CA: Rand Education.

Stanovich, K. (1986). Matthew effects in reading: Some consequences of individual differences in the acquisition of literacy. *Reading Research Quarterly, 21*, 360–407.

Street, B. V. (1995). *Social literacies: Critical approaches to literacy in development, ethnography, and education*. New York: Longman.

Strickland, D., & Alvermann, D. (Eds.). (2004). *Bridging the literacy achievement gap, grades 4–12.* New York: Teachers College Press.

Sturtevant, E. G. (1997). Teaching contexts and literacy decisions in mathematics and science: A focus on three beginning teachers during years 1 and 2. In C. Kinzer, K. A. Hinchman, & D. J. Leu (Eds.), *Inquiries in literacy theory and practice: The forty-seventh yearbook of The National Reading Conference* (pp. 237–249). Chicago: The National Reading Conference.

Sturtevant, E. G. (2003). *The literacy coach: A key to improving teaching and learning in secondary schools.* Retrieved December 6, 2003, from http://www.all4ed.org/publications/reports.html

Sunderman, G. L., Amoa, M., & Meyers, T. (2001). California's reading initiative: Constraints on implementation in the middle and high schools. *Educational Policy, 15,* 674–698.

Sweet, A. P., & Snow, C. (2002). Reconceptualizing reading comprehension. In C. C. Block, L. B. Gambrell, & M. Pressley (Eds.), *Improving comprehension instruction: Rethinking research, theory, and classroom practice* (pp. 17–53). San Francisco: Jossey-Bass.

Symonds, K. W. (n.d.). *Literacy coaching: How school districts can support a long-term strategy in a short-term world.* Retrieved November 8, 2003, from http://www.basrc.org/Pubs&Docs/LiteracyCoaching.pdf

Tatum, A. W. (2000). Against marginalization and criminal reading curriculum. *Journal of Adolescent & Adult Literacy, 43,* 570–572.

Taylor, C. (1992). *The house that crack built.* San Francisco, CA: Chronicle Books, LLC.

Tchudi, S. N., & Huerta, M. C. (1983). *Teaching writing in the content areas: Middle school/junior high.* Washington, DC: National Education Association.

Teachers of English to Speakers of Other Languages. (2001). *ESL Standards for pre-K–12 students.* Retrieved July 6, 2004, from http://www.tesol.org/assoc/k12standards/it/01.html

Thorpe, L., & Wood, D. (2000). Cross-age tutoring for young adolescents. *The Clearing House, 73,* 239–242.

Tichenor, M., Bock, A. M., & Sumner, M. A. (1999). Enhancing literacy of an at-risk group: A reading incentive program for teen parents and their babies. *Reading Improvement, 36,* 134–142.

Tichenor, M., & Heins, E. (2000). Study groups: An inquiry-based approach to improving schools. *The Clearing House, 36,* 134–142.

Tierney, R. J., & Shanahan, T. (1991). Research on the reading–writing relationship: Interactions, transactions, and outcomes. In R. Barr, M. L. Kamil, P. B. Mosenthal, & P. D. Pearson (Eds.), *Handbook of reading research* (Vol. 2, pp. 246–280). New York: Longman.

Tyner, K. (1998). *Literacy in a digital world: Teaching and learning in the age of information.* Mahwah, NJ: Lawrence Erlbaum Associates.

U.S. Department of Education. (2002). *National assessment of educational progress in reading.* Retrieved February 28, 2004, from http://nces.ed.gov/nationsreportcard/reading/results2002/

Vacca, R. T., & Alvermann, D. E. (1998). The crisis in adolescent literacy: Is it real or imagined? *NASSP Bulletin, 82*(600), 4–9.

Vacca, R. T., & Vacca, J. L. (2004). *Content area reading.* New York: Allyn & Bacon.

Valenzuela, A. (1999). *Subtractive schooling: U.S.–Mexican youth and the politics of caring.* Albany, NY: SUNY Press.

Van Sledright, B. A. (2004). What does it mean to read history? Fertile ground for cross-disciplinary collaborations? *Reading Research Quarterly, 39,* 342–346.

Vaughn, S., Moody, S. W., & Schumm, J. S. (1998). Broken promises: Reading instruction in the resource room. *Exceptional Children, 64,* 211–225.

Vogt, M. E., & Shearer, B. A. (2003). *Reading specialists in the real world: A sociocultural view.* Boston: Pearson Education.

Vyas, S. (2004). Exploring bicultural identities of Asian high school students through the analytic window of a literature club. *Journal of Adolescent & Adult Literacy, 48,* 12–23.

Vygotsky, L. (1986). *Thought and language.* Cambridge, MA: MIT Press.

Wade, S. E., & Moje, E. B. (2000). The role of text in classroom learning. In M. L. Kamil, P. B. Mosenthal, P. D. Pearson, & R. Barr (Eds.), *Handbook of reading research* (Vol. 3, pp. 609–627). Mahwah, NJ: Lawrence Erlbaum Associates.

Wasley, P. A., Hampel, R. L., & Clark, R. W. (1997). *Kids and school reform.* San Francisco: Jossey-Bass.

Westheimer, J., & Kahne, J. (2003). Reconnecting education to democracy: Democratic dialogues. *Phi Delta Kappan, 85*(1), 9–21.

Westheimer, J., & Kahne, J. (2004). What kind of citizen? The politics of educating for democracy. *American Educational Research Journal, 41,* 237–269.

Wilkinson, L., & Silliman, E. (2000). Classroom language and literacy learning. In M. L. Kamil, P. B. Mosenthal, P. D. Pearson, & R. Barr (Eds.), *Handbook of reading research, III* (pp. 337–360). Mahwah, NJ: Lawrence Erlbaum Associates.

Worthy, J., Broaddus, K., & Ivey, G. (2001). *Pathways to independence: Reading, writing, and learning in grades 3–8.* New York: Guilford.

Worthy, J., Moorman, M., & Turner, M. (1999). What Johnny likes to read is hard to find in school. *Reading Research Quarterly, 34,* 12–53.

Young, J. P. (2000). Boy Talk: Critical literacy and masculinities. *Reading Research Quarterly, 35,* 312–337.

Zirkel, S. (2002). Is there a place for me? Role models and academic identity among white students and students of color. *Teachers College Record, 104,* 357–376.

APPENDIX
Additional Resources

PROFESSIONAL ORGANIZATIONS

Council for Exceptional Children
1110 North Glebe Rd., Suite 300
Arlington, VA 22201-5704
http://www.cec.sped.org/

International Reading Association
Headquarters Office
800 Barksdale Rd.
Newark, DE 19714-8139
http://www.reading.org/

National Council of Social Studies
8555 Sixteenth St.
Silver Spring, MD 20910
http://www.ncss.org/

National Council of Teachers of English
1111 W. Kenyon Rd.
Urbana, IL 61801-1096
http://www.ncte.org/

National Council of Teachers of Mathematics
1906 Association Dr.
Reston, VA 20191-1502
http://www.nctm.org/

National Middle School Association
4151 Executive Parkway, Suite 300
Westerville, OH 43081
http://www.nmsa.org/

National Reading Conference
7044 S. 13th St.
Oak Creek, WI 53154
http://www.nrconline.org/

National Science Teachers Association
Arlington, VA
http://www.nsta.org/

Teachers of English to Speakers of Other Languages, Inc.
700 South Washington St., Suite 200
Alexandria, VA 22314
http://www.tesol.org/

JOURNALS

English Education
English Journal
Journal of Adolescent and Adult Literacy
Journal of Literacy Research
Middle School Journal
Reading Online: http://www.readingonline.org/
Reading Research and Instruction
Reading Research Quarterly
Reading and Writing Quarterly
Voices from the Middle

OTHER INTERNET RESOURCES

Alliance for Excellent Education
www.all4ed.org

International Reading Association Position Statement on Adolescent
Literacy
http://www.reading.org/resources/issues/positions_adolescent.html

*Link to final Reading Report, Reading for Understanding: Toward a R&D
Program in Reading Comprehension*
http://www.rand.org/multi/achievementforall/reading/readreport.html

National Institute for Literacy
http://www.nifl.gov/
*Administered by the Secretaries of Education, Labor, and Health and Human
Services*

National Middle School Association and the International Reading Association Joint Position on Supporting Adolescent Literacy
http://www.nmsa.org/news/final_position_paper_2_boards.pdf

National Reading Panel
http://www.nationalreadingpanel.org/

Rand Reading Study Group
http://www.rand.org/multi/achievementforall/reading/

NATIONAL STANDARDS AND GOALS

National Council for Agricultural Education
*Strategies for Teaching Reading in Secondary Agriscience: a Blueprint for
Research and Practice*
http://www.teamaged.org/ReadingResearchReportDec03.pdf

National Council of Teachers of English/International Reading
Association
Standards for the English Language Arts
http://www.ncte.org/about/over/standards

National Council of Teachers of Mathematics
Principles and Standards for School Mathematics
http://www.nctm.org/standards/

National Educational Technology Standards Project
http://cnets.iste.org/ncate/#standards

National Science Education Standards
http://www.nap.edu/readingroom/books/nses/html/

National Standards for Social Studies Teachers
www.socialstudies.org/standards/teachers/vol1/

National Standards for Visual Arts Education
www.getty.edu/artsednet/resources/Scope/Standards/index.html

Author Biographies

Elizabeth G. Sturtevant is an Associate Professor at George Mason University in Fairfax, Virginia, where she teaches master's and doctoral courses and serves as Coordinator of the Literacy Program Area. Previously a high school reading specialist and middle-school social studies teacher, she earned her PhD from Kent State University in 1992. She currently serves as co-editor of the *Journal of Literacy Research* and was co-editor of the College Reading Association *Yearbook* for 8 years. Her interests include adolescent literacy, teacher development, literacy in developing countries, and literacy coaching. Her work includes *Content Literacy: A Case-Based Inquiry Approach* (Merrill/Prentice-Hall), *The Literacy Coach: A Key to Improving Teaching and Learning in Secondary Schools* (Alliance for Excellent Education), various book chapters, and articles in publications such as *Reading Research and Instruction*, the *Journal of Literacy Research*, the NASSP *Bulletin*, the *Journal of Educational Research*, and the National Reading Conference *Yearbook*. She served as co-chair of the International Reading Association's Commission on Adolescent Literacy from 2000 to 2004 and travels frequently to Macedonia as part of an IRA international development project, providing support to secondary teachers.

Fenice B. Boyd is an Assistant Professor of Literacy Education in the Department of Learning and Instruction at the University at Buffalo, SUNY. She teaches master's and doctoral courses focused on reading comprehension research, adolescent literacy, language arts methods, young adult literature, and language, literacy, and culture. Her research centers on adolescents who struggle with literacy learning and schooling, students' responses to young adult and multicultural literature, issues of diversity, and, most recently, using multiple text types to enhance comprehension strategies. She has published in such journals as *Reading Research and Instruction, Reading & Writing Quarterly,* and the *Journal of Adolescent and Adult Literacy.* She is the co-editor of *Multicultural and Multilingual Literacy and Language: Contexts and Practices.*

William G. Brozo is a Professor of Literacy in the Graduate School of Education at George Mason University. He earned his bachelor's degree from the University of North Carolina and his master's and doctorate from the University of South Carolina. He has taught reading and language arts in junior and senior high school in the Carolinas. He is the author of numerous articles on literacy development for children and young adults. His books include *To Be a Boy, To Be a Reader: Engaging Teen and Preteen Boys in Active Literacy* (International Reading Association); *Readers, Teachers, Learners: Expanding Literacy Across the Content Areas* (Merrill/Prentice-Hall); and *Setting the Pace: A Speed, Comprehension and Study Skills Program* (Merrill). He serves on the editorial review boards of *Reading Research Quarterly, Reading Research and Instruction,* and the *Journal of Adolescent & Adult Literacy.* He writes a regular column for the International Reading Association's *Thinking Classroom* entitled "Strategic Moves," and he is also a past member of IRA's Commission on Adolescent Literacy and current member of the PISA/PIRLS Task Force. As an International Development Division–IRA volunteer, he travels regularly to Macedonia, where he provides technical support to secondary teachers.

Kathleen A. Hinchman is an Associate Professor and chair of the Reading and Language Arts Center at Syracuse University. Once a middle-school teacher, she now teaches undergraduate and graduate classes in childhood, adolescent, and adult literacy. Her research is concerned with adolescent literacy and literacy teacher education. With a wide array of book chapters and articles, she has published in such journals as *The Reading Teacher, Language Arts, Reading Research Quarterly, Journal of Literacy Research,* and *Reading Research and Instruction.* She has co-authored or co-edited *Struggling Adolescent Readers: A Collection of Teaching Strategies, Starting Out: A Guide to Teaching Adolescents Who Struggle With Reading and Writing, Reconceptualizing the Literacies in Adolescents' Lives,* and the National Reading Conference *Yearbook.*

David W. Moore is a Professor of Education at Arizona State University, where he teaches secondary school teacher-education courses in classroom instruction and management and specializes in adolescent literacy. His vita shows a 25-year publication record that balances research reports, professional articles, book chapters, and books. Noteworthy co-authored items include an International Reading Association position statement on adolescent literacy and a *Handbook of Reading Research* chapter on secondary school reading. Recent co-authored books include *Developing Readers and Writers in the Content Areas: K–12* (4th ed.) and *Starting Out: A Guide to Teaching Adolescents Who Struggle With Reading.* He co-chaired the International Reading Association's Commission on Adolescent Literacy from 2000 to 2004.

Donna E. Alvermann is Distinguished Research Professor of Language and Literacy Education at the University of Georgia. Formerly a classroom teacher in Texas and New York, her research focuses on youths' multiple literacies in and out of school. From 1992 to 1997, she co-directed the National Reading Research Center, funded by the U.S. Department of Education. With over 100 articles and chapters in print, her books include *Content Reading and Literacy: Succeeding in Today's Diverse Classrooms* (4th ed.), *Popular Culture in the Classroom: Teaching and Researching Critical Media Literacy, Bridging the Literacy Achievement Gap, Grades 4–12,* and *Adolescents and Literacies in a Digital World.* A past president of the National Reading Conference (NRC), co-chair of the International Reading Association's Commission on Adolescent Literacy, and member of the 2009 NAEP Reading Framework, she currently edits *Reading Research Quarterly* and serves on the Adolescent Literacy Advisory Group of the Alliance for Excellent Education. She was elected to the Reading Hall of Fame in 1999 and is the recipient of NRC's Oscar Causey Award for Outstanding Contributions to Reading Research, the Albert Kingston Award for Distinguished Service, College Reading Association's Laureate Award, and the H. B. Herr Award for Contributions to Research in Reading Education.

ADDITIONAL CONTRIBUTORS

Patricia L. Anders is a Professor and Head of the Department of Language, Reading and Culture in the College of Education at the University of Arizona. The focus of her research and teaching is adolescent literacy and professional development.

Thomas W. Bean is a Professor of Reading/Literacy and Coordinator of Doctoral Studies at the University of Nevada, Las Vegas. His research interests include qualitative case studies of content-area teachers' beliefs and practices using multiple texts and research on young adult literature set in international war zones.

George G. Hruby is an Assistant Professor of Reading and Literacy in the Department of Secondary Education, Utah State University. His research interests include adolescent literacy development, educational research method and theory, and educational neuroscience.

Judith Irvin is a Professor at Florida State University in Tallahassee. She has authored and co-authored many books and articles on adolescent literacy and also serves as the executive director of the National Literacy Project, a nonprofit organization dedicated to school- and district-wide approaches to improving middle- and high school student literacy.

Gay Ivey is an Associate Professor of Reading Education at James Madison University. Her research and teaching interests include reconceptualizing content area classrooms in the middle and secondary grades to make them more responsive to the needs of inexperienced readers and writers.

Guofang Li is an Assistant Professor of Education at SUNY at Buffalo. Her research interests include home and community literacy practices of immigrant and minority groups, the interrelationship between minority literacy practices and mainstream schooling, and second-language and literacy education.

Josephine Peyton Marsh (formerly Josephine Peyton Young) is an Associate Professor of Language and Literacy at Arizona State University, where she teaches courses in adolescent literacy. Her past experiences as a high school reading teacher influence her research interest in adolescent literacy and her commitment to working with teachers in schools to find ways to engage adolescents in literacy and learning.

Elizabeth Birr Moje is an Arthur F. Thurnau Professor of Educational Studies in the Literacy, Language, and Culture program and the Joint Program in English and Education at the University of Michigan, where she teaches undergraduate and graduate courses in literacy and cultural theory and in qualitative research methods. Moje conducts research in the Detroit Public Schools and surrounding communities, focusing on the intersections between young people's literacy practices in their everyday lives and the practices they are asked to engage in as part of secondary school content area learning, supported by NICHD/OVAE/OSERS, the National Science Foundation, and the William T. Grant Foundation.

Richard T. Vacca is a Professor Emeritus from Kent State University and currently works with school districts and universities throughout the United States on issues related to adolescent literacy and learning. He is the author of numerous books, chapters, and articles, and in 1996–1997 he served as the 42nd president of the International Reading Association.

Author Index

Subject Index